Study Guide to Accompany Schiller

ESSENTIALS OF ECONOMICS

Prepared by

Michael M. Tansey

Rockhurst College

and

Lawrence F. Ziegler

University of Texas at Arlington

McGRAW-HILL, INC.

NEW YORK ST LOUIS SAN FRANCISCO AUCKLAND BOGOTA CARACAS

LISBON LONDON MADRID MEXICO MILAN MONTREAL NEW DELHI

PARIS SAN JUAN SINGAPORE SYDNEY TOKYO TORONTO

Study Guide to Accompany Schiller: ESSENTIALS OF ECONOMICS

234567890 SEM SEM 909876543

ISBN 0-07-056295-4

The editors were Jim Bittker and Elaine Rosenberg.
The production supervisor was Kathryn Porzio.
Semline, Inc., was printer and binder.

Contents

To the Instructor v

To the Student vii

Acknowledgments ix

SECTION   I   BASICS

1. An Overview 1
2. Supply and Demand 17
3. The U. S. Economy 41
4. Consumer Demand 57

SECTION   II   MICROECONOMICS

5. Supply Decisions 73
6. Competition 89
7. Monopoly 111
8. The Labor Market 131
9. Government Intervention 149

SECTION   III   MACROECONOMICS

10. The Business Cycle 165
11. Aggregate Supply and Demand 181
12. Fiscal Policy 197
13. Money and Banks 209
14. Monetary Policy 221
15. Economic Growth 235
16. Theory and Reality 249

SECTION   IV   INTERNATIONAL

17. International Trade 265

To the Instructor

This *Study Guide* is an important part of the complete and fully integrated textbook package called *Essentials of Economics*. Students who use this *Study Guide* on a continuous basis should be able to remember what they have read in their textbook and heard in your lecture. It should enable them to apply to examinations the principles they learn and, more importantly, should help them recognize the same principles at work in their daily experiences. Each section of each chapter has a particular objective, which is described in the following paragraphs.

The *Quick Review* and *Learning Objectives* sections provide brief summaries of the basic contents of the corresponding text chapters and outline the important areas of the *Study Guide*. Each learning objective is keyed to specific pages in the text and to questions and problems that follow. Look at Chapter 1 for examples.

Economic terminology is often an obstacle to new students in economics. Thus the *Key-Term Review* section of the *Study Guide* provides practice in the use of terminology. This section helps the students to link economic terms to the appropriate economic concepts. The *Study Guide* attempts to reinforce the terminology by systematic and inventive repetition.

The *True or False* and *Multiple Choice* sections help the student advance from memorizing terminology to applying the economic principles in a familiar problem-solving setting. This will help greatly in their preparation for exams.

The *Problems and Applications* section lets students discover economic principles for themselves. Students not only learn the techniques that economists use, but they also discover the basis for the economic principles they have learned.

The section called *Common Errors* reflects our feeling that, semester after semester, students have difficulty with the same concepts and make the same mistakes; hence, the name *Common Errors*. We've tried to draw attention to some of these problem areas and provide explanations using the appropriate economics principles. You may wish to add some of your own.

Another unique feature of this *Study Guide* is what we call the "media exercise." The media exercises are contained in the *Problems and Applications* section of each chapter. Each one directs the student to reread a certain Headline article from those interspersed throughout the text. The students then answer a series of questions based on the article, using the economic principles explained in the chapter. The media exercises help students see economic principles at work in the world around them, and make them aware of how to get the "economics" out of a critical reading of the "news" long after they leave the economics classroom.

The *Study Guide* provides an attractive alternative to memorization: it directs the student in applying economic principles. The exercises and crossword puzzles should actually stimulate interest in economics. We have found that our students showed great satisfaction from the discovery of the ideas embedded in the exercises as well as the neatness of completed problems and mathematical calculations. The exercises focusing on current or historic events also generated interest among the students and some of our students enjoyed making up their own crossword puzzles.

To the Student

This *Study Guide* is designed to be used with *Essentials of Economics, First Edition*, by Bradley R. Schiller. Working through the *Study Guide* should reinforce what you have learned in the textbook and help you to recognize economic principles in your daily experiences.

Note the following sections of each of the chapters:

- The *Quick Review* provides a brief summary of the concepts in the corresponding text chapter. If you are not comfortable with the terminology and concepts in this review, you should reread the appropriate sections of the text chapter.
- The *Learning Objectives* focus on the basic information in each text chapter and provide outlines for material to be covered in the *Study Guide.* The learning objectives are keyed to questions and problems that follow, and to pages in the text. If you have difficulty with a particular idea you can quickly find the text material and review it.
- The *Key-Term Review* gives you practice in the use of terminology in the specific chapters.
- The *True or False* and *Multiple Choice* questions test your understanding of the basic economic principles discussed in the text chapter.
- The *Problems and Applications* section contains one or more real-world problems, which allow you to work out, in a practical way, the economic principles that you have been studying.
- Nearly all chapters contain a "media exercise" that refers you to specific Headline articles reprinted in the text. These exercises will assist you in developing your critical thinking skills.
- The *Common Errors* section identifies some of the errors that students often make and explains the correct principles. This is a very effective way to help you discover and correct your mistakes.
- Answers to *all* problems, exercises, and questions are provided at the end of each chapter of the *Study Guide,* so you can quickly check your answers and go back and review where necessary.

Acknowledgments

We wish to acknowledge the support of the McGraw-Hill staff. They are terrific. We especially thank Jim Bittker, economics editor, for being responsive to our requests and for the calm and friendly manner in which he dispatched his responsibilities. Elaine Rosenberg, editing supervisor, is a real professional. We thank her for her no-nonsense approach and for her skillful management of a difficult project. Carole Schwager is a superb copy editor, and we thank her for her meticulous work.

The manuscript was typed by Alice Gould. We appreciate the care she took in her work and her contributions to the layout and style of the book. Finally, we acknowledge the efforts of Raphael Arinaitwe, a student at Rockhurst College, who read the text manuscript and the *Study Guide* manuscript several times. Bryce Jones, professor of economics at Rockhurst College, has provided valuable commentary and support for many years. We thank him for that.

Michael M. Tansey
Lawrence F. Ziegler

CHAPTER   1

An Overview

Quick Review

The output of the U.S. economy is approaching $6 trillion per year. This is simply the economist's way of summarizing the total volume of goods and services produced in the economy by market participants like you and me. In other words, "The economy is us."

Although our annual production of goods and services is impressive, our resources are not sufficient to satisfy all of our wants. Society's wants are infinite and insatiable while our available resources are relatively fixed. This is the problem of "scarcity." As a result, we (like all societies) are forced to choose which goods and services will be produced and which will not. Economists illustrate these choices by drawing a production-possibilities curve. This curve shows the combinations of goods and services a society could produce if it were operating efficiently and all of its resources were fully employed. The production-possibilities curve is the menu of different output choices from which society can choose. The limits to output choices are dictated by available factors of production and technology.

Every society has to decide what goods and services it wants to produce. In the United States our choices are determined predominately by the market mechanism. Through the market mechanism the production and consumption decisions of individuals directly affect the allocation of resources. These individual decisions are supplemented with generous doses of public-sector activity. When the market mechanism fails to provide goods and services efficiently and equitably—a situation called "market failure"—the public sector must provide assistance. Market systems do not automatically generate pollution-control mechanisms which assure us of clean air and water. Such market imperfections must be overcome by government activity. In some economies the market mechanism was not allowed to work efficiently. Planned (or command) economies, like that of the Soviet Union, were good examples of this. Even in mixed economies "government failure" can make things worse.

In studying the economy, it is useful to break economics into two categories: microeconomics and macroeconomics. Microeconomics focuses on a specific individual, firm, industry, or government agency; macroeconomics focuses on the entire economy.

Learning Objectives

After reading Chapter 1 and doing the following exercises, you should:	True or false	Multiple choice	Problems and applications	Common errors	Pages in the text
1. Know that the science of economics is concerned with "scarcity" of factors of production.	1, 2, 3, 4, 12	1, 2, 3, 5		1	5-9
2. Be familiar with the ideas of several important writers on the subject of resource allocation.	5, 17	2, 18, 19, 21, 23, 24			4-5
3. Understand why the WHAT, HOW, and FOR WHOM questions arise in every society.	9	5			6-12
4. Understand opportunity costs and how to represent them.	12	3, 6, 7, 8	1, 2, 3		8
5. Be able to draw and interpret a production-possibilities curve.	4, 11, 16	10, 11	1, 2, 3	2	6-9
6. Be able to demonstrate growth, decline, and technological change by shifting the production-possibilities curve.	11, 13, 14, 16	10, 11	1, 2, 3		8-10
7. Know how the market mechanism allocates resources to solve the WHAT, HOW, and FOR WHOM questions.	6, 7, 8, 18, 19	4, 24			10
8. Be able to differentiate between microeconomics and macroeconomics; positive and normative economics.	15, 18	13, 14, 22		3	13-14
9. Understand why large-scale central planning failed.		15, 16, 17			10-11
10. Understand the importance of the *ceteris paribus* assumption in economic analysis.	10, 20	22			14-15

Key-Term Review

Review the following terms; if you are not sure of the meaning of any term, write out the definition and check it against the Glossary in the text.

ceteris paribus	macroeconomics	mixed economy
economics	market failure	opportunity cost
factors of production	market mechanism	production possibilities
government failure	microeconomics	scarcity
laissez faire		

Fill in the blank following each of the statements below with the appropriate term from the list above.

1. A Latin phrase meaning "all other things being equal" is .... 1. _____

2. The branch of economics that focuses on the activities of individual decision-making units is .... 2. _____

3. When economists say that to have more schools we must give up houses, they are are illustrating the principle of .... 3. _____

4. When market prices signal what goods and services should be produced, the allocation of resources is being accomplished by the .... 4. _____

5. Those things that are transformed into final goods and services desired by society are .... 5. _____

6. The branch of economics that focuses on the behavior of the entire economy is .... 6. _____

7. A curve showing the various combinations of goods and services that a society can produce with its scarce resources is a _____ curve. ...... 7. _____

8. The policy of nonintervention by government in the market mechanism is known as .... 8. _____

9. When laissez faire leads to increased pollution, then pollution is an example of .... 9. _____

10. The science that studies how societies allocate scarce resources is .... 10. _____

11. Some of the resource allocation in the United States is done through the public sector, indicating that we have a .... 11. _____

12. When our wants exceed the available resources to satisfy them, there is...................... 12. _____

13. Public-sector intervention that fails to improve economic outcomes is an example of .... 13. _____

3

True or False: *Circle your choice.*

T F 1. Since students do not pay tuition in elementary school, there is no scarcity in offering education from society's point of view.

T F 2. Goods are scarce because society's desire for them exceeds society's ability to produce them.

T F 3. If a commodity has a market price that is greater than zero, it must be scarce.

T F 4. A production-possibilities curve can be drawn only if a scarce resource prevents production of as much of a commodity as society desires.

T F 5. Adam Smith observed how markets enable individuals to pursue their self-interest.

T F 6. The U.S. economy is referred to as a mixed economy because a large fraction of our resources are allocated by the public sector (government).

T F 7. The policy of laissez faire means that the government leaves the economy alone.

T F 8. In the U.S. market system, the government gives the signals for deciding how to use resources.

T F 9. The distribution of income largely determines the kinds of goods and services the economy will produce.

T F 10. The task of economic theory is to explain and predict the economic behavior of economic resources.

T F 11. One reason that the production-possibilities curve is bowed out is that the efficiency with which resources can be used in production varies from industry to industry.

T F 12. If the economy is fully and efficiently employing its resources, then the only way to acquire more of one good is to accept less of something else.

T F 13. Technological advance shifts the production-possibilities curve inward.

T F 14. When the economy experiences declining productivity, then the production-possibilities curve is likely to be shifting inward.

T F 15. Microeconomics focuses on the economy as a whole.

T F 16. The slope of the production-possibilities curve is related to the idea of opportunity cost.

T F 17. Karl Marx believed that socialism would eventually be replaced by capitalism.

T F 18. Pollution is an example of market failure.

T F 19. Inequities can result from either market failure or government failure.

T F 20. Positive economics deals with "what is," and normative economics deals with "what ought to be."

Multiple Choice: *Select the correct answer.*

_____ 1. Which of the following best describes the subject matter included in principles of economics?
(a) How the economy allocates its scarce resources.
(b) How households make decisions.
(c) How governments make choices about resources.
(d) How society purchases resources.

2. Which of the following best describes the term "resource allocation"?
   (a) Which goods and services society will produce with available land, labor, and capital.
   (b) How society spends the income of individuals.
   (c) How society purchases resources.
   (d) How one spends one's income.

3. In economics, what does scarcity mean?
   (a) That when there is a shortage of a particular good, the price will fall.
   (b) That very few buggy whips are being manufactured nowadays.
   (c) That society's desires exceed the want-satisfying capability of the resources available to satisfy those desires.
   (d) None of the above.

4. Which of the following *best* describes the way resources are allocated in the U.S. economy?
   (a) By tradition.
   (b) By command
   (c) By markets.
   (d) By government.

5. Which of the following are considered scarce in the U.S. economy?
   (a) Hamburgers.
   (b) Automobiles.
   (c) Petroleum products.
   (d) All of the above.

6. I plan on going to a $5 movie this evening instead of studying for an exam. The total opportunity cost of the movie:
   (a) Depends on how I score on the exam.
   (b) Is $5.
   (c) Is what I could have purchased with the $5 plus the study time I forgo.
   (d) Is the forgone studying I could have done in the same time.

7. The opportunity cost of installing a traffic light at a dangerous intersection is:
   (a) Negative, since it will reduce the number of accidents.
   (b) The cost of the stoplight plus the cost savings from a reduction in the number of accidents.
   (c) The time lost by drivers who approach the intersection when the light is red.
   (d) The best possible alternative bundle of other goods or services that must be forgone in order to build and install the traffic light.

8. The frequently used phrase "time is money" is a way of stating:
   (a) The idea of opportunity cost.
   (b) Everyone has a price.
   (c) People work for free.
   (d) Money is an economic goal.

5

9. Which of the following events would cause the production-possibilities curve to shift *inward?*
    (a) The labor supply grows.
    (b) New factories are built.
    (c) A technological breakthrough occurs.
    (d) None of the above.

10. Which of the following events would cause the production-possibilities curve to shift *outward?*
    (a) The economy grows.
    (b) A new, strong plastic is developed for use in building houses.
    (c) More women enter the labor force.
    (d) All of the above would cause such a shift.

11. The *slope* of the production-possibilities curve provides information about:
    (a) The growth of the economy.
    (b) Technological change in the economy.
    (c) Opportunity costs in the economy.
    (d) All of the above.

12. *The General Theory of Employment, Interest, and Money* was written by:
    (a) Karl Marx.
    (b) John Maynard Keynes.
    (c) Adam Smith.
    (d) None of the above.

13. Which of the following are major goals of the economy?
    (a) Full employment.
    (b) Price stability.
    (c) An equitable distribution of income.
    (d) All of the above.

14. Macroeconomics focuses on the performance of:
    (a) Individual consumers.
    (b) Firms.
    (c) Government agencies.
    (d) None of the above.

15. The most likely source of the failure of communism in the Soviet Union was the problem of:
    (a) Inadequate land, labor, and capital.
    (b) Centralization of decision making.
    (c) Devastation from World War II.
    (d) The focus on too few social goals.

16. The collapse of communism is evidence of:
    (a) Government failure.
    (b) Market failure.
    (c) The failure of a mixed economy.
    (d) *Ceteris paribus.*

17. Which of the following is a typical source of government failure?
    (a) Bureaucratic delays.
    (b) Shortages.
    (c) Inefficient incentives.
    (d) All of the above.

18. Who first wrote of the "invisible hand" of the marketplace as being more efficient than government at allocating resources?
    (a) Adam Smith.
    (b) John Maynard Keynes.
    (c) Karl Marx.
    (d) Boris Yeltsin.

19. Who wrote *The Wealth of Nations*?
    (a) Karl Marx.
    (b) Adam Smith.
    (c) John Maynard Keynes.
    (d) None of the above.

20. *The General Theory of Employment, Interest and Money*:
    (a) Had a central thesis based on class warfare.
    (b) Made the case for laissez faire.
    (c) Argued that the government sector played a necessary role in stabilizing the economy.
    (d) Discussed the relationship of wages and interest in determining the distribution of income.

21. Which of the following contains a name, word, or term that does not belong with the others?
    (a) Adam Smith, Karl Marx, Mikhail Gorbachev.
    (b) Laissez faire, market mechanism, Adam Smith.
    (c) John Maynard Keynes, government intervention, economic stabilization.
    (d) Classical economics, Adam Smith, market mechanism.

22. Which of the following is a positive statement?
    (a) The market mechanism is superior to central planning in allocating resources.
    (b) The cost of a Stealth bomber can be computed as the amount of housing forgone.
    (c) It costs too much to produce Stealth bombers.
    (d) *The Wealth of Nations* is more difficult to read than *Das Kapital*.

23. Who is associated with the statement, "The whole world of experience has demonstrated the viability and effectiveness of the market economy"?
    (a) Adam Smith.
    (b) Mikhail Gorbachev.
    (c) John Maynard Keynes.
    (d) Karl Marx.

_____ 24. Who spoke of the role of government as an "invisible hand" which would allocate resources in an efficient and equitable manner?
(a) Karl Marx.
(b) Adam Smith.
(c) John Maynard Keynes.
(d) None of the above.

Problems and Applications

Exercise 1

This exercise is similar to the problem at the end of Chapter 1 in the text. It provides practice in drawing and interpreting a production-possibilities curve and demonstrating shifts of such a curve.

1. A production-possibilities schedule showing the production alternatives between corn and lumber is presented in Table 1.1. Graph combination A in Figure 1.1 and label it. Do the same for combination B. In going from combination A to combination B, the economy has sacrificed _____ billion board feet of lumber production per year and has transferred the land to production of _____ billion bushels of corn per year. The opportunity cost of corn in terms of lumber is _____ board feet per bushel.

Table 1.1

Combination	Quantity of corn (billions of bushels per year)	Quantity of lumber (billions of board feet per year)
A	0	50
B	1	48
C	2	44
D	3	38
E	4	30
F	4	20
G	6	0

2. In answering Question 1 you determined the opportunity cost of corn when the economy is initially producing corn (combination A). Using the information in Table 1.1, graph the rest of the production-possibilities combinations in Figure 1.1 and label each of the points with the appropriate letter.

Figure 1.1

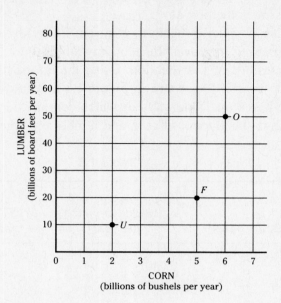

3. When Table 1.2 is completed, it should show the opportunity cost of corn at each possible combination of lumber and corn production in the economy. Opposite "1st billion bushels" insert the number of board feet per year of lumber sacrificed when the economy shifts from combination A to combination B. Complete the table for each of the remaining combinations.

Table 1.2

Corn production (billions of bushels per year)	Opportunity cost of corn in terms of lumber (billions of board feet per year)
1st billion bushels	
2nd billion bushels	
3rd billion bushels	
4th billion bushels	
5th billion bushels	
6th billion bushels	

9

4. In Table 1.2, as more corn is produced (as the economy moves from combination A toward combination G), the opportunity cost of corn _____ (falls, rises, remains the same), which illustrates the law of _____ .

5. Suppose that lumber companies begin to clear-cut forest areas instead of cutting them selectively. Clear-cutting improves the economy's ability to produce lumber but not corn. Table 1.3 describes such a situation. Using the information in Table 1.3, sketch the new production-possibilities curve in Figure 1.1 as you did the initial production-possibilities curve based on Table 1.2. For which combination does the use of clear-cutting fail to change the amount of corn and lumber produced? _____

Table 1.3

Combination	Corn (billions of bushels per year)	Lumber (billions of board feet per year)
A′	0	75
B′	1	72
C′	2	66
D′	3	57
E′	4	45
F′	4	30
G′	6	0

6. After the introduction of clear-cutting the new production-possibilities curve is (outside, inside, the same as) the earlier curve. The opportunity cost of corn has (increased, decreased) as a result of clear-cutting.

7. Study your original production-possibilities curve in Figure 1.1 and decide which of the combinations shown (U, F, O) demonstrates each of the following. (*Hint:* Check the answers at the end of the chapter to make sure you have diagramed the production-possibilities curve in Figure 1.1 correctly.)
   (a) Society is producing at its maximum potential. Combination_____.
   (b) Society has some unemployed or underemployed resources. Combination _____.
   (c) Society cannot produce this combination. Combination _____.
   (d) Society might be able to produce this combination if technology improved but cannot produce it with current technology. Combination _____.
   (e) If society produces this combination, some of society's wants will go unsatisfied unnecessarily. Combination _____.

Exercise 2

The following exercise shows how to recognize and infer the concept of production possibilities from statements made by public officials.

In a speech before the American Society of Newspaper Editors on April 16, 1953, President Eisenhower stated:

Every gun that is made, every warship launched, every rocket fired signifies, in the final sense, a theft from those who hunger and are not fed, those who are cold and not clothed. This world in arms is not spending money alone. It is spending the sweat of its laborers, the genius of its scientists, the hopes of its children. . . . This is not a way of life at all in any true sense. Under the cloud of threatening war, it is humanity hanging from a cross of iron.

Answer the following questions on the basis of the preceding quotation:
1. What *factors of production* did Eisenhower point to as the resources that limit our production possibilities?
   (a) Guns, warships, rockets.
   (b) Food, clothes.
   (c) Money.
   (d) Laborers, scientists, and the hopes of our children.
2. What are the final goods and services that society desires?
   (a) Guns.   (c) Clothes.
   (b) Warships.   (d) All of the above.
3. What labels should be placed on one of the axes of the production-possibilities curve that Eisenhower has implicitly described?
   (a) Guns, warships, rockets, and other armaments.
   (b) Laborers, scientists, and other labor.
   (c) Money.
   (d) None of the above.
4. Which of the following is the opportunity cost of armaments (guns, warships, and rockets)?
   (a) The amount of clothing or food given up to produce a given quantity of armaments.
   (b) The dollar value of armaments absorbed in providing national defense.
   (c) The amount of money that Congress appropriates for purchasing armaments.
   (d) None of the above.
5. Implicitly, President Eisenhower recommended that there be greater:
   (a) Expenditure on armaments relative to clothing.
   (b) Expenditure on clothing and on food relative to armaments.
   (c) Development of labor, genius, and hopes to make more armaments, food, and clothing possible.
   (d) Expenditure of money for all of society's needs.
6. If Eisenhower's speech resulted in a cutback in the production of armaments and greater production of food and clothing, then, assuming the law of increasing opportunity costs applies, the opportunity cost of:
   (a) Both armaments and clothing-food should rise.
   (b) Both armaments and clothing-food should fall.
   (c) Armaments should fall while the opportunity cost of food-clothing should rise.
   (d) Armaments should rise while the opportunity cost of food-clothing should fall.

Exercise 3

Newspapers contain a great deal of information about the tradeoffs involved in producing different combinations of goods and services. To describe tradeoffs, the articles should provide certain information. By using one of the articles in the text, this exercise will show the kind of information to look for. If your professor makes a newspaper assignment from the *Instructor's Manual*, this exercise will provide an example of how to do it.

Reread the Headline article on page 9 in Chapter 1 of the text entitled "The Peace Dividend."

1. How many pairs of goods are matched to illustrate the tradeoff between the goals of the defense buildup and the nondefense buildup?

2. What "resources" do the tradeoff examples suggest are in limited supply?

3. List all of the quotations that explicitly refer to this resource.

4. What passages in the article indicate a possible shift of the production-possibilities curve or a movement along it? The shift or movement may have occurred already, may be occurring now, or may occur in the future.

Common Errors

The first statement in each "common error" below is incorrect. Each incorrect statement is followed by a corrected version and an explanation.

1. Words mean the same thing in economics that they do in our everyday conversation. WRONG!
Words used in everyday conversation *very often* have different meanings when they are used in economics. RIGHT!

You'll have to be very careful here. Words are used with precision in economics. You'll have difficulty if you confuse their everyday meanings with their economic meanings. For example, the term "capital" in economics means simply "man-made instruments of production." In everyday usage it may mean money, machines, a loan, or even the British response to the question "How are you feeling?"

2. Economic models are abstractions from the real world and are therefore useless in predicting and explaining economic behavior. WRONG!

Economic models are abstractions from the real world and *as a result* are useful in predicting and explaining economic behavior. RIGHT!

You have to be willing to deal with abstractions if you want to get anything accomplished in economics. By using economic models based on specific assumptions, we can make reasonable judgments about what's going on around us. We try not to disregard any useful information. However, to try to include everything (such as what cereal we like for breakfast) would be fruitless. For example, the production-possibilities frontier is an abstraction. No economist would argue that it is an economy! But it certainly is useful in focusing on public-policy choices, such as the choice between guns and butter.

3. Because economics is a "science," all economists should come up with the same answer to any given question. WRONG!

Economics is a science, but there is often room for disagreement in trying to answer a given question. RIGHT!

Economics is a social science, and the entire society and economy represent the economist's laboratory. Economists cannot run the kind of experiments on the economy that are done by physical scientists. As a result, two economists may attack a given problem or question in different ways using different models. They may come up with different answers, but since there is no answer book, you cannot say which is right. The solution is, then, to do more testing, refine our models, compare results, and so on. By the way, the recent space probes have given physicists cause to reevaluate much of their theory concerning the solar system, and there is much controversy concerning what the new evidence means. But physics is still a science, as is economics!

■ ANSWERS ■

Key-Term Review

1. *ceteris paribus*
2. microeconomics
3. opportunity cost
4. market mechanism
5. factors of production
6. macroeconomics
7. production-possibilities
8. laissez faire
9. market failure
10. economics
11. mixed economy
12. scarcity
13. government failure

True or False

1. F	5. T	9. T	12. T	15. F	18. T
2. T	6. T	10. F	13. F	16. T	19. T
3. T	7. T	11. T	14. T	17. F	20. T
4. T	8. F				

Multiple Choice

1. a	6. c	10. d	14. d	18. a	22. b
2. a	7. d	11. c	15. b	19. b	23. b
3. c	8. a	12. b	16. a	20. c	24. d
4. c	9. d	13. d	17. d	21. a	
5. d					

Problems and Applications

Exercise 1

1. 2, 1, 2

2. **Figure 1.1 Answer**

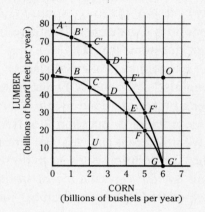

3. **Table 1.2 Answer**

Corn production (billions of bushels per year)	Opportunity cost of corn in terms of lumber (billions of board feet per year)
1st billion bushels	2
2nd billion bushels	4
3rd billion bushels	6
4th billion bushels	8
5th billion bushels	10
6th billion bushels	20

4. rises, increasing opportunity costs
5. See Figure 1.1 answer; combination *G*.
6. outside, increased
7. a, *F;* b, *U;* c, *O;* d, *O;* e, *U*

14

Exercise 2

1. d   3. a   5. b
2. d   4. a   6. c

Exercise 3

1. 7
2. The article focuses on the budget limitation. The budget limitation, in turn, reflects the economy's limited resources.
3. "resources," "peace dividend," $120 billion, $40 billion, $25 billion, $5 billion, $532 million, $2.6 million, and $1 million.
4. "Reverse the military build up" and "could allow the United States to cut $120 billion" both suggest reduced military spending. The passage "This 'peace dividend' represents resources that could be allocated to other uses" suggests greater non-military spending. These two changes suggest a movement along the production-possibilities curve.

CHAPTER 2

Supply and Demand

Quick Review

Every economy must answer the same basic questions:
- **WHAT** goods and services should the economy produce?
- **HOW** should they be produced?
- **FOR WHOM** should they be produced?

In the U.S. economy we rely heavily on markets to answer these questions. In this chapter we focus on markets and market participants and seek answers to three subsidiary questions:
- What determines the price of a good or service?
- How does the price of a product affect its production or consumption?
- Why do prices and production levels often change?

Let's look at some market participants and see how they interact. Households and firms exchange factors of production in factor markets and goods and services in product markets. The quantity supplied of factors or products in a market is the quantity that sellers are willing and able to sell at a particular price. Market prices are likely to affect the quantity supplied. Economists represent the relationship between price and the quantity supplied in a supply schedule or supply curve. Supply represents the ability and willingness to sell specific quantities of a good at alternative prices in a given time period, *ceteris paribus*.

The quantity demanded of factors or products in a market is the quantity that buyers are willing and able to buy at a particular price. When prices fall, people tend to buy more. Economists represent the relationship between price and the quantity purchased in the form of a demand schedule or demand curve. Demand is the ability and willingness to buy specific quantities of a good at alternative prices in a given time period, *ceteris paribus*. Demand and supply do not determine what is actually exchanged, nor do they tell why an exchange occurs.

Market-supply and market-demand curves can be used to find the equilibrium price and rate of production in a market. A market-supply curve is the sum of the supply curves of the sellers in the market. Similarly, a market-demand curve is the sum of the individual demand curves of buyers in the market. When the market-demand curve intersects the market-supply curve, the market is in equilibrium. The market mechanism moves price toward the equilibrium price level:

1. If the market price is above the equilibrium price, surpluses appear. To get rid of the surplus, sellers lower prices and production rates. Buyers buy more at lower prices.

2. If the market price is below equilibrium price, shortages occur. Buyers bid up the price of the commodity and sellers raise production rates in response to the increased price.

In both cases price and production rates change until the market reaches the equilibrium price and equilibrium production rate. This is the price and production rate that clears the market. The market mechanism is not perfect and may fail if there are externalities, and it may not allocate income in a desirable way, but it does answer the questions what to produce, how to produce, and for whom to produce.

Market-demand and market-supply curves shift for a variety of reasons. Changes in the price or availability of other goods, tastes, income, expectations, and the price of a given good can alter market demands. Changes in resource prices, in technology, in expectations, in taxes, and in the number of sellers can alter market supply. With each shift the market finds its way through trial and error back to equilibrium. Governments sometimes feel compelled to interfere with the market mechanism by establishing minimum prices (price floors) or maximum prices (price ceilings) for certain things. No matter how laudable the goals of the program for which they are instituted, intractable surpluses result from price floors and intractable shortages from price ceilings. In some cases the results have been so perverse that they represent government failure, that is, public-sector intervention which moves society away from, rather than toward, preferred economic outcomes.

Learning Objectives

After reading Chapter 2 and doing the following exercises, you should:	True or false	Multiple choice	Problems and applications	Common errors	Pages in the text
1. Know the basic questions in economics and how the U.S. economy answers the questions.	1, 14				25-29
2. Be able to describe the different types of markets and the participants in those markets.	2	4, 9			26-27
3. Understand how a demand schedule represents demand and how a supply schedule represents supply.	5, 6	23	1, 3, 4	1, 5, 6	29-36
4. Be able to define and graph supply and demand curves.	3, 4, 7, 8	5, 23	1, 4	1	30-34, 36-37
5. Know why supply and demand curves shift.	16, 17, 18	8, 12, 16, 18, 20, 22	2, 3, 4, 5	7	32-34

Learning Objectives (cont'd.)	True or false	Multiple choice	Problems and applications	Common errors	Pages in the text
6. Know the difference between individual demand and market demand and between individual supply and market supply.	8	17	1, 3		34-37
7. Be able to describe how and why markets move toward equilibrium.	9, 10, 11, 13, 14, 15	10, 11, 19	4, 5	2, 3, 4	38-42
8. Be able to explain shortages and surpluses and the effects of price ceilings and price floors.	10, 12	11, 15	3, 4, 5		42-44
9. Know what causes movements along demand and supply curves.	19, 20	13, 14, 15	4, 5	5, 6	33-37
10. Understand the concept of laissez faire.		1			45-46

Key-Term Review

Review the following terms; if you are not sure of the meaning of any term, write out the definition and check it against the Glossary in the text.

ceteris paribus	laissez faire	market surplus
demand	law of demand	opportunity cost
demand curve	law of supply	price ceiling
demand schedule	market demand	price floor
equilibrium price	market mechanism	product market
factor market	market shortage	shift in demand
government failure	market supply	supply

Fill in the blank following each of the statements below with the appropriate term from the list above.

1. The sum of the quantities demanded by all of the individual buyers in a market at every price is called .... 1. _____

2. The relationship between prices and the quantity a buyer is willing and able to purchase at those prices is shown in tabular form as a .... 2. _____

3. The value of the next most desirable use of resources is called the .... 3. _____

4. By adding together all the quantities that individual suppliers are willing and able to sell at different prices, you can find .... 4. _____

5. A French term meaning "let alone" is .... 5. _____

6. What a buyer is willing and able to buy at various prices per unit of time, *ceteris paribus* .... 6. _____

7. What a seller is willing and able to sell at various prices per unit of time, *ceteris paribus* .... 7. _____

8. When quantity demanded equals quantity supplied, this correspondence establishes the .... 8. _____

9. Changes in tastes, income, or prices of other goods may cause a .... 9. _____

10. The quantities that buyers are willing and able to buy at various prices are shown graphically as a .. 10. _____

11. When prices are determined by buyers and sellers in a market, the economy is using the _____ 11. _____ to allocate resources.

12. A decline in market prices below the market equilibrium level causes a .... 12. _____

13. Finished goods are exchanged in a .... 13. _____

14. A rise in market price above the market-equilibrium price level causes a .... 14. _____

15. Resources are exchanged for money in a .... 15. _____

16. A Latin phrase meaning "all other things remaining equal" is .... 16. _____

17. The idea that quantity demanded increases as price falls, *ceteris paribus,* is known as the .... 17. _____

18. The idea that quantity supplied increases when price increases, *ceteris paribus*, is known as the ... 18. _____

19. Attempts by government to hold certain prices down with a _____ or prop prices up with ... 19. _____ a _____ lead to shortages and surpluses ...... _____ respectively.

20. A term that describes government interference with markets that worsens economic outcomes is .... 20. _____

True or False: *Circle your choice.*

T   F   1. In a market economy, prices are determined by the consumer; in a planned or command economy, prices are determined by the seller.

T F   2. People who are producers at work may be consumers when they go to the store to buy groceries.

T F   3. Supply curves reflect the potential behavior only of the sellers or producers of a good or service, not of buyers.

T F   4. Demand curves reflect potential behavior only of buyers of a good or service, not sellers.

T F   5. Transactions in a command economy reflect the willingness and ability of sellers to supply a product.

T F   6. Transactions in a command economy reflect the willingness and ability of buyers to demand a product.

T F   7. The demand curve shows how much of a good a buyer will actually buy at a given price.

T F   8. A market-demand curve can always be found by adding, horizontally, the demand curves of all of the buyers in a given market.

T F   9. The equilibrium price occurs at the price where the market supply and market demand curves intersect.

T F 10. In a command economy the market moves the price toward the equilibrium price.

T F 11. The equilibrium price can be determined through the process of trial and error by both the buyers and the sellers in a market.

T F 12. There are never shortages or surpluses when the price in a market is equal to the equilibrium price for the market.

T F 13. At the equilibrium price, sellers receive signals to increase production rates while buyers receive signals to increase purchases in a given time period.

T F 14. The people who demand goods and services are constrained by their incomes from achieving the goal of satisfying their desires for goods and services.

T F 15. An economy run with a laissez-faire policy permits the invisible hand to direct prices for all goods and services toward their equilibrium levels.

T F 16. When the number of suppliers in a market changes, the market-supply curve for goods and services also changes, even if the individual supply curves of original suppliers do not shift.

T F 17. Changes in technology, prices of resources, taxes, and expectations cause market-supply curves to shift.

T F 18. Changes in variables that shift individual demand curves (such as tastes and income) also shift market-demand curves.

T F 19. Price ceilings result in surpluses.

T F 20. To be effective, price floors should be set below equilibrium prices, and price ceilings should be set above equilibrium prices.

Multiple Choice: *Select the correct answer.*

_____ 1. A laissez-faire policy may not create as much satisfaction as might otherwise be obtainable because of the existence of:
  (a) Public goods, inequitable distributions of income, and market power of businesses.
  (b) Public goods, government intervention, and competitiveness of businesses.
  (c) Government intervention, welfare for the poor, and lobbying by unions and businesses.
  (d) Government taxation, government regulation, and government enterprise.

_____ 2. The principal actors in an economy are all constrained from achieving their goals:
  (a) Consumers by income, businesses by profits, and government by taxes.
  (b) Consumers by available goods and services, businesses by scarce resources, government by resources not used in businesses.
  (c) Consumers by the satisfaction derived from purchasing goods and services, businesses by profits, and government by the general welfare.
  (d) Consumers by available goods and services, businesses by scarce resources, and government by the general welfare.

_____ 3. The goals of the principal actors in the economy are:
  (a) Income for consumers, profits for business, and taxes for government.
  (b) Goods and services for consumers, scarce resources for businesses, and resources not used by businesses for government.
  (c) Satisfaction from the purchase of goods and services for consumers, profits for businesses, and general welfare for government.
  (d) Available goods and services for consumers, scarce resources for businesses, and general welfare for government.

_____ 4. The three factors of production are:
  (a) Labor, natural resources, and equipment.
  (b) Rent, wages, and profit.
  (c) Land, labor, and capital.
  (d) None of the above.

_____ 5. The emphasis on "willingness and ability" in the definitions of supply and demand warns us that supply and demand do not necessarily tell us:
  (a) The actual quantities produced and bought in a market.
  (b) The reasons that a particular quantity is demanded or supplied.
  (c) Who actually produces or receives the quantity demanded or supplied.
  (d) All of the above.

_____ 6. Market-supply and market-demand curves are similar in that both:
  (a) Involve the willingness and ability of a supplier to sell a product or service.
  (b) Involve the willingness and ability of a buyer to buy a product or service.
  (c) Have price on the y-axis and production rate (quantity) on the *x*-axis.
  (d) Can be derived by adding vertically all of the supply and demand curves of the individuals in the market.

_____ 7. Equilibrium prices include:
    (a) List prices that firms post on their products or in catalogs to inform the buyer of the price that is being offered.
    (b) Bid prices of buyers to inform the seller of the highest price that a buyer is willing and able to pay for a product.
    (c) Transaction prices that leave no shortages or surpluses at the end of the transaction period.
    (d) Prices at which there is excess supply.

_____ 8. A downward shift in demand and a leftward shift in demand are both characterized by (two answers):
    (a) A smaller quantity demanded at every price.
    (b) A greater quantity demanded at every price.
    (c) A higher price at each quantity demanded.
    (d) A lower price at each quantity demanded.

_____ 9. The goal of the supplier of a product or service in a market economy is:
    (a) The use of scarce resources subject to the constraint of taxes.
    (b) The use of scarce resources subject to the constraint of available profit.
    (c) Profits subject to the constraint of scarce resources.
    (d) Profits subject to the constraint of income.

_____ 10. The equilibrium price in a market is found where:
    (a) The market-supply curve intersects the market-demand curve.
    (b) The market-supply curve intersects the y-axis.
    (c) The market-demand curve intersects the y-axis.
    (d) The market-supply curve intersects the x-axis.

_____ 11. An effective price floor results in black market pressures:
    (a) To reduce prices because of surpluses.
    (b) To raise prices because of surpluses.
    (c) To reduce prices because of shortages.
    (d) To raise prices as a result of surpluses.

_____ 12. A movement along the supply curve is the same as:
    (a) A shift in the supply curve.
    (b) A change in the quantity supplied.
    (c) A change in the quantity demanded.
    (d) All of the above.

_____ 13. The determinant of demand that does not shift a demand curve is:
    (a) Income.
    (b) Taste.
    (c) The price of the good itself.
    (d) The prices of other goods.

_____ 14. According to the law of demand, the quantity of a good demanded in a given time period:
    (a) Increases as its price rises, _ceteris paribus._
    (b) Decreases as its price falls, _ceteris paribus._
    (c) Increases as its price falls, _ceteris paribus._
    (d) Does none of the above.

15. A market shortage is:
   (a) The amount by which the quantity demanded exceeds the quantity supplied at a given price.
   (b) Excess demand.
   (c) A situation in which market price does not equal equilibrium price, so that people cannot buy all of the goods that they are willing and otherwise able to buy.
   (d) All of the above.
16. A shift in demand is defined as a change in the:
   (a) Quantity demanded.
   (b) Quantity demanded due to a change in price.
   (c) Quantities demanded at alternative prices.
   (d) Equilibrium quantity.
17. Market supply represents:
   (a) The total quantity of a good that sellers are willing and able to sell at alternative prices in a given time period, *ceteris paribus*.
   (b) The horizontal sum of individual supply curves.
   (c) The combined willingness and ability of market suppliers to sell goods and services at various prices, in a given time period, *ceteris paribus*.
   (d) All of the above.
18. A downward shift in the supply curve and a rightward shift in the supply curve are both characterized by:
   (a) A smaller quantity supplied and a greater price.
   (b) A greater quantity supplied and a greater price.
   (c) A smaller quantity supplied and a lower price.
   (d) A greater quantity supplied and a lower price.
19. By definition, the equilibrium price in a market:
   (a) Occurs when the supply and demand curves are the same, *ceteris paribus*.
   (b) Is the price at which the quantity of a good or service demanded in a given time period equals the quantity supplied.
   (c) Is the market price.
   (d) All of the above.
20. Which of the following would generally cause an increase in the demand for automobiles?
   (a) A decrease in the price of automobiles.
   (b) An increase in consumers' income.
   (c) The new models are perceived as ugly compared to old models.
   (d) Consumer expectation that the price of automobiles will be lower next year.
21. Which of the following would you expect to cause a decrease in the demand for automobiles?
   (a) A rise in the price of gasoline.
   (b) Consumer expectation that the price of automobiles will be lower next year.
   (c) Consumer expectation that a significant recession will develop that could last for a year.
   (d) All of the above.

_____ 22. Which of the following would not cause the market supply of telephones to increase?
  (a) Telecommunications are deregulated, and anyone who wants to can produce and sell telephones.
  (b) A new and cheaper technology for producing plastics is developed.
  (c) A reduction in the demand for telephones causes their prices to fall.
  (d) Taxes levied on telephone production are reduced.

_____ 23. Which of the following best provides an example of the law of supply?
  (a) Falling labor costs cause an increase in supply.
  (b) An improved technology shifts the supply curve to the right.
  (c) Some producers leave the industry, and the supply curve shifts upward.
  (d) Demand falls and the quantity supplied decreases.

_____ 24. Which of the following groupings contains a word which does not belong?
  (a) Market economy, command economy, mixed economy.
  (b) Laissez faire, _ceteris paribus,_ market economy.
  (c) Technology, factor prices, number of sellers.
  (d) Tastes, income, expectations.

Problems and Applications

Exercise 1

This exercise provides practice in graphing demand and supply curves for individual buyers and sellers as well as graphing market-demand and market-supply curves.

1. Suppose you were willing and able to buy 20 gallons of gasoline per week if the price were $1 per gallon, but if the price were $3 per gallon you would be willing and able to buy only the bare minimum of 10 gallons. Complete the demand schedule in Table 2.1.

Table 2.1. Your demand schedule for gasoline

Price (dollars per gallon)	Quantity (gallons per week)
$1	_____
3	_____

25

2. Use your demand schedule for gasoline in Table 2.1 to diagram the demand curve in Figure 2.1. Assume your demand curve is a straight line.

Figure 2.1. Your demand curve for gasoline

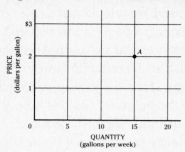

If you have drawn your demand curve correctly, it should go through point *A*

3. Suppose that 999 other people in your town have demand curves for gasoline that are just like yours in Figure 2.1. Fill out the town's market-demand schedule in Table 2.2 at each price. (Remember to include your own quantity demanded along with everyone else's at each price.)

Table 2.2. Market-demand schedule for gasoline in your town

Price (dollars per gallon)	Quantity (gallons per week)
$1	_____
3	_____

4. Using the market-demand schedule in Table 2.2, draw the market-demand curve for gasoline for your town in Figure 2.2. Assume that the curve is a straight line, and label it *D*.

Figure 2.2. Market-supply and demand curves for gasoline in your town

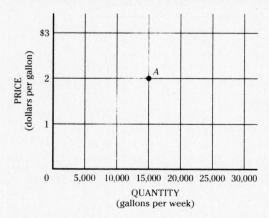

If you have drawn the demand curve correctly, it should pass through point *A*.

26

5. Suppose the friendly neighborhood gas station is not willing to sell anything at $1 per gallon, but at $3 it would be willing to sell 1,500 gallons per week. Fill in the supply schedule for this gas station in Table 2.3.

Table 2.3. Supply schedule for neighborhood gas station

Price (dollars per gallon)	Quantity (gallons per week)
$1	_____
3	_____

6. Graph the supply curve in Figure 2.3 based on the information in Table 2.3 and label it *S*. Assume that the supply curve is a straight line through both points.

Figure 2.3. Supply curve for neighborhood gas station

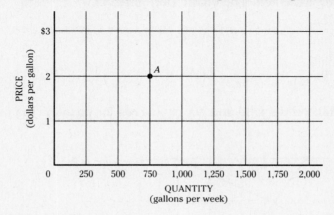

7. Suppose that 19 other gas stations in your town have the same supply schedule as your neighborhood gas station (Table 2.3). Fill out the market-supply schedule for gasoline of the 20 gas stations in your town in Table 2.4.

Table 2.2. Market-demand schedule for gasoline in your town

Price (dollars per gallon)	Quantity (gallons per week)
$1	_____
3	_____

8. Using the market-supply schedule in Table 2.4, draw the market-supply curve for gasoline for your town in Figure 2.2. Assume that the market-supply curve is a straight line. If you have drawn the curve correctly, it should pass through point *A*. Label the supply curve *S*

27

9. The equilibrium price for gasoline for your town's 20 gas stations and 1,000 buyers of gasoline (see Figure 2.2) is:
   (a) Above $2.
   (b) Exactly $2.
   (c) Below $2.
10. At the equilibrium price there are:
    (a) Shortages.
    (b) Surpluses.
    (c) Excess inventories.
    (d) None of the above.

Exercise 2

This exercise shows the market mechanics at work in shifting market-demand curves.
1. In Figure 2.4, the supply (S_1) and demand (D_1) curves for gasoline as they might appear in your town are presented. The equilibrium price is:
   (a) $3 per gallon.
   (b) $2 per gallon.
   (c) $1 per gallon.
   (d) $0 per gallon.

Figure 2.4. Market-demand and supply curves for gasoline in your town

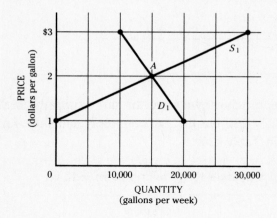

2. Assume that one-half of the people in your town move away. Because of this suppose that the remaining buyers are willing and able to buy only half as much gasoline at each price as was bought before. Draw the new demand curve in Figure 2.4 and label it D_2.
3. T   F   When the number of buyers in a market changes, the market-demand curve for goods and services shifts.
4. When half of the buyers move from your town, the equilibrium price:
   (a) Rises above the old equilibrium price.
   (b) Equals the old equilibrium price.
   (c) Falls below the old equilibrium price.
   (*Hint:* See the second demand curve, D_2, in Figure 2.4.)

28

5. If the old market price ($2) doesn't change to the new equilibrium price, there will be:
   (a) A larger quantity demanded than would be supplied at the new equilibrium price.
   (b) A smaller quantity demanded than would be supplied at the new equilibrium price.
6. If the market price does not adjust to the new equilibrium price after the potential buyers leave, there will be:
   (a) A market shortage.
   (b) A market surplus.
   (c) Neither shortage nor surplus.
7. When there is a surplus in a market, prices are likely to fall:
   (a) Because buyers do not wish to buy as much as sellers want to sell.
   (b) Because sellers are likely to offer discounts to eliminate expensive excess inventories.
   (c) Because buyers who cannot buy commodities at the current market price are likely to make offers to buy at lower prices that sellers will accept.
   (d) For all of the above reasons.
8. Whenever there is a leftward shift of the market-demand curve, market forces should push:
   (a) Market prices upward and market quantity downward.
   (b) Market prices upward and market quantity upward.
   (c) Market prices downward and market quantity upward.
   (d) Market prices downward and market quantity downward.
9. Whenever there is a rightward shift of the market-demand curve, market forces should push:
   (a) Market prices upward and market quantity downward.
   (b) Market prices upward and market quantity upward.
   (c) Market prices downward and market quantity upward.
   (d) Market prices downward and market quantity downward.

Exercise 3

This exercise gives practice in computing market-demand and market-supply curves using the demand and supply curves of individuals in a market. It is similar to the problem at the end of Chapter 2 in the textbook.

1. Table 2.5 shows the weekly demand and supply schedules for various individuals. Fill in the total market quantity that these individuals demand and supply.

Table 2.5. Individual demand and supply schedules

	Price			
	$4	$3	$2	$1
Buyers				
Al's quantity demanded	2	3	5	6
Betsy's quantity demanded	2	2	2	3
Casey's quantity demanded	1	2.5	3	3.5
Total market quantity demanded	___	___	___	___
Sellers				
Alice's quantity supplied	8	3	2	0
Butch's quantity supplied	7	5	4	0
Connie's quantity supplied	9	7	3	0
Ellen's quantity supplied	6	5	1	0
Total market quantity supplied	___	___	___	___

Use the data in Table 2.5 to answer Questions 2-4.

2. Construct and label market-supply and market-demand curves in Figure 2.5.
3. Identify the equilibrium price and label it *EQ* in Figure 2.5.
4. What is the amount of shortage (surplus) that would exist at a price of $1?

Figure 2.5. Market-supply and market-demand curves for buyers and sellers

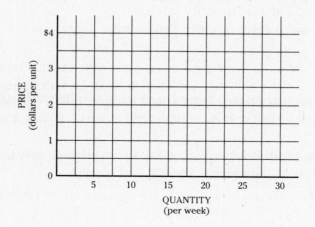

Exercise 4

This exercise provides several examples of events that would shift demand or supply curves. It is similar to the exercise at the end of Chapter 2 in the text.

Choose the letter of the appropriate diagram in Figure 2.6 that best describes the type of shift that would occur in each of the following situations. The shifts are viewed as occurring in the market for U.S. defense goods. (*Hint:* Ask yourself if the change occurs initially through the buyers or the

Exercise 4

This exercise provides several examples of events that would shift demand or supply curves. It is similar to the exercise at the end of Chapter 2 in the text.

Choose the letter of the appropriate diagram in Figure 2.6 that best describes the type of shift that would occur in each of the following situations. The shifts are viewed as occurring in the market for U.S. defense goods. (*Hint*: Ask yourself if the change occurs initially through the buyers or the sellers. Then look for the determinant that is changing. Finally, ask yourself how the quantity or price should change due to the hypothesized event. Use common sense. With these three pieces of information it should be possible to determine the shift that occurs. The nonprice determinants of demand are tastes and preferences, incomes, buyer expectations, prices and availability of other goods, and number of buyers. The nonprice determinants of supply are technology, price and availability of resources, expectations, taxes, and number of suppliers.)

Figure 2.6 . Shifts of curves

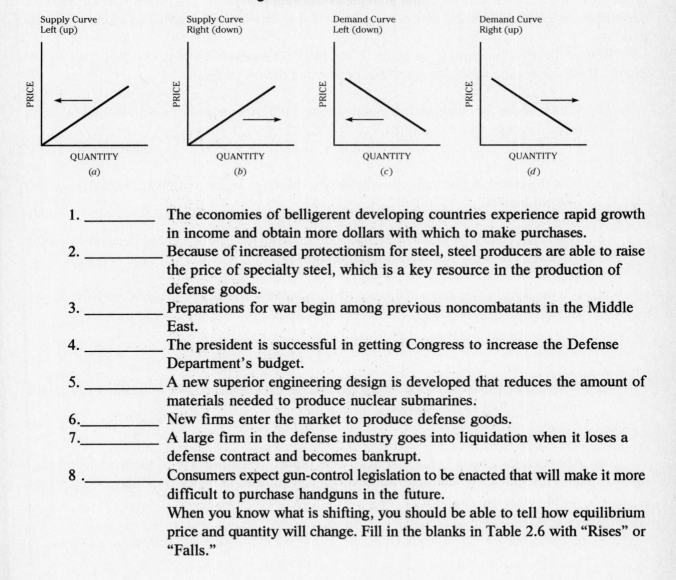

1. _____ The economies of belligerent developing countries experience rapid growth in income and obtain more dollars with which to make purchases.

2. _____ Because of increased protectionism for steel, steel producers are able to raise the price of specialty steel, which is a key resource in the production of defense goods.

3. _____ Preparations for war begin among previous noncombatants in the Middle East.

4. _____ The president is successful in getting Congress to increase the Defense Department's budget.

5. _____ A new superior engineering design is developed that reduces the amount of materials needed to produce nuclear submarines.

6. _____ New firms enter the market to produce defense goods.

7. _____ A large firm in the defense industry goes into liquidation when it loses a defense contract and becomes bankrupt.

8. _____ Consumers expect gun-control legislation to be enacted that will make it more difficult to purchase handguns in the future.

When you know what is shifting, you should be able to tell how equilibrium price and quantity will change. Fill in the blanks in Table 2.6 with "Rises" or "Falls."

31

Table 2.6. Response of equilibrium price and quantity to shifts in market supply and demand

Type of shift (ceteris paribus)	Equilibrium price	Equilibrium quantity
Market supply shifts leftward	_____	_____
Market supply shifts rightward	_____	_____
Market demand shifts leftward	_____	_____
Market demand shifts rightward	_____	_____

Exercise 5

The media often provide information about supply and demand shifts. Using one of the articles in the text, this exercise will show the kind of information to look for. If your professor makes a newspaper assignment from the *Instructor's Manual*, this exercise will provide an example of how to do it.

Reread the Headline article on page 39 in Chapter 2 entitled "Surplus Punches Hole in Oil Price". Then answer the following questions concerning the oil market:

1. Which of the four diagrams in Figure 2.6 (p. 31) best represents the shift caused by Iraq's rebuilding of its port facilities?

a   b   c   d   (circle one)

2. Find the sentence that indicates whether the market is an international, national, regional, or local market.

3. What single word or phrase describes the change in the determinant of demand or supply that has caused the shift you chose in Figure 2.6?

4. Is it the buyer or the seller of crude oil who is initially affected by the change? How do you know?

5. What phrase (no more than a sentence) indicates the change in price or quantity that results from rebuilding export facilities?

6. Although the article indicates prices were headed down because of the market surplus, does it provide any indication about which determinants of demand and supply caused the world surplus to develop?

Crossword Puzzle

Select the economic term in the following list that corresponds with each of the definitions and descriptions below. Then fit the term or one of the words within it into the crossword puzzle at the numbers indicated. Some of the words in the list do not fit the puzzle.

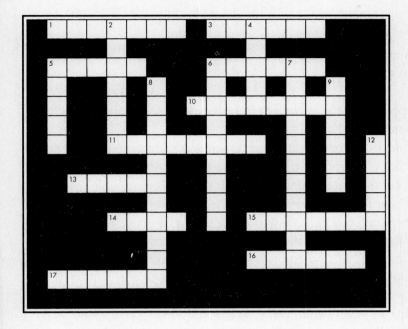

ceteris paribus
command
 economy
demand
demand curve
demand
 schedule
equilibrium
 price
factor market
government
 failure
invisible hand
laissez faire
market
 demand
market
 mechanism

market
 shortage
market supply
market surplus
opportunity
 cost
price ceiling
price floor
product
 market
shift in
 demand
shift in supply
supply

Across

1. What occurs when market price is above the market-equilibrium price level.
3. Where resources are exchanged for money.
5. A French way of saying "let alone."
6. The total quantity that all sellers in a market are willing and able to make available at various prices.
10. A table that shows the relationship between prices and the quantities a buyer is willing and able to buy at various prices.
11. What occurs when market price is below the market-equilibrium price level.
13. Changes in tastes, incomes, or expectations cause this to happen.
14. What guides market prices if the government does not interfere.
15. Intervention that does not improve market outcomes.
16. The total quantity demanded by all of the individual buyers in a market at every price.
17. The quantities a seller is willing and able to sell at various prices.

Down

2. A Latin term meaning "all other things being equal."
4. A graph representing the quantities that buyers are willing to buy at various prices, *ceteris paribus.*
5. A government limitation on prices set above the market-equilibrium price.
6. When prices are determined by buyers and sellers in a market, the economy is using this.

7. When quantity demanded equals quantity supplied, this is established.
8. The value of the best alternative that must be forgone as a result of the decision to use resources in a particular way.
9. What a buyer is willing and able to buy at various prices.
12. A government limitation on prices set below the market-equilibrium price.

Common Errors

The first statement in each "common error" below is incorrect. Each incorrect statement is followed by a corrected version and an explanation.

1. If a large number of people petition the government in order to get something, then there is a large demand for that item. WRONG!
If a large number of people desire a commodity *and have the ability to pay for it,* then there is a large demand for that commodity in a particular time period. RIGHT!
People want something, but there is no "demand" for it unless they are able to pay for it. Economists use the word "demand" in a way that is quite different from normal usage. People who want (desire; have preferences, a taste or a liking for) a commodity are seen as going to a market to purchase the commodity with money or through bartering. As economists use the word, "demand" has no connotation of stridency or imperiously claiming the right to something when a person hasn't the ability to buy it.

2. Market price is the same thing as equilibrium price. WRONG!
The market price moves by trial and error (via the market mechanism) toward the equilibrium price. RIGHT!
When demand and supply curves shift, the market is temporarily out of equilibrium. The price may move along a demand or supply curve toward the new equilibrium.

3. Since the quantity bought must equal the quantity sold, every market is always in equilibrium by definition. WRONG!
Although quantity bought equals quantity sold, there may be shortages or surpluses. RIGHT!
Although the quantity *actually* bought does equal the quantity *actually* sold, there may still be buyers who *are willing and able* to buy more of the good at the market price (shortages exist) or sellers who are willing and able to sell more of the good at the market price (surpluses exist). If the market price is above the equilibrium price, there will be queues of goods (inventories). Prices will be lowered by sellers toward the equilibrium price. If the market price is below the equilibrium price, there will be queues of buyers (shortages). Prices will be bid up by buyers toward the equilibrium price.

4. The intersection of the supply and demand curves determines how much of a good or service will actually be exchanged and the actual price of the exchange. WRONG!
The intersection of supply and demand curves shows only where buyers and sellers *intend* and have the *ability* to exchange the same amount of a commodity. RIGHT!

34

Many institutional interferences may prevent the market from ever reaching the equilibrium point, where supply and demand curves intersect. All that can be said is that, given a free market, prices and production will tend to move toward equilibrium levels.

5. A change in price changes the demand for goods by consumers. WRONG!
A change in price changes the quantity demanded by consumers in a given time period. RIGHT!
   Economists differentiate between the terms "quantity demanded" and "demand." A change in the quantity demanded usually refers to a movement along the demand curve due to a change in price or production rate. A change in demand refers to a shift of the demand curve due to a change in incomes, tastes, prices or variability of other goods, or expectations.

6. A change in price changes the supply of goods produced by a firm. WRONG!
A change in price changes the quantity of a good supplied by a firm in a given time period. RIGHT!
   Economists differentiate between the terms "quantity supplied" and "supply." A change in the quantity supplied usually refers to a movement along a supply curve due to a change in price or production rate. A change in supply refers to a shift of the supply curve due to a change in technology, prices of resources, number of sellers, other goods, expectations, or taxes.

7. A rise in the supply curve is the same as an increase in supply. WRONG!
An upward shift in the supply curve implies a decrease in supply. RIGHT!
   In Figure 2.7 the rise of the supply curve from S_1 to S_2 will result in a fall in quantity from Q_1 to Q_2 at any price, P^*. Supply is *lower*. A fall in the supply curve means an increase in supply.

Figure 2.7

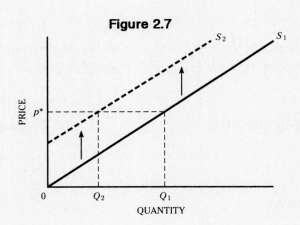

Be careful: When a shift in the supply curve is mentioned, it may help to think of the shift as a movement to the left or right, not up or down.

8. Surpluses and shortages are determinants of demand and supply that shift demand and supply curves. WRONG!

Surpluses and shortages often result from shifts of demand or supply curves, but they do not cause such shifts themselves. RIGHT!

Surpluses or shortages may appear in a market if the market price does not adjust to the equilibrium price. If there is a shift in demand or supply, shortages or surpluses may temporarily result until the market price reaches its equilibrium.

■ ANSWERS ■

Key-Term Review

1. market demand
2. demand schedule
3. opportunity cost
4. market supply
5. laissez faire

6. demand
7. supply
8. equilibrium price
9. shift in demand
10. demand curve

11. market mechanism
12. market shortage
13. product market
14. market surplus
15. factor market

16. *ceteris paribus*
17. law of demand
18. law of supply
19. price ceiling
    price floor
20. government failure

True or False

1. F	4. T	7. F	10. F	13. F	16. T	19. F
2. T	5. F	8. T	11. T	14. T	17. T	20. F
3. T	6. F	9. T	12. T	15. T	18. T	

Multiple Choice

1. a	4. c	7. c	10. a	13. c	16. c	19. b	22. c
2. b	5. d	8. a, d	11. a	14. c	17. d	20. b	23. d
3. c	6. c	9. c	12. b	15. d	18. d	21. d	

24. b *Ceteris paribus* does not indicate if markets are allowed to work or not. Other topics include (a) structure for controlling the economy, (c) determinants of supply, and (d) determinants of demand.

Problems and Applications

Exercise 1

1. **Table 2.1 Answer**

p	q
$1	20
3	10

2. **Figure 2.1 Answer**

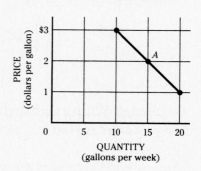

36

3. Table 2.2 Answer

p	q
$1	20,000
3	10,000

4. Figure 2.2 Answer

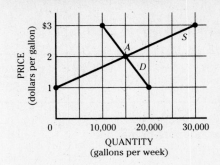

5. Table 2.3 Answer

p	q
$1	0
3	1,500

6. Figure 2.3 Answer

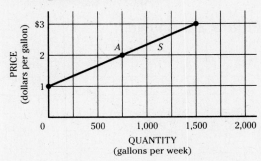

7. Table 2.4 Answer

p	q
$1	0
3	30,000

8. See Figure 2.2 answer.
9. b
10. d

Exercise 2

1. b

2. Figure 2.4 Answer

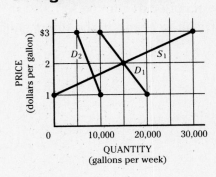

3. T
4. c
5. b
6. b
7. d
8. d
9. b

Exercise 3

1. Table 2.5 Answer

	Price			
	$4	$3	$2	$1
Buyers Total market quantity demanded	5	7.5	10	12.5
Sellers Total market quantity supplied	30	20	10	0

2. Figure 2.5 Answer

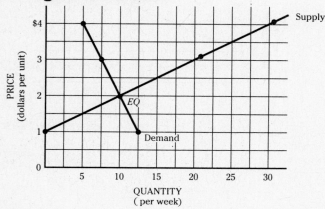

QUANTITY (per week)

3. See point *EQ* in Figure 2.5.

4. Since the quantity supplied is zero at a price of $1, the *shortage* is the same as the quantity demanded (12.5 units).

Exercise 4

1. d A rise in income shifts the demand curve upward (to the right).
2. a An increase in the price of a resource shifts the supply curve upward (to the left).
3. d An increase in the number of buyers shifts the demand curve upward (to the right).
4. d A larger budget (income) for defense shifts the demand curve upward (to the right).
5. b An improvement in technology shifts the supply curve downward (to the right.)
6. b An increase in the number of suppliers shifts the supply curve downward (to the right).
7. a A decrease in the number of suppliers shifts the supply curve to the left.
8. d Buyers' expectations that guns will be more difficult to obtain in the future shift the demand curve upward (to the right) today.

9. Table 2.6 Answer

Type of shift (ceteris paribus)	Equilibrium price	Equilibrium quantity
Market supply shifts leftward	Rises	Falls
Market supply shifts rightward	Falls	Rises
Market demand shifts leftward	Falls	Falls
Market demand shifts rightward	Rises	Rises

Exercise 5

1. b   Supply shifts to the right because there will be more oil available at every price.
2. The fact that the Gulf war and United Nations embargoes can affect West oil prices suggests an international market. Also, the article describes a world surplus.
3. The first sentence states "restoring the capability of supplying another 1 million barrels a day."
4. Iraq is a seller of oil. The article specifically says its rebuilding increases its capability of "supplying" oil.
5. Quantity (see quotation in #3 above).
6. No, the article gives no information on the major theme of the article, "surplus punches hole in oil price." Such incomplete information is likely when the media deliberately keep news short. Incompleteness is an important reason for using the *Wall Street Journal, New York Times, Business Week*, and other news sources that provide more background information.

Crossword Puzzle Answer

Across

1. market *surplus*
3. *factor* market
5. laissez *faire*
6. *market* supply
10. demand *schedule*
11. *market shortage*
13. *shift* in demand
14. invisible *hand*
15. government *failure*
16. market *demand*
17. *supply*

Down

2. ceteris *paribus*
4. demand *curve*
5. price *floor*
6. market *mechanism*
7. *equilibrium* price
8. *opportunity* cost
9. *demand*
12. *price* ceiling

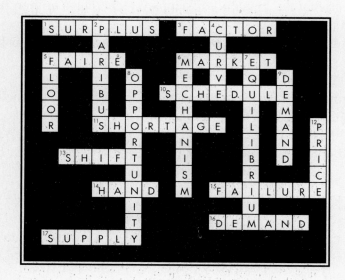

40

CHAPTER 3

The U.S. Economy

Quick Review

The economy must answer the WHAT, HOW, and FOR WHOM questions. Specifically, it determines:

- WHAT goods and services are produced?
- HOW are the goods and services produced?
- FOR WHOM are the goods and services produced?

To know how the economy answers these questions, we must be able to measure economic activity. The most frequently used measure of output is the gross domestic product (GDP), which is the total market value of all final services produced in a country during a given period of time. The GDP measurements are routinely adjusted for inflation using a price index. The inflation-adjusted GDP is the value of output measured in constant prices and is called the "real" GDP.

By making comparisons with other economies we can often get a picture of how our own economy ranks. The U.S. output is approximately one-fourth of the world's total output. The U.S. GDP per capita is about five times the world's average. The high level of U.S. GDP per capita reflects high productivity because we have an abundance of resources, an educated labor force, modern technology, and skilled managers of American workers.

The major uses of total output are categorized according to the four major market participants: consumers, business firms, government, and foreign buyers and sellers. Consumer goods and services continue to be the largest component of America's GDP. Investment goods account for only 15 percent of total output. Small businesses like proprietorships and partnerships outnumber corporations nearly 5 to 1, but corporations produce nearly 90 percent of total output. The service industries continue to grow faster than goods-producing industries.

Personal income is unequally distributed among households. Wages and salaries make up nearly three-fourths of total income in the United States. The households in the highest income class receive nearly ten times more than the average low-income household, and the tax system does not dramatically redistribute income. However, government transfer payments (like social security and welfare, which are the largest income transfers) do significantly redistribute income and thereby alter the answer to the FOR WHOM question. Overall, the income transfer system gives lower income households greater command over goods and services than the market itself would provide but is still unable to eliminate poverty and income inequality.

Learning Objectives

After reading Chapter 3 and doing the following exercises, you should:	True or false	Multiple choice	Problems and applications	Common errors	Pages in the text
1. Understand that every economy must answer the WHAT, HOW, and FOR WHOM questions.	17, 18, 19				51
2. Understand how an economy's gross domestic product (GDP) is the answer to the WHAT question.	1, 9, 14, 15, 16	9, 10	1	1, 2	52-54
3. Be able to calculate GDP by analyzing the expenditures made by the market participants.	10, 11, 12		1, 2	2	54-57
4. Be able to distinguish between the types of expenditures made by the market participants.	1		2		54-57
5. Understand that the answer to the HOW question deals with the efficiency with which the GDP is produced.		11			57
6. Be able to articulate the importance of several historical economic trends in the U.S. economy.	3, 4, 7, 13	1, 12, 13			57-59
7. Know the differentiating characteristics of partnerships, proprietorships, and corporations and their role in the U.S. economy.					59-61
8. Be able to discuss the FOR WHOM question using the functional distribution of income and the personal distribution of income.	16, 17, 18, 19	14, 16	4		61-65
9. Know the impact of the tax and transfer system in answering the FOR WHOM question.	2, 5, 6, 8, 20, 21, 22, 23	3, 4, 5, 6, 7, 8, 15	3		65-66

Key-Term Review

Review the following terms; if you are not sure of the meaning of any term, write out the definition and check it against the Glossary in the text.

economic growth

exports

factors of production

functional distribution of income

gross domestic product

imports

income transfers

in-kind income

investment

per capita GDP

personal distribution of income

productivity

progressive tax

real GDP

regressive tax

Fill in the blank following each of the statements below with the appropriate term from the list above.

1. Multiplying the quantities of all new final goods and services produced by their prices makes it possible to compute their total market value, which is called the .... 1. _____

2. The _____ has been corrected for price ... 2. _____
   increases and an increase in this quantity over time indicates that there is _____. .... _____

3. As output expands, households receive higher incomes and purchase more_____ from ... 3. _____
   foreign countries.

4. To make comparisons of economic welfare between different countries, GDP is divided by a country's population; the result is called the .... 4. _____

5. The _____ include capital, labor and ..... 5. _____
   land.

6. The purchase of new capital is referred to as _____. It helps to increase ....6. _____
   _____ which is the amount of output ..... _____
   produced per unit of labor.

7. As labor productivity increases, American _____ can become more competitive ... 7. _____
   in foreign markets.

8. The _____ shows how income is .... 8. _____
   divided among the factors of production.

9. The _____ shows how income is .... 9. _____
   divided among income classes.

10. Because many households fall below the poverty line, the government makes _____ .10. _____
    to those who need help.

11. _____ is provided directly by government ..... 11. _____
    to those in need without going through the marketplace.

12. When people with higher taxable incomes
    pay a larger percentage of that income in
    taxes, the government is using a .... 12. _____
13. However, governments often find it easier to
    collect a sales tax, which tends to be a .... 13. _____

True or False: *Circle your choice.*

T F 1. The term "public sector" refers only to federal government purchases of goods and services.

T F 2. Income transfers are payments to individuals for which nothing is currently rendered in return.

T F 3. When federal government expenditures exceed federal tax revenues, the national debt grows.

T F 4. State and local government employment exceeds federal government employment.

T F 5. The federal income tax is progressive because the tax rates increase as taxable income increases.

T F 6. Progressive tax rates mean a larger fraction of income is taken in the form of taxes as income increases.

T F 7. The federal government's share of the U.S. economy has grown in both relative and absolute terms since the 1950s.

T F 8. State and local property taxes tend to be regressive.

T F 9. Per capita GDP is commonly used to compare economic welfare across international boundaries.

T F 10. Comparisons of per capita GDP across international boundaries do not provide information on the distribution of GDP within each country.

T F 11. In periods of rising prices, real GDP will rise more slowly than GDP in current dollars.

T F 12. In periods of falling prices, GDP in current dollars must be inflated to obtain real GDP.

T F 13. The United States is among the leading Western countries in improving average yearly productivity.

T F 14. When an economy moves from a point within its production-possibilities curve to a point on its production-possibilities curve, no economic growth takes place.

T F 15. Once an economy is on its production-possibilities curve, further increases in output require an expansion of productive capacity.

T F 16. Growth in GDP per capita is achieved when population grows more rapidly than GDP.

T F 17. Wealth and income are the same thing.

T F 18. A person can have a great deal of wealth but have very little income.

T F 19. Income is a flow and wealth is a stock.

T F 20. Marginal tax rates must increase as income increases for a tax to be progressive, *ceteris paribus.*

T F 21. The functional distribution of income focuses on the size of the shares going to labor, capital, and land.

T   F   22.   The top 20 percent of income recipients in the United States get about one-fifth of the total income.

T   F   23.   Since income is simply a dollar measure of output produced, the functional distribution of income is synonymous with the personal distribution of income.

Multiple Choice: *Select the correct answer.*

_____   1.   When federal government expenditures exceed federal government revenues, the effect is:
(a) To increase federal government borrowing.
(b) To increase the national debt.
(c) To increase the interest expense on the federal government's debt, *ceteris paribus*.
(d) All of the above.

_____   2.   The opportunity costs of public-sector activity:
(a) Can be measured in terms of the private-market activity forgone.
(b) Are represented as the slope of a production-possibilities curve showing public versus private goods.
(c) Reflect the limited resources available for public and private activity.
(d) All of the above statements are true.

_____   3.   Which of the following can be classified as a regressive tax?
(a) The federal corporate income tax.
(b) The federal personal income tax.
(c) The federal gasoline tax.
(d) All of the above.

_____   4.   Which of the following is an example of a progressive tax?
(a) The excise tax on distilled spirits.
(b) The federal tax on gasoline.
(c) The federal personal income tax.
(d) None of the above.

_____   5.   A tax is regressive if it takes a:
(a) Larger number of dollars as income rises.
(b) Larger number of dollars as income falls.
(c) Smaller fraction of income as income falls.
(d) Smaller fraction of income as income rises.

_____   6.   The social security tax is:
(a) A progressive tax at all income levels.
(b) A regressive tax above a certain income level.
(c) A proportional tax at all income levels.
(d) None of the above.

_____   7.   Suppose that if your income is $10,000, your tax is $1,000, but if your income is $50,000, your tax is $4,000. Such a tax is:
(a) Regressive.
(b) Progressive.
(c) Proportional.
(d) Not enough information is given to answer the question.

8. The tuition paid by college students is a:
   (a) Progressive tax.
   (b) Regressive tax.
   (c) Flat rate tax.
   (d) Price of a scarce good.

9. If both the prices and the quantities of all final goods and services produced doubled from one year to the next and population remained constant, then:
   (a) GDP in current dollars would be four times as large in the second year as in the first.
   (b) Real GDP would be twice as large in the second year as in the first.
   (c) On the average, the population could be twice as well off in the second year as in the first.
   (d) All of the above would be the case.

10. In periods of rising prices, percentage increases in GDP will:
    (a) Exceed percentage increases in real GDP.
    (b) Equal percentage increases in real GDP.
    (c) Be less than percentage increases in real GDP.
    (d) Not enough information is given to answer the question.

11. Which of the following would likely contribute to an improvement in the productivity of labor?
    (a) Greater expenditures on training and education.
    (b) Policies to stimulate the saving and investment process.
    (c) Greater expenditures on research and development.
    (d) All of the above.

12. Which of the following contributes to advances in productivity?
    (a) Improvement in management.
    (b) Increases in capital per worker.
    (c) Spending on research and development.
    (d) All of the above.

13. Which of the following may be cited as a cause of the U.S. economy's poor performance in advancing labor productivity?
    (a) A relatively low saving rate.
    (b) Changes in the age-sex composition of the labor force.
    (c) The trend away from manufacturing and toward services in our industrial structure.
    (d) All of the above.

14. The personal distribution of income is basically the answer to:
    (a) The WHAT question for society.
    (b) The HOW question for society.
    (c) The FOR WHOM question for society.
    (d) None of the above.

15. Which of the following is typically a progressive tax?
    (a) A sales tax.
    (b) A property tax.
    (c) The social security tax.
    (d) None of the above.

16. The market mechanism in the United States generates a distribution of income that is viewed as:
    (a) Equal, since everyone gets the same income.
    (b) Equitable, since public policy does not tamper with it.
    (c) Both equal and equitable, since they mean the same thing.
    (d) Inequitable, apparently, since we change it through activities of the public sector.

Problems and Applications

Exercise 1

This exercise shows the relationship between nominal GDP and real GDP, and it provides practice in computing percentage changes over time.

Each January the president has the Council of Economic Advisers prepare an economic report on the state of the U.S. economy called *The Economic Report of the President.* National-income accounts* form the basis of much of the analysis that goes into this report. It summarizes the essential features of the economy's performance and the policy initiatives that are likely to be undertaken. This exercise shows the kind of information that is developed for this publication.

Table 3.1 presents the Commerce Department's estimates of GDP.

1. Table 3.1 shows the real GDP and a price index for each of the years indicated. Calculate nominal GDP (GDP unadjusted for price changes for each year), and write it in the appropriate column.

---

*The Commerce Department provides information on the national accounts in the *Survey of Current Business, Statistical Abstract of the United States,* and other readily available publications.

Table 3.1. Real GDP and per capita GDP, 1980-91

(1) Year	(2) Price index	(3) Real GDP (in billions of dollars per year)	(4) Nominal GDP (in billions of dollars per year)	(5) Percentage growth in nominal GDP	(6) Percentage growth in real GDP	(7) U.S. population (in millions)	(8) Real GDP per capita
1980	71.7	3,776.3	$_____			227.8	$_____
1981	78.9	3,843.1	_____	_____	_____	230.1	_____
1982	83.8	3,760.3	_____	_____	_____	232.5	_____
1983	87.2	3,906.6	_____	_____	_____	234.8	_____
1984	91.0	4,148.5	_____	_____	_____	237.0	_____
1985	94.4	4,279.8	_____	_____	_____	239.3	_____
1986	96.9	4,404.5	_____	_____	_____	241.6	_____
1987	100.0	4,539.9	_____	_____	_____	243.9	_____
1988	103.9	4,718.6	_____	_____	_____	246.3	_____
1989	108.4	4,836.9	_____	_____	_____	248.8	_____
1990	112.9	4,884.9	_____	_____	_____	251.5	_____
1991	117.0	4,848.4	_____	_____	_____	254.2	_____

Source: *The Economic Report of the President,* 1992.

2. From the information in Table 3.1, calculate the percentage growth in nominal and real GDP for each of the years 1980-91 and insert your answers in the appropriate columns. Use the following formula:

$$\text{Percentage growth in real GDP} = \frac{\text{GDP}_{n+1} - \text{GDP}_n}{\text{GDP}_n} \times 100\%$$

where n = beginning year
$n + 1$ = next year

For example, from 1987 to 1988 the real GDP increased by the following percentage:

$$\frac{\text{GDP}_{n+1} - \text{GDP}_n}{\text{GDP}_n} \times 100\% = \frac{\$4,718.6 - \$4,540.0}{\$4,718.6} \times 100\% = 3.8\%$$

3. T   F   When nominal GDP grows, real GDP must grow.
4. By what nominal dollar amount did nominal GDP grow from 1980 to 1991? $_____
5. By what constant-dollar amount did real GDP grow from 1980 to 1991? $_____
6. The U.S. population for the years 1980-91 is presented in column 7 of Table 3.1. Calculate the real GDP per capita in column 8.
7. T   F   When real GDP rises, real GDP per capita must also rise.

48

Exercise 2

This problem is designed to help you learn the way the national-income aggregates are determined and to reinforce your understanding of their relationship to one another.

Table 3.2. U.S. national-income aggregates, 1991 (billions of dollars per year)

Expenditure categories		Percent of total output
Personal consumption expenditures	$3,886.5	_____
Gross private domestic investment	725.3	_____
Exports	593.3	_____
Imports	620.4	_____
Federal government purchases	445.1	_____
State and local government purchases	641.8	_____

Source: *The Economic Report of the President,* 1992.

1. Calculate the percent of total output accounted for by each of the expenditure categories in Table 3.2. Then check your answers using Figure 3.3 on page 56 in the text. Figures will not be exact due to rounding.

2. Are net exports ($X - M$) positive or negative in Table 3.2? _____

3. T   F   When net exports are negative, an economy consumes more than it produces.

Exercise 3

The following problem shows how to determine whether a tax is progressive or regressive. The problem is similar to the one at the end of Chapter 3 in the text.

Suppose that Table 3.3 describes the spending and saving behavior of individuals at various income levels.

1. Assume that a tax of 40 percent is levied on savings and calculate the following:
   (a) The amount of taxes paid at each income level (column 3 of Table 3.3).

   (b) The fraction of income paid in taxes at each income level (column 4 of Table 3.3).

Table 3.3. Taxes on income and savings

(1) Income	(2) Total savings	(3) Savings tax (at 40 percent)	(4) Savings tax as percentage of income	(5) Income tax (at 10 percent)
$ 1,000	$ -50	$ _____	_____%	$_____
2,000	0	_____	_____	_____
3,000	50	_____	_____	_____
5,000	100	_____	_____	_____
10,000	1,000	_____	_____	_____
100,000	20,000	_____	_____	_____

2. Is the tax on savings progressive or regressive in relation to income?

3. Alternatively, assume that a flat-rate income tax of 10 percent is levied. Compute the amount of taxes paid at each income level (column 5 of Table 3.3).

4. Work problem 4 at the end of Chapter 3 in the text and then consider these questions: Which of the following—a flat-rate income tax, a tax on savings, or a tax on spending— would provide:

    (a) The greatest incentive for taxpayers to earn higher incomes?

    (b) The most equitable outcome if society wishes to redistribute income to the poor?

    (c) The most equitable outcome if society assumes that everyone should make the same percentage contribution to the maintenance of our government?

Exercise 4

This exercise provides practice in analyzing the personal distribution of both income and wealth.

The Federal Reserve Board conducts a survey of consumer finances every three years. They measure household wealth by computing each household's "net worth." In 1983, the richest 1 percent of American households had 31 percent of the wealth. By 1989, the richest 834,000 households, which constituted 1 percent of total U.S. households, had $5.74 trillion of the $15.5 trillion of total income, while the poorest 90 percent of the households had only $4.8 trillion.

1. What was the percentage of wealth owned by the richest 1 percent of the households in 1989?_____

2. T   F   From 1983 to 1989 the rich got richer.

3. What was the percentage of wealth owned by the poorest 90 percent of the households in 1989?_____

4. What is the total number of households? _____

5. Suppose we define the "next richest group" as the number of households who are not in the poorest 90 percent, or in the richest 1 percent, of all households. Determine the f following about this next richest group:

    (a) How many households are in this group?_____

    (b) How much wealth (in dollars) does this next richest group have?_____

    (c) What is the average wealth per household in this next richest group? _____

50

6. The same report showed that the top 1 percent of households had 10 percent of the income, the 9 percent next richest had 20 percent of the income, and the poorest 90 percent had 70 percent of the income. If these data were consistent and comparable with the income groups in Table 3.4 in the textbook on page 63, compute the percentage of income earned by the:

    (a) Richest 10 percent of households _____

    (b) Next richest 10 percent of households _____

7. There is _____ (greater, less, the same) inequality in the personal distribution of wealth than the personal distribution of income. How do you know? _____
_____

Common Errors

The first statement in each "common error" below is incorrect. Each incorrect statement is followed by a corrected version and an explanation.

1. Income and output are two entirely different things. WRONG!
   Income and output are two sides of the same coin. RIGHT!
       This is fundamental. Every time a dollar's worth of final spending takes place, the seller must receive a dollar's worth of income. It could not be otherwise. Remember, profits are used as a balancing item. Don't confuse the term "income" with the term "profit." Profits can be negative, whereas output for the economy cannot.

2. Comparisons of per capita GDP between countries tell you which population is better off. WRONG!
   Comparisons of per capita GDP between countries are only indicators of which population is better off. RIGHT!
       Simple comparisons of per capita GDP ignore how the GDP is distributed. A country with a very high per capita GDP that is unequally distributed may well provide a standard of living that is below that of another country with a lower per capita GDP which is more equally distributed. There are other problems with comparisons of per capita GDP as a result of exchange-rate distortions, and differences in mix of output in two countries, and how the economy is organized. GDP per capita is an indicator only of the amount of goods and services each person could have, not what they do have.

3. Income and wealth are the same thing. WRONG!
   Income and wealth mean distinctly different things. RIGHT!
       The distinction between income and wealth is critical to sound economic analysis. Income is a flow and has a time dimension. For example, one states one's income in dollars per year. Wealth is a stock and is measured at a point in time; for example, you may say you have $5,000 in your savings account today. Some people with apparently great wealth may have very little income, as in the case of someone who owns land known to contain oil. On the other hand, someone who has much income may have little wealth; some famous entertainers earn large incomes, save little (accumulate no wealth), and wind up

in bankruptcy. Of course, wealth and income may go hand in hand: the incomes of some oil magnates flow from their wealth. But clearly the two terms imply different things about one's economic well-being and command over goods and services.

4. Equity and equality of income distribution mean the same thing. WRONG!
Equity and equality of income distribution mean different things. RIGHT!

Many arguments over the division of the income pie, whether at the national level, the corporate level, or the university level, are laced with the terms *equity* and *equality* used interchangeably. They are not interchangeable. Equality of income distribution means that each person has an equal share. Equity of income distribution implies something about fairness. In a free society some will surely be more productive than others at doing what society wants done. The brain surgeon's services have greater value than the hairdresser's. The surgeon's income will exceed that of the hairdresser—that is, they'll be unequal. But is that inequitable? This is a matter of judgment. It's safe to say, however, that if one were not allowed to keep some of the rewards for being more productive than average, our economy would suffer. An equitable distribution of income in our society will require some inequality. How much? There is no sure answer to that question, only a series of compromises.

■ ANSWERS ■

Key-Term Review

1. gross domestic product	5. factors of production	9. personal distribution
2. real GDP	6. investment	of income
economic growth	productivity	10. income transfers
3. imports	7. exports	11. in-kind income
4. per capita GDP	8. functional distribution	12. progressive tax
	of income	13. regressive tax

True or False

1. F	5. T	9. T	12. F	15. T	18. T	21. T
2. T	6. T	10. T	13. F	16. F	19. T	22. F
3. T	7. F	11. T	14. F	17. F	20. T	23. F
4. T	8. T					

Multiple Choice

1. d	4. c	7. a	10. a	13. d	15. d
2. d	5. d	8. d	11. d	14. c	16. d
3. c	6. b	9. d	12. d		

Problems and Applications

Exercise 1

1. Table 3.1 Answer

(1) Year	(2) Price index	(3) Real GDP (in billions of dollars per year)	(4) Nominal GDP (in billions of dollars per year)	(5) Percentage growth in nominal GDP	(6) Percentage growth in real GDP	(7) U.S. population (in millions)	(8) Real GDP per capita
1980	71.7	3,776.3	$2,707.6	–	–	227.8	$16,577
1981	78.9	3,843.1	3,032.2	12.0	1.8	230.1	16,702
1982	83.8	3,760.3	3,151.1	3.9	-2.2	232.5	16,173
1983	87.2	3,906.8	3,406.7	8.1	3.9	234.8	16,639
1984	91.0	4,148.5	3,775.1	10.8	6.2	237.0	17,504
1985	94.4	4,279.8	4,040.1	7.0	3.2	239.3	17,885
1986	96.9	4,404.5	4,268.0	5.6	2.9	241.6	18,231
1987	100.0	4,540.0	4,540.0	6.4	3.1	243.9	18,614
1988	103.9	4,718.6	4,902.6	8.0	3.9	246.3	19,158
1989	108.4	4,836.9	5,243.2	6.9	2.5	248.8	19,441
1990	112.9	4,884.9	5,515.1	5.2	1.0	251.5	19,423
1991	117.0	4,848.4	5,672.6	2.9	-0.8	254.2	19,073

Source: *The Economic Report of the President,* 1992.

2. See Table 3.1 answer, columns 5, 6
3. F
4. $2,965.0 billion
5. $1,072.1 billion
6. See Table 3.1 answer, column 8
7. F

Exercise 2

1. Table 3.2 Answer

Expenditure categories		Percent of total output
Personal consumption expenditures	$3,886.5	68.9
Gross private domestic investment	725.3	12.9
Exports	593.3	10.8
Imports	620.4	11.1
Federal government purchases	445.1	7.5
State and local government purchases	641.8	11.2

Source: *The Economic Report of the President,* 1992.

2. Negative
3. T

53

Exercise 3

1a and b.   See columns 3 and 4.

Table 3.3 Answer

(1)	(2)	(3)	(4)	(5)
		Savings tax	Savings tax as	Income tax
Income	Total savings	(at 40 percent)	percentage of income	(at 10 percent)
$ 1,000	$ -50	$ -20	2.0%	$ 100
2,000	0	0	0.0	200
3,000	50	20	0.67	300
5,000	100	40	0.8	500
10,000	1,000	400	4.0	1,000
100,000	20,000	8,000	8.0	10,000

2. Progressive. With greater income a higher percentage of income goes to taxes (from 0 to 8 percent in column 4).
3. See Table 3.3 answer, column 5.
4. (a) A regressive tax such as the tax on spending would provide an incentive for people to earn higher incomes because a smaller percentage of their income will be taxed at higher income levels.
   (b) A progressive tax such as the tax on saving would provide the most equitable outcome if society wishes to redistribute income to the poor.
   (c) If equity is defined in terms of equal contribution in terms of percentage of income to the maintenance of government, then the flat-rate income tax would be most equitable.

Exercise 4

1. 37% (= 5.74/15.5)
2. T
3. 31% (= 4.8/15.5)
4. If 1% of the households consists of 834,000 households, then the total number must be 100 times that number, or 83,400,000 households.
5. (a) Middle-class households are 9% (=100% - 90% - 1%) of the total (83,400,000), which is 7,506,000.
   (b) $4.96 trillion (=$15.5 - $5.74 - $4.8 trillion).
   (c) $660,000 per household.

6. (a) Since the highest 1% has 10% of the income and the next 9% have 20% of the income, the richest 10% of households have 30% of the income.
   (b) Since the richest 10% have 30% of the income, and the richest 20% have 46.3% of the income (according to Table 3.4 in the textbook), the second richest 10% earns the difference of 16.3% (=46.3% - 30%).
7. Greater. The richest 1% of households has a much larger percentage (37%) of the wealth than of the income (10%).

CHAPTER 4

Consumer Demand

Quick Review

Demand and supply were introduced in Chapter 2 to demonstrate how markets operate. In this chapter we look at demand in greater depth. (Supply is considered in Chapter 5.) Specifically, the chapter looks at the following questions:
- How do we decide how much of any good to buy?
- How does a change in price affect the quantity we purchase or the amount of money we spend on a good?
- What factors other than price affect our consumption patterns?

Other concepts are developed too, but these three questions organize our early discussion.

Demand refers to the willingness and ability of buyers to buy goods and services. It has nothing to do with the sellers of those goods or services or even with the availability of the goods or services. It refers only to buyers. In fact, demand can exist even if there are no purchases by buyers at all.

Demand for goods and services is more than just the desire for goods and services. When people starve as a result of a drought, they have the desire for food but not the ability to pay for it. Demand reflects both the willingness and the ability to buy goods and services. Consumers' tastes, their incomes, the prices (and availability) of other goods, and people's expectations (about tastes, incomes, and prices) determine what individuals are willing and able to buy. If any of these determinants of demand change, then the demand curve shifts. Shifts in the demand curve are likely to cause changes in price and quantities purchased in the marketplace. To understand the market, we must look carefully at tastes, incomes, prices, and expectations.

Utility theory helps to clarify much of what we know about consumer tastes and preferences. Consumers buy only those things that give them satisfaction or utility. As a consumer consumes more and more of any one product, other goods and services begin to look relatively more desirable. Here we see the law of diminishing marginal utility at work: as we consume more of a product, we receive smaller and smaller increments of pleasure from it.

The law of diminishing marginal utility translates readily into the law of demand. The law of demand asserts that we will be willing to buy increasing quantities of a product as its price falls; that is, an inverse relationship exists between quantity demanded and price. This law is graphically illustrated by a downward-sloping demand curve. The demand curve itself relates the quantity of a good demanded to its price, under the assumption that all other things are held constant *(ceteris paribus)*. The downward slope of the demand curve indicates that larger quantities of a good will be purchased at lower prices.

The demand curve gives information about the total revenue that a firm could receive. By computing the price elasticity of demand, the firm can even determine how its total revenue changes for a given change in price and how responsive quantity demanded is to a change in price.

Learning Objectives

After reading Chapter 4 and doing the following exercises, you should:	True or false	Multiple choice	Problems and applications	Common errors	Pages in the text
1. Be able to distinguish the demand for a good from the desire for it.	1	17			72-75
2. Know how the law of diminishing marginal utility and the law of demand relate to each other.	2, 5, 6, 7, 11	1, 2, 3, 5, 9, 19	2	1, 5	75-77
3. Be able to draw a demand curve from a demand schedule and create a demand schedule by looking at a demand curve.	3, 7	21	1	2	75-78
4. Be able to distinguish between a change in demand (a shift of the curve) and a change in quantity demanded (a movement along the demand curve).	3, 4, 12, 16	4, 5, 14, 21		7	80
5. Be able to show how any change in the price of a good, in the price of other goods, in incomes, tastes, or expectations will affect the demand curve.	13, 14, 16	4, 11, 12, 14, 15, 18, 19	3	6	80
6. Be able to compute the price elasticity of demand between two points on the demand curve.	8, 9, 10, 15		10	3, 4	78-80
7. Be able to determine on the basis of the elasticity of demand what will happen to total revenue when prices change.	15	6 ,7, 8, 13			80-82

Learning Objectives (con't.)	True or false	Multiple choice	Problems and applications	Common errors	Pages in the text
8. Know the determinants of elasticity and how they influence the elasticity coefficient.		20			82-83

Key-Term Review

Review the following terms; if you are not sure of the meaning of any term, write out the definition and check it against the Glossary in the text.

ceteris paribus	law of diminishing marginal utility	total revenue
demand	marginal utility	total utility
demand curve	market demand	utility
law of demand	price elasticity of demand	

Fill in the blank following each of the statements below with the appropriate term from the list above.

1. The total quantity of goods and services that the buyers in a market are willing and able to buy at alternative prices, *ceteris paribus,* is the .... 1. _____

2. "All other determinants of demand are held constant" is expressed by the phrase .... 2. _____

3. The change in quantity demanded in response to a change in price illustrates the .... 3. _____

4. If a firm raises prices 10 percent but people buy 20 percent less of its product, the firm experiences a decline in .... 4. _____

5. The decline in revenue because of the price increase could have been anticipated if the firm had known its .... 5. _____

6. As you drink more and more soda, you begin to feel less comfortable, in accordance with the .... 6. _____

7. The various quantities that people are willing and able to purchase at various prices in a given time period, *ceteris paribus,* is known as .... 7. _____

8. The inverse relationship of quantity and price is expressed graphically in a .... 8. _____

9. The satisfaction a person gains from consuming an extra unit of a product is .... 9. _____

10. Satisfaction is also known as .... 10. _____

11. The amount of satisfaction obtained from your
entire consumption of a product is known as ....11. _____

True or False: *Circle your choice.*

T F   1. It is not possible to draw a demand curve for a good or service if the good or service is not available at any price.

T F   2. The law of demand differs from the law of diminishing marginal utility in that it considers what a person is able to pay for a good or service, not just the person's desire for a good or service.

T F   3. In order to find the demand curve for a consumer, we can design an experiment in which all determinants of demand are held constant except for price. We locate the demand curve by observing the quantity of a good or service that the consumer is willing and able to buy at each price.

T F   4. A change in the quantity demanded occurs only when the demand curve shifts.

T F   5. According to the law of diminishing marginal utility, the total utility we obtain from a product decreases as we consume more of it.

T F   6. In general, that total utility we derive from consuming all products increases with the number of products we obtain.

T F   7. If the law of demand holds, the demand curve of a consumer must slope downward to the right.

T F   8. If demand is elastic, a rise in price raises total revenue.

T F   9. If the elasticity of demand is equal to 1, then a 1 percent increase in price will shift the demand curve 1 percent to the left.

T F   10. Since a flat (horizontal) demand curve is inelastic, consumers are unlikely to change their purchasing habits when the price changes.

T F   11. According to the law of demand, quantity demanded rises as price rises.

T F   12. When there are food riots because people are starving, the demand for food is increasing.

T F   13. By the law of demand, when people expect the price of a commodity to rise in the future, they buy less of the commodity in the present.

T F   14. When a buyer purchases a good, the demand for the good falls by the amount of the purchase.

T F   15. Elasticity of demand is constant along straight-line demand curves.

T F   16. A successful advertising campaign induces consumers to buy less of the product at any given price than before.

Multiple Choice: *Select the correct answer.*

_____ 1. The law of demand says that, *ceteris paribus:*
(a) The lower the price, the less buyers will purchase.
(b) The lower the price, the more buyers will purchase.
(c) The lower the income of a buyer, the more the buyer will purchase.
(d) The lower the income of a buyer, the less the buyer will purchase.

2. Which of the following statements exemplifies the law of diminishing marginal utility?
   (a) Garbage gives me no satisfaction, so I won't spend my income for any of it.
   (b) The more soda I drink, the more I want to drink.
   (c) The more I go to school, the more I want to do something else.
   (d) Since we need water more than we need diamonds, water is more valuable.

3. *Ceteris paribus* means (in demand theory):
   (a) Nothing is allowed to change.
   (b) The determinants of demand may change, but all else must be held constant.
   (c) Only one determinant (for example, price) is being changed while all other determinants remain unchanged.
   (d) Consumers try to keep all things constant so that prices will be lower.

4. Demand for soda would remain unchanged with:
   (a) A change in consumer income.
   (b) A change in the price of a substitute, such as mineral water.
   (c) A change in the price of soda itself.
   (d) A change in taste for soda.

5. A decline in the price of a good, *ceteris paribus,* causes:
   (a) A change in the demand for the good.
   (b) A change in quantity demanded of the good.
   (c) Both a and b.
   (d) None of the above.

6. Total revenue declines when demand is:
   (a) Elastic and price rises, causing a demand shift.
   (b) Elastic and price rises, causing a movement along the demand curve.
   (c) Inelastic and price rises, causing a demand shift.
   (d) Inelastic and price rises, causing a movement along the demand curve.

7. One of the airline industry's arguments against deregulation of air fares was that the resulting fall in prices would lower airline total revenue. Instead, total revenue rose. Assuming the increase in total revenue was due solely to the lower fares, it can be concluded that:
   (a) Airline representatives thought demand for plane trips was elastic.
   (b) Quantity demanded of airline service increased by a greater percentage than the percentage fall in price.
   (c) Demand for airline service increased with the fall in prices.
   (d) Airlines were more profitable after deregulation.

8. Each member of a union pays dues of 5 percent of his or her wage. In a contract negotiation the union succeeds in raising wages. But it finds that total union dues have actually decreased after the increased wage settlement. This is consistent with which of the following statements?
   (a) The demand for the labor services of union members is elastic.
   (b) Because of automation, more workers are hired.
   (c) Because of a recession, more workers are hired elsewhere.
   (d) It is consistent with all of the above statements.

9. Both the law of demand and the law of diminishing marginal utility:
   (a) State that quantity and price are inversely related.
   (b) Reflect declining increments of satisfaction from consuming additional units of product.
   (c) Reflect both the willingness and the ability of buyers to buy goods and services.
   (d) Can be illustrated by means of demand curves.

10. The concept of elasticity:
   (a) Compares the absolute change in quantity demanded with the percentage change in price.
   (b) Provides evidence on the way total revenue changes when price changes.
   (c) Shows what the slope of the demand curve is.
   (d) Does both a and b.

11. When a man is fired from his job and is unable to find another job:
   (a) His demand curve for goods should shift to the left.
   (b) His demand curve for goods should shift to the right.
   (c) He will move up along his demand curve.
   (d) He will move down along his demand curve.

12. When an employee is fired and cannot find work, the determinant of his or her demand for goods that has changed is:
   (a) Income.
   (b) Prices of related goods.
   (c) Tastes and preferences.
   (d) Technology.

13. If a state legislature wishes to raise revenue by increasing certain excise taxes, it would increase excise taxes on goods that:
   (a) Are illegal.
   (b) Are bought by rich people.
   (c) Have inelastic demand.
   (d) Have elastic demand.

14. A politician states that price controls would induce people to increase their demand, with resultant benefits to both firms and consumers. Which of the following criticisms of this claim is valid?
   (a) If demand for goods is inelastic, firms may receive lower total revenues.
   (b) The quantity demanded of goods will change, but demand will not change.
   (c) Businesses need to know how costs will change before they increase production.
   (d) All of the above criticisms are valid.

15. If consumers expect automakers to offer rebates next month, they will:
   (a) Increase their demand for cars today.
   (b) Decrease their demand for cars today.
   (c) Keep demand the same but increase the quantity demanded of cars.
   (d) Keep demand the same but decrease the quantity demanded of cars.

16. If a firm finds that demand for its product has become inelastic, it can:
   (a) Raise total revenue by lowering price.
   (b) Raise total revenue by raising price.
   (c) Lower total costs by lowering price.
   (d) Lower total costs by raising production rates.

17. Status and ego considerations in consumption are:
    (a) Economic determinants of demand.
    (b) Sociopsychiatric explanations of demand.
    (c) An example of income.
    (d) All of the above.
18. One Headline article in the text differentiates the spending habits of women and men: "Advertising for medical services and gifts may find a more receptive audience among women, whereas some restaurants may want to target men." What determinant of demand would most likely be involved?
    (a) Income.
    (b) Tastes.
    (c) Expectations.
    (d) Other goods (availability and prices).
19. *Ceteris paribus* means (in demand theory):
    (a) Nothing is allowed to change.
    (b) The determinants of demand may change, but all else must be held constant.
    (c) Only one determinant is being changed while all other determinants remain unchanged.
    (d) Consumers try to keep all things constant so that prices will be lower.
20. *Ceteris paribus,* as the number of substitutes for a good increases:
    (a) The absolute value of the price elasticity of demand should become more positive.
    (b) The price elasticity of demand should move closer to zero.
    (c) The cross-price elasticity of demand should become more negative.
    (d) The cross-price elasticity of demand should become less negative.
21. A change in a determinant of demand for a good causes:
    (a) A shift in demand.
    (b) A change in marginal utility.
    (c) A change in a consumer's willingness or ability to buy the good.
    (d) All of the above.

Problems and Applications

Exercise 1

This exercise will help you to draw demand curves from demand schedules. It should also give you practice in constructing market-demand curves.
1. Market demand is:
   (a) The total quantity of a good or service that people are willing and able to buy at alternative prices in a given period of time, *ceteris paribus.*
   (b) The sum of individual demands.
   (c) Represented as the horizontal sum of individual demand curves.
   (d) All of the above.
2. Table 4.1 presents a *hypothetical* demand schedule for cars manufactured in the United States.

Table 4.1. Demand for U.S. cars

Price	Number of new U.S. cars (millions per year)
$10,000	9.0
9,000	10.0

Graph this demand curve in Figure 4.1.

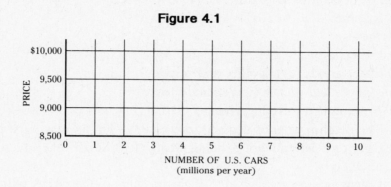

Figure 4.1

3. Table 4.2 presents a similar demand schedule for imported cars.

Table 4.2. Demand for foreign cars

Price	Number of new foreign cars (millions per year)
$10,000	1.0
9,000	2.0

Graph this demand curve in Figure 4.2.

Figure 4.2

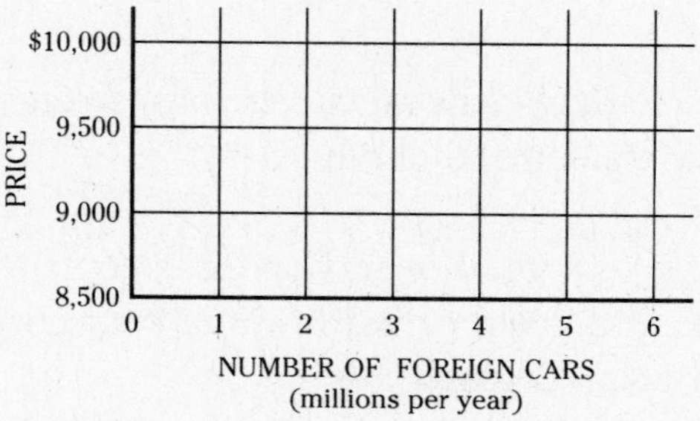

4. Suppose that foreign-car prices are always kept competitive with domestic-car prices, so that they are the same. In Table 4.3 indicate the number of cars (both foreign and domestically produced) at the two prices shown.

64

Table 4.3. Market demand for new cars

Price	Number of new U.S. cars (millions per year)
$10,000	_____
9,000	_____

5. In Figure 4.3 draw the domestic market demand curve for both foreign and domestic cars.

Figure 4.3

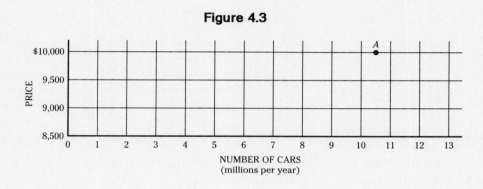

NUMBER OF CARS
(millions per year)

Exercise 2

This exercise shows the relationship between total and marginal utility. It also gives practice in identifying the law of diminishing marginal utility.

Suppose there are two types of entertainment you enjoy—an evening at home with friends and an "event" entertainment, such as a sports event or a rock concert. The number of times that you experience each type of entertainment during a month determines the total utility of each type of entertainment for that month. Suppose Table 4.4 represents the total utility you achieve from consuming various quantities of the two types of entertainment.

Table 4.4. Total and marginal utility of two types of entertainment per month

Days of entertainment per month	Evening at home		Event	
	Total utility	Marginal utility	Total utility	Marginal utility
0	0	_____	0	_____
1	180	_____	600	_____
2	360	_____	1,200	_____
3	530	_____	1,680	_____
4	670	_____	2,040	_____
5	810	_____	2,400	_____
6	950	_____	2,760	_____
7	1,050	_____	3,120	_____
8	1,150	_____	3,120	_____
9	1,250	_____	3,120	_____
10	1,250	_____	3,120	_____
11	1,150	_____	2,920	_____
12	1,030	_____	2,700	_____

1. Compute the marginal utility of each type of entertainment by completing Table 4.4.
2. The law of diminishing marginal utility means:
   (a) The total utility of a good declines as more of it is consumed in a given time period.
   (b) The marginal utility of a good declines as more of it is consumed in a given time period.
   (c) The price of a good declines as more of it is consumed in a given period of time.
   (d) All of the above.
3. The law of diminishing marginal utility is in evidence in Table 4.4:
   (a) For both types of entertainment.
   (b) For home entertainment only.
   (c) For event entertainment only.
   (d) For neither type of entertainment.

(*Hint*: You should be able to tell by looking at the marginal utility columns in Table 4.4. Does the marginal utility become smaller as you go down the column?)

4. In Figure 4.4 graph the total utility curve for evenings at home.

Figure 4.4

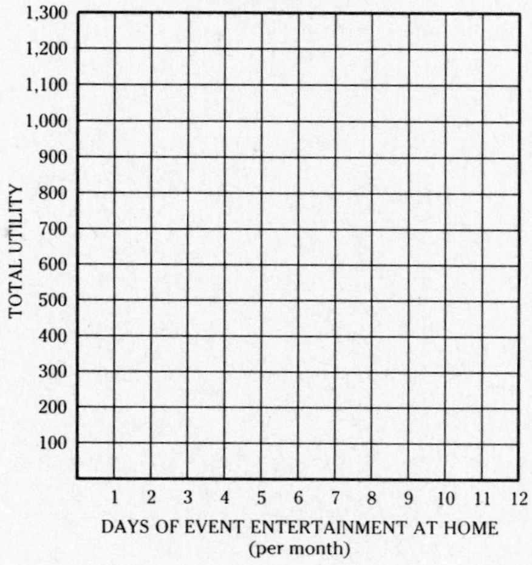

DAYS OF EVENT ENTERTAINMENT AT HOME
(per month)

66

5. In Figure 4.5 graph the marginal utility curve for evenings at home.

Figure 4.5

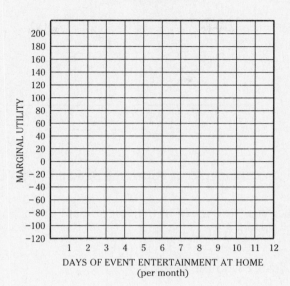

6. On the basis of the two graphs, marginal utility becomes zero only when:
   (a) Total utility is zero.
   (b) Total utility reaches a maximum.
   (c) Total utility is rising.
   (d) Total utility is falling.
7. When total utility is rising, then:
   (a) Marginal utility is rising.
   (b) Marginal utility is negative.
   (c) Marginal utility is positive.
   (d) Marginal utility is zero.

Exercise 3

The media often provide information that suggests shifts in a market-demand curve or a movement along such a curve. By using one of the articles in the text, this exercise will show the kind of information to look for. If your professor makes a newspaper assignment for this chapter from the *Instructor's Manual,* this exercise will provide an example of how to do it.

Reread the Headline article on page 80 in Chapter 4 entitled "Changing Consumption". Then answer the following questions.

1. Which of the four diagrams in Figure 4.6 best represents the movement or shift of cigarette demand due to government efforts to restrict cigarette advertising, to force manufacturers to issue health warnings, and to undertake antismoking campaigns? a b c d (circle one)

Figure 4.6

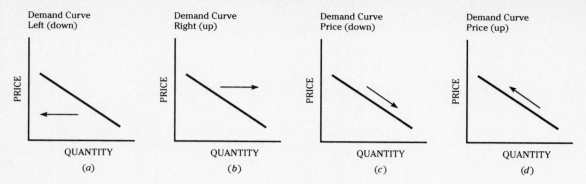

2. What phrase indicates the *market* in which the demand shift occurs?

3. What passage describes the change in the determinant of demand or price that caused the shift you chose in Figure 4.6?

4. What passage indicates who the buyer is?

5. Where does the article mention a change in price or quantity that resulted from the shift in demand or that caused the movement along the demand curve?

Common Errors

The first statement in each "common error" below is incorrect. Each incorrect statement is followed by a corrected version and an explanation.

1. The law of demand and the law of diminishing marginal utility are the same. WRONG! The law of demand and the law of diminishing marginal utility are not the same. RIGHT!
   Do not confuse utility and demand. Utility refers only to expected satisfaction. Demand refers to both preferences and ability to pay. This distinction should help you to keep the law of diminishing marginal utility separate from the law of demand.
2. Figures 4.7a and 4.7b represent simple graphs drawn from a demand schedule.

Figure 4.7a

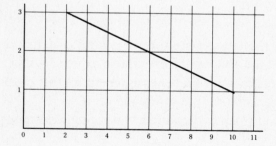

Price ($ per unit)	Output Quantity per unit of time
10	1
2	3

WRONG!

68

Figure 4.7b

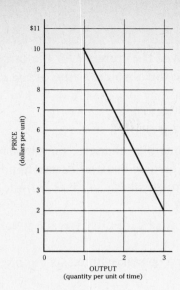

OUTPUT
(quantity per unit of time)

Price ($ per unit)	Output Quantity per unit of time
10	1
2	3

RIGHT!

The first graph has been drawn without any units indicated. It is something of an accidental tradition in economics to show price on the *y*-axis and quantity on the *x*-axis. This convention is sometimes confusing to mathematicians, who want to treat quantity as a function of price, according to the definition in the text. In Figure 4.8a the axes have been reversed and incorrect points have been chosen.

Be careful! When you are drawing a new graph, make a special effort to understand the units that are placed on the axes. Also make sure you know the kinds of units in which each axis is measured. If you are drawing a graph from a table (or schedule), you can usually determine what should be on the axes by looking at the heading above the column from which you are reading the numbers.

Make sure price is shown on the *y*-axis (vertical) and quantity on the *x*-axis (horizontal). If you mix up the two, you may confuse a graph showing perfectly elastic demand with one showing perfectly inelastic demand.

3. The formula for the price elasticity of demand is

$$\frac{\text{Change in price}}{\text{Change in quantity}}$$

WRONG!

The formula for the price elasticity of demand is

$$\frac{\text{Percentage change in quantity}}{\text{Percentage change in price}}$$

RIGHT!

The concept of elasticity allows us to compare relative changes in quantity and price without having to worry about the units in which they are measured. In order to do this, we compute percentage changes of both price and quantity. A change in price *causes* people to change the quantity they demand in a given time period. By putting the quantity changes in the numerator, we can see that if the quantity response is very large in relation to a price change, the elasticity will also be very large. If the quantity response is small in relation to a price change, then demand is inelastic (elasticity is small).

69

Be careful! Do not confuse slope and elasticity. The formula for the slope of the demand curve is the *wrong* formula shown above. The formula for the price elasticity of demand is the *right* formula. Remember to take the absolute value of the elasticity too.

4. A flat demand curve has an elasticity of zero. WRONG!
A flat demand curve has an infinite elasticity. RIGHT!

   When price remains constant even when quantity changes, the elasticity formula requires us to divide by a zero price change. In fact, as demand curves approach flatness, the elasticity becomes larger and larger. By agreement we say it is infinite.

5. The person for whom a good or service has the greatest utility has the greatest desire for more of it. WRONG!
The good that has the greatest marginal utility for a person, with respect to price, is the good of which he or she desires more. RIGHT!

   Utilities of one good for many people cannot be compared. Utilities of various goods for one person can be compared. Marginal utility with respect to price, however, is the best indicator of how to make a choice; not total utility.

6. An expected price change has the same effect as a change in the current price. WRONG!
An unexpected price change shifts the demand curve, whereas a current price change is a movement along the demand curve. RIGHT!

   If prices are expected to rise in the near future, people will demand more of the commodity today in order to beat the rise in price. Demand increases and the quantity demanded will rise. However, if the price rises today, by the law of demand people reduce the quantity demanded! Furthermore, demand itself does not change. A current price change and an expected price change have very different effects.

7. When a buyer buys a good, the demand for the good decreases. WRONG!
When a buyer buys a good, demand is not affected. RIGHT!

   Demand refers only to the willingness and ability of a buyer to buy. The potential for purchase, not the actual purchase, is the focus of demand. Demand is defined over a given period of time. If a buyer buys a good during that period of time, he or she is still counted as demanding the good—even after it is purchased.

■ ANSWERS ■

Key-Term Review

1. market demand
2. *ceteris paribus*
3. law of demand
4. total revenue
5. price elasticity of demand
6. law of diminishing marginal utility
7. demand
8. demand curve
9. marginal utility
10. utility
11. total utility

True or False

1. F	4. F	7. T	10. F	13. F	15. F
2. T	5. F	8. F	11. F	14. F	16. F
3. T	6. T	9. F	12. F		

Multiple Choice

1. b	5. b	9. b	13. c	16. b	19. c
2. c	6. b	10. b	14. d	17. b	20. a
3. c	7. b	11. a	15. b	18. b	21. d
4. c	8. a	12. a			

Problems and Applications

Exercise 1

1. d

2. Figure 4.1 Answer

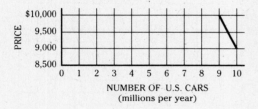

NUMBER OF U.S. CARS
(millions per year)

3. Figure 4.2 Answer

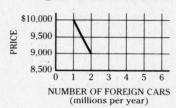

NUMBER OF FOREIGN CARS
(millions per year)

4. Table 4.3 Answer

Price	Number of new U.S. cars (millions per year)
$10,000	10.0
9,000	12.0

5. Figure 4.3 Answer

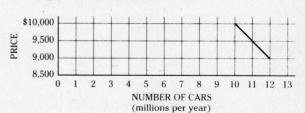

NUMBER OF CARS
(millions per year)

Days of entertainment per month	Evening at home Marginal utility	Event Marginal utility
0	–	–
1	180	600
2	180	600
3	170	480
4	140	360
5	140	360
6	140	360
7	100	360
8	100	0
9	100	0
10	0	0
11	-100	-200
12	-120	-220

2. b

3. a

4. **Figure 4.4 Answer**

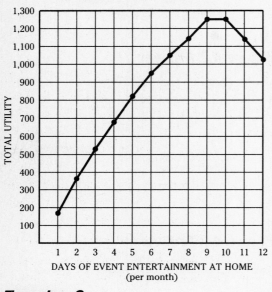

DAYS OF EVENT ENTERTAINMENT AT HOME
(per month)

5. **Figure 4.5 Answer**

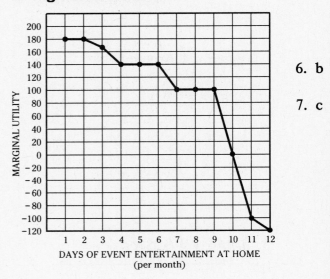

DAYS OF EVENT ENTERTAINMENT AT HOME
(per month)

6. b

7. c

Exercise 3

1. a

2. "Nations around the world" suggests the international market for cigarettes. However, the government's actions to restrict cigarette sales suggest some very narrow, local markets for cigarettes such as "military facilities" and "public transportation."

3. The demand determinant indicated is "tastes" for the actions taken by the government in the second paragraph.

4. There are frequent references to buyers including "Fidel Castro," "countrymen," "2 million Americans," "6000,000 teenagers . . . ."

5. The change in tastes leads to a lower quantity of cigarette purchases as indicated with the example of Fidel Castro in Cuba. Both price and quantity changes are mentioned in reference to price increases resulting from taxation.

CHAPTER 5

Supply Decisions

Quick Review

In this chapter we attempt to identify the costs of producing goods and services. We begin by looking at some basic questions:

- What limits a firm's ability to produce?
- What costs are incurred in producing a good?
- How do costs change when output increases?

Business managers must know how costs change when output is changed. Without such knowledge they cannot determine the output that they would be willing and able to supply in the marketplace. Costs can be computed for different levels of production if management keeps track of all factors that are used in producing the output. The production function establishes the quantity that can be produced from a given amount of factors. The production function is, therefore, the cornerstone for the computation of a firm's costs at different output levels.

The law of diminishing returns says that the marginal physical product of any factor decreases as more of it is used to produce output when other factors are held constant. This concept has important implications for the behavior of cost. In the short run (when firms are unable to vary some factors of production), the law of diminishing returns causes the marginal costs of production to rise with increased output. In effect, the variable factors of production are limited by the fixed factors, which cannot be expanded. The production decision is how much output to produce with existing capacity and technology.

In the long run, all factors are variable. An investment decision includes decisions on fixed factors such whether to build, buy, or lease plant and equipment. In the long run (when there are no fixed factors), changes in average total cost may occur when the rate of output is increased.

Certain rules relate the cost curves, in both the long run and short run. Whenever the marginal curve is below the average curve, then the average curve falls as output increases. However, if the marginal curve is above the average curve, the average curve will be rising. The marginal cost curve always intersects the average variable cost curve and the average total cost curve at their lowest points.

Learning Objectives

After reading Chapter 5 and doing the following exercises, you should:	True or false	Multiple choice	Problems and applications	Common errors	Pages in the text
1. Know the relationship between the production function and the firm's ability to produce goods and services.	2, 3, 4, 17	2, 6, 16	1		89-93
2. Understand the relationship between the production function and the short-run cost curves.	1, 5, 8, 9, 10, 12	2, 6, 10	1	2	90
3. Understand the nature and determinants of marginal productivity.	6, 17	3		3	92-93
4. Be able to draw a graph relating the marginal physical product and total product curves.	7, 17	4, 6		3	91
5. Be able to define and explain the law of diminishing returns.	13	5, 7		1	92-93
6. Understand the difference between variable costs and fixed costs.	8, 9, 10	1, 8, 9, 11, 12, 13, 16	3		93-94
7. Know how to define and calculate the total, average, and marginal costs of production and be able to show their relationship to marginal productivity.	8, 9, 10	1, 8, 10 11, 12, 13	3		93-99
8. Understand the relationship between average and marginal cost curves.	14, 15	14	2		95-97
9. Understand the distinction between economic costs and accounting costs.	11, 16		4		100-101
10. Know the distinction between the long run and the short run.	1, 13, 18	1, 5, 15			101-102

Learning Objectives *(con't.)*	True or false	Multiple choice	Problems and applications	Common errors	Pages in the text
11. Be able to distinguish the factors which are relevant to the production decision from those which are relevant to the investment decision.	18	15	3		101-102
12. Understand the impact of technological improvements on the production function.	2, 17	2			103

Key-Term Review

Review the following terms; if you are not sure of the meaning of any term, write out the definition and check it against the Glossary in the text.

average total cost (ATC)
economic cost
factors of production
fixed costs
investment decision
law of diminishing returns

long run
marginal cost (MC)
marginal physical product (MPP)
production decison
production function

profit
short run
supply
total cost
variable cost

Fill in the blank following each of the statements below with the appropriate term from the list above.

1. The _____ converts .... 1. _____
_____ into maximum possible .... _____
output that can be produced with the available technology.

2. The change in total output associated with one additional unit of input is known as the .... 2. _____

3. When the marginal physical product of a variable input begins to decline, it is the result of the .... 3. _____

4. The_____ is the market value of ... 4. _____
inputs used to produce any output, whether the costs are explicitly paid by the producer or not.

75

5. By adding_____, which do not .... 5._____
   change with the rate of output, to _____, _____
   which do change with the rate of output,
   one can calculate the _____, which ..... _____
   reflects the total value of all inputs used to
   produce a given output.
6. The addition to total cost incurred if the firm
   produces an additional unit of output is called .. 6. _____
7. Dividing total cost by the quantity of output
   produced yields the .... 7. _____
8. The difference between total revenue and
   total cost is known as .... 8. _____
9. A firm makes the decision to_____ an ... 9. _____
   additional unit when it makes the _____ _____
   in the _____ in which some.......... _____
   factors are fixed.
10. The firm makes the_____ in the .... 10. _____
    _____ when all factors are variable.... _____

True or False: *Circle your choice.*

T   F   1. The shape of the short-run cost curves is determined by the production function, with
           input prices held constant.
T   F   2. The production function shows the maximum amount of a particular good or service
           that can be produced with given combinations of resources.
T   F   3. The production function is synonymous with the production-possibilities curve.
T   F   4. If resources are combined inefficiently, society is producing at a point inside the
           production-possibilities curve.
T   F   5. If any factor of production is fixed in a firm's decision-making process, then the firm
           is making a short-run decision.
T   F   6. Marginal physical product is the addition to total output associated with a one-unit
           increase in all required inputs.
T   F   7. Total output may continue to rise even though marginal physical product is
           declining.
T   F   8. Marginal cost is the increase in total cost required to hire one more unit of input.
T   F   9. Total cost refers to the market value of all resources used in producing a good or
           service.
T   F 10. Fixed costs are those costs that do not change with the rate of production.
T   F 11. Normal profit is an economic cost of production.
T   F 12. If output is reduced to zero, total cost falls to zero in the short run.
T   F 13. The law of diminishing returns eventually causes both marginal cost and variable
           cost to diminish.
T   F 14. When marginal cost is rising, average total cost must be rising.
T   F 15. When marginal cost is below average total cost, average total cost will always fall.

T   F   16. When a factor of production is paid an explicit wage, both the accountant and the economist will include it in their cost calculations.

T   F   17. Improved technology shifts the total product curve upward and the total cost curve downward.

T   F   18. The production decision is a long-run supply decision.

Multiple Choice: *Select the correct answer.*

_____ 1. Which of the following is not held constant when drawing short-run cost curves?
(a) Technology.
(b) Input prices.
(c) Fixed factors.
(d) Output.

_____ 2. A production function shows:
(a) The minimum amount of output that can be obtained from alternative combinations of inputs.
(b) The maximum quantities of inputs required to produce a given quantity of output.
(c) The maximum quantity of output that can be obtained from alternative combinations of inputs.
(d) None of the above.

_____ 3. Productivity is a measure of:
(a) Output per unit of input.
(b) Input per unit of output.
(c) Output per dollar of input.
(d) Input per dollar of output.

_____ 4. Marginal physical product is:
(a) The change in total input required to produce one additional unit of output.
(b) The change in total output associated with one additional unit of a variable input.
(c) The number of units of output obtained from all units of input employed.
(d) Another name for total output.

_____ 5. The law of diminishing returns occurs with each additional unit of variable input when:
(a) Total output begins to decline.
(b) Marginal physical product becomes negative.
(c) Total output begins to rise.
(d) Marginal physical product begins to decline.

_____ 6. Declining marginal productivity is the result of:
(a) Inefficiency in the production process.
(b) The use of inferior factors of production.
(c) Laziness.
(d) A rising ratio of variable input to fixed input.

7. The law of diminishing returns:
   (a) Operates in few societies.
   (b) Operates in every production process.
   (c) Does not apply to command economies.
   (d) Can be rendered inoperative with good management techniques.

8. Marginal cost:
   (a) Is the change in total cost from producing one additional unit of output.
   (b) Is the change in total variable cost from producing one additional unit of output.
   (c) Rises because of declining marginal productivity.
   (d) All of the above.

9. Which of the following would most likely be a fixed cost?
   (a) The cost of property insurance.
   (b) The cost of water used in the production process.
   (c) The cost of labor used in the production process.
   (d) The cost of electricity used in the production process.

10. Rising marginal costs result from:
    (a) Rising prices of fixed and variable inputs.
    (b) Rising prices of variable inputs only.
    (c) Falling marginal physical product.
    (d) None of the above.

11. Which of the following costs must remain constant at all levels of output?
    (a) Total costs.
    (b) Variable costs.
    (c) Fixed costs.
    (d) Marginal costs.

12. Which of the following must be variable costs?
    (a) Total costs.
    (b) Economic costs.
    (c) Accounting costs.
    (d) Marginal costs.

13. Which of the following can you compute if you know total cost at all levels of output?
    (a) Fixed cost.
    (b) Variable cost.
    (c) Marginal cost.
    (d) All of the above.

14. Which one of the following curves must be rising when marginal cost is above it?
    (a) Average total cost curve.
    (b) Marginal revenue curve.
    (c) Marginal physical product curve.
    (d) All of the above.

15. A production decision is:
    (a) A short-run choice involving both fixed and variable costs.
    (b) A short-run choice involving only variable costs.
    (c) A long-run choice involving both fixed and variable costs.
    (d) A long-run choice involving only variable costs.

16. Which of the following groupings contains a word or phrase that does not belong?
    (a) Implicit cost, explicit cost, economic cost.
    (b) Average total cost, total cost, marginal cost.
    (c) Rising marginal cost, falling marginal physical product, law of diminishing returns.
    (d) Marginal revenue, marginal cost, production function.

Problems and Applications

Exercise 1

This exercise shows how to compute and graph the marginal physical product of a factor of production. It also demonstrates the law of diminishing returns.

In the textbook, an example of jeans production was used to show how many sewing machines and workers were needed per day to produce various quantities of jeans per day. The table (5.1 on page 90 in the text) is reproduced here as Table 5.1.

Table 5.1. The production of jeans (pairs per day)

Capital input (sewing machines per day)	Labor input (workers per day)							
	0	1	2	3	4	5	6	7
0	0	0	0	0	0	0	0	0
1	0	15	34	44	48	50	51	46
2	0	20	46	64	72	78	81	80
3	0	21	50	73	82	92	99	102

1. Suppose a firm had only two sewing machines and could vary only the amount of labor input. On the basis of Table 5.1, fill in column 2 of Table 5.2 to show how much can be produced at different levels of labor input when there are only two sewing machines.

Table 5.2. The production of jeans with two sewing machines

(1) Labor input (workers per day)	(2) Production of jeans (pairs per day)	(3) Marginal physical product (pairs per worker)
0	_____	_____
1	_____	_____
2	_____	_____
3	_____	_____
4	_____	_____
5	_____	_____
6	_____	_____
7	_____	_____

2. Graph the total output curve in Figure 5.1.

Figure 5.1

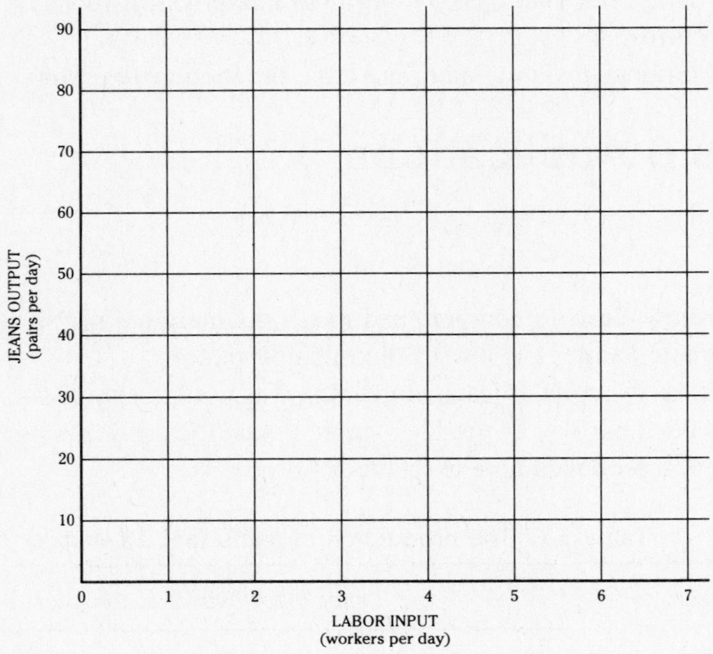

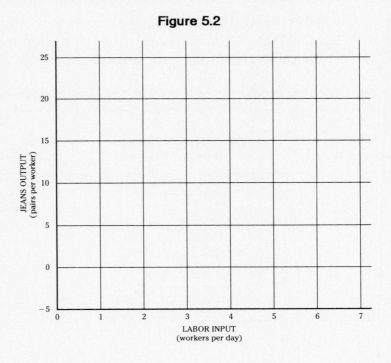

3. Compute the marginal physical product of each extra worker per day. (*Hint:* See Figure 5.2 in the text.) Place the answers in column 3 of Table 5.2.
4. Graph the marginal physical product curve in Figure 5.2.

Figure 5.2

5. The law of diminishing returns states that the marginal physical product of a factor:
   (a) Will become negative as output increases.
   (b) Will decline as output increases.
   (c) Will increase and then decline as output increases.
   (d) Will decline as the amount of a factor used increases.
6. At what amount of labor input does the law of diminishing returns first become apparent in Figure 5.2?
   (a) 0-1 (b) 1-2 (c) 2-3 (d) 3-4
7. In Figure 5.1 at 3 units of labor, total output:
   (a) Is rising with increased labor usage.
   (b) Is falling with increased labor usage.
   (c) Remains constant with increased labor.
8. T F When marginal physical product declines, total output declines.

Exercise 2

This exercise shows the relationship between average and marginal cost curves. Although this example is confined only to average and marginal costs, it can also be applied to average and marginal revenue, average and marginal product, and average and marginal utility.

1. Complete Table 5.3.

Table 5.3. Falling average total cost

Quantity (items per year)	Total cost (TC) (dollars per year)	Average total cost (ATC) (dollars per item)	Marginal cost (MC) (dollars per item)
0	$ 0	$_____	$_____
2	8	_____	_____
4	12	_____	_____
6	15	_____	_____

(*Remember:* MC is the cost of producing one more unit, so you must divide the change in total cost by the *difference* in output rate.)

2. Graph average total cost and marginal cost in Figure 5.3. Label them ATC_1 and MC_1.

Figure 5.3

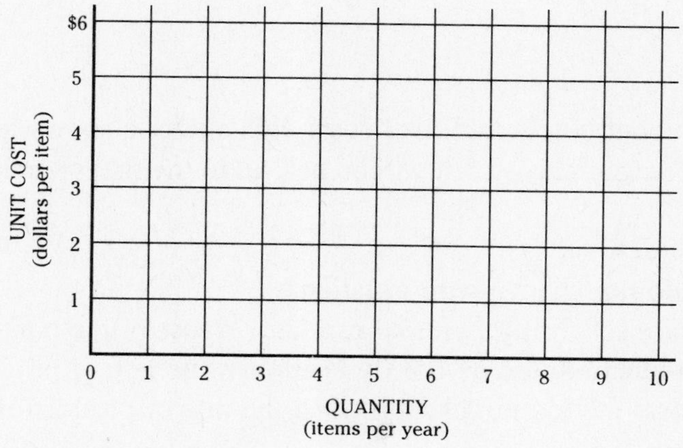

81

3. Complete Table 5.4.

Table 5.4. Constant average total cost

Quantity (items per year)	Total cost (TC) (dollars per year)	Average total cost (ATC) (dollars per item)	Marginal cost (MC) (dollars per item)
0	$ 0	$_____	$_____
1	5	_____	_____
2	10	_____	_____
3	15	_____	_____
4	20	_____	_____
5	25	_____	_____

4. Graph average total cost and marginal cost in Figure 5.3. Label them ATC_2 and MC_2.
5. Complete Table 5.5.

Table 5.5. Rising average total cost

Quantity (items per year)	Total cost (TC) (dollars per year)	Average total cost (ATC) (dollars per item)	Marginal cost (MC) (dollars per item)
0	$ 0.0	$_____	$_____
1	0.5	_____	_____
2	2.0	_____	_____
3	4.5	_____	_____
4	8.0	_____	_____
5	12.5	_____	_____

6. Graph average total cost and marginal cost in Figure 5.3. Label them ATC_3 and MC_3.
7. When the average total cost curve is rising, the marginal cost curve is (above, below, the same as) the average total cost curve.
8. When the average total cost curve is falling, the marginal cost curve is (above, below, the same as) the average total cost curve.
9. When the average total cost curve is flat, the marginal cost curve is (above, below, the same as) the average total cost curve.

Correctly answered, Problems 6-9 summarize the relationship of the average total cost curve to the marginal cost curve. These rules are a fast way of checking whether the curves you draw on an examination are correct.

Exercise 3

Using information about output and total costs, this exercise shows how to compute average total, fixed, variable, and marginal costs. It will be helpful in the first exercise at the end of Chapter 5 in the text.

1. Fixed costs are defined as:
    (a) Costs that do not change with inflation.
    (b) Costs that are set firmly (without escalator clauses) in a contract.
    (c) Costs of production that do not change when the rate of production is altered.
    (d) Average costs that do not change when the rate of production is altered.

2. Variable costs include:
   (a) Costs of production that change when the rate of production is altered.
   (b) All costs in the long run.
   (c) The difference between total and fixed costs.
   (d) All of the above.
3. Suppose you decide to go into the parachute business. Table 5.6 shows the expenses you would find in your income statement at various rates of production.

Table 5.6. Expense statements for parachute business (dollars per week)

Weekly expense	Parachutes produced per week							
	0	100	200	300	400	500	600	700
Leased prod. facilities	$1,400	$1,400	$1,400	$1,400	$1,400	$1,400	$1,400	$1,400
Sewing machines	600	600	600	600	600	600	600	600
Nylon	0	400	1,150	1,700	2,450	3,200	4,650	6,300
Utilities (electricity, etc.)	0	100	150	200	250	300	350	400
Labor	0	500	500	500	500	1,000	1,000	1,000
Testing and certification	1,000	1,000	1,000	1,000	1,000	1,000	1,000	1,000

Which items are fixed costs?_____
4. Complete Table 5.7 using the information in Table 5.6.

Table 5.7. Summary, expenses for parachute business

Costs	Parachutes produced per week							
	0	100	200	300	400	500	600	700
Fixed costs (dollars per week)	$_____	$_____	$_____	$_____	$_____	$_____	$_____	$_____
Variable costs (dollars per week)	_____	_____	_____	_____	_____	_____	_____	_____
Total costs (dollars per week)	_____	_____	_____	_____	_____	_____	_____	_____
Average total costs (dollars per parachute)	_____	_____	_____	_____	_____	_____	_____	_____
Marginal cost (dollars per parachute)	_____	_____	_____	_____	_____	_____	_____	_____

5. In Figure 5.4 draw the average total cost and marginal cost curves. Label them ATC and MC, respectively. You should find the MC and ATC curves intersecting at point B.

Figure 5.4

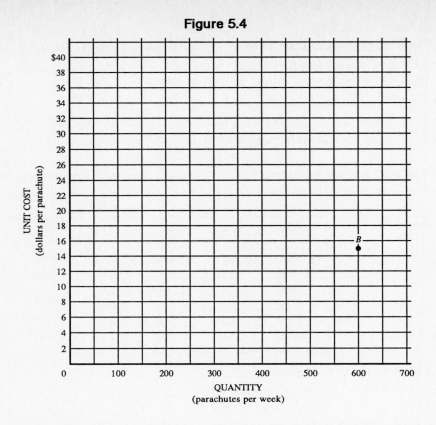

QUANTITY
(parachutes per week)

6. T F Since there are no variable costs, the cost curves in Figure 5.4 represent your firm's long-run costs.

7. What is the output at which the lowest unit cost is first attained? _____

Exercise 4

This exercise should test your knowledge of the economic definitions of profit, interest, and rent.

Table 5.8 contains the annual revenues and costs faced by a firm.

Table 5.8. Costs and revenues (millions of dollars per year)

Costs		Revenues	
Wages and salaries	$100	Sales	$420
Materials	90		
Leased equipment	30		
Rented property and buildings	50		
Payments on money borrowed to buy inventories of materials	10		

In order to begin operations, the firm has to raise capital by issuing stock. The firm uses the money to finance inspections, licenses, and patents. However, the stockholders might have used their money elsewhere; the opportunity cost of these funds is $109 million per year. Furthermore, there is an

84

owner-manager of the firm who could receive income for his services elsewhere; the opportunity cost of his services is $1 million per year

1. Accountants would compute the annual profit, or net revenue, of the firm to be:
   (a) $140 million.   (b) $30 million.   (c) $110 million.   (d) $40 million.
2. The annual normal profit of the firm would be:
   (a) $140 million.   (b) $30 million.   (c) $110 million.   (d) $40 million.
3. Annual economic profit would be:
   (a) $140 million.   (b) $30 million.   (c) $110 million.   (d) $40 million.
4. Annual explicit costs would be:
   (a) $280 million.   (b) $390 million.   (c) $270 million.   (d) $380 million.
5. Annual implicit costs would be:
   (a) $1 million.   (b) $10 million.   (c) $109 million.   (d) $110 million.
6. Annual labor costs would be:
   (a) $1 million.   (b) $100 million.   (c) $101 million.   (d) $130 million.

Common Errors

The first statement in each "common error" below is incorrect. Each incorrect statement is followed by a corrected version and an explanation.

1. Total output starts falling when diminishing returns occur. WRONG!
   Diminishing returns set in when marginal physical product begins to decline. RIGHT!
   The law of diminishing returns describes what happens to *marginal physical product*, not total output. Marginal physical product will typically begin to decline long before total output begins to decline. For total output to decline, the marginal physical product must be negative.

2. The marginal cost curve rises because factor prices rise when more of a good is produced. WRONG!
   The marginal cost curve rises because the marginal productivity of the variable factor declines. RIGHT!
   The marginal cost curve moves in the opposite direction to the marginal product curve. Changes in factor prices would shift the whole marginal cost curve but would not explain its shape and would not affect the marginal product curve.

3. Marginal physical product begins to decline because inferior factors must be hired to increase output. WRONG!
   Declining marginal physical product occurs even if all of the factors are of equal quality. RIGHT!
   Many people incorrectly attribute diminishing returns to the use of inferior factors of production. Diminishing returns result from an increasing ratio of the variable input to the fixed input. There is always a point where the variable input begins to have too little of the fixed input to work with. Result? Diminishing marginal product! The quality of the factors has nothing to do with it. Generally, factors of production are considered homogeneous in economics.

■ ANSWERS ■

Key-Term Review

1. production function
   factors of production
2. marginal physical product (MPP)
3. law of diminishing returns
4. economic cost

5. fixed costs
   variable cost
   total cost
6. marginal cost (MC)
7. average total cost (ATC)

8. profit
9. supply
   production decision
   short run
10. investment decision
    long run

True or False

1. T	4. T	7. T	10. T	13. F	15. T	17. T
2. T	5. T	8. F	11. T	14. F	16. T	18. F
3. F	6. F	9. T	12. F			

Multiple Choice

1. d	4. b	7. b	9. a	11. c	13. d	15. a
2. c	5. d	8. d	10. c	12. d	14. a	
3. a	6. d					

16. (d) "production function" is not a curve or "marginal revenue" is not considered in supply. Other subjects include (a) economic costs, (b) cost calculations, and (c) implications of the law of diminishing returns.

Problems and Applications

Exercise 1

1. See Table 5.2 answer, column 2
3. See Table 5.2 answer, column 3.

Table 5.2 Answer

(1)	(2)	(3)
0	0	--
1	20	20
2	46	26
3	64	18
4	72	8
5	78	6
6	81	3
7	80	- 1

2. **Figure 5.1 Answer**

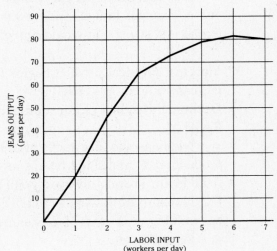

4. Figure 5.2 Answer

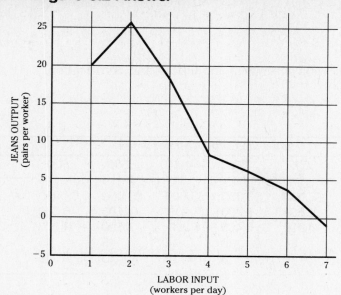

LABOR INPUT
(workers per day)

5. d
6. c
7. a
8. F

Exercise 2

1. Table 5.3 Answer

TC	ATC	MC
$ 0	$--	$--
8	4	4
12	3	2
15	2.5	1.5

2. See lines ATC_1 and MC_1 in Figure 5.3 answer.

Figure 5.3 Answer

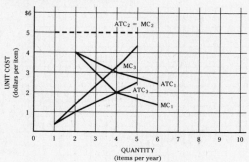

QUANTITY
(items per year)

3. Table 5.4 Answer

TC	ATC	MC
$ 0	$--	$--
5	5	0.5
10	5	1.5
15	5	2.5
20	5	3.5
25	5	4.5

4. See lines ATC_2 and MC_2 in Figure 5.3 answer.

5. Table 5.5 Answer

TC	ATC	MC
$ 0.0	$ --	$--
0.5	0.5	0.5
2.0	1.1	1.5
4.5	1.5	2.5
8.0	2.0	3.5
12.5	2.5	4.5

6. See lines ATC_3 and MC_3 in Figure 5.3 answer.
7. above
8. below
9. the same as

87

Exercise 3

1. c
2. d
3. leased production facilities, sewing machines, and testing and certification

4. **Table 5.7 Answer**

				Parachutes produced per week				
Costs	0	100	200	300	400	500	600	700
Fixed costs	$3,000	$3,000	$3,000	$3,000	$3,000	$3,000	$3,000	$ 3,000
Variable costs	0	1,000	1,800	2,400	3,200	4,500	6,000	7,700
Total costs	3,000	4,000	4,800	5,400	6,200	7,500	9,000	10,700
Average total costs	—	40	24	18	15.5	15	15	15.3
Marginal cost	—	10	8	6	8	13	15	17

5. **Figure 5.4 Answer**

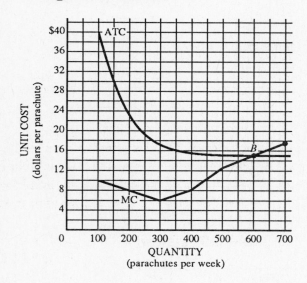

6. F
7. 500 parachutes, where ATC reaches $15

Exercise 4 (answers in millions of dollars per year)

1. (a) Total revenues - total cost = $420 - $280 = $140.
2. (c) Opportunity costs of stockholders + opportunity costs of owner-manager = $109 + $1 = $110.
3. (b) Net revenues - normal profits = $140 - $110 = $30.
4. (a) Wages and salaries + materials + leased equipment + property and buildings + payments on borrowed money = $100 + $90 + $30 + $50 + $10 = $280.
5. (d) Opportunity costs of stockholders + opportunity costs of owner-manager = $109 + $1 = $110.
6. (c) Wages and salaries + opportunity costs of owner-manager = $100 + $1 = $101.

CHAPTER 6

Competition

Quick Review

The perfectly competitive model is a standard by which all other market structures are judged. Other models are labeled efficient or inefficient, depending on how their long-run equilibrium price and output compare with what would be achieved in a competitive market.

The essence of a competitive market is that the actors are powerless to influence product prices and resource flows. They are powerless because such a market is characterized by (1) a product that is homogeneous, (2) a large number of very small buyers and sellers, (3) prices that are free of artificial restrictions, and (4) an absence of barriers to entry into or exit from the market.

In this chapter we discuss three principal questions:
- What are the unique characteristics of competition?
- How can a competitive firm maximize profits?
- How are the quantity and price of a good determined in a competitive market?

Of course, firms sometimes incur losses. In that case, the market has sent a signal that some firms should leave the market. Supply is thereby reduced, price rises, *ceteris paribus*, and long-run market equilibrium is established at a higher price. Resources that leave the market will move to higher-valued uses elsewhere.

Firms in a competitive market are called "price takers." The price that they "take" is the price established by the market at equilibrium. Equilibrium occurs at the quantity and price at which the supply and demand curves cross each other. Each firm is so small relative to the market that changes in any individual firm's output have no effect on market price.

Therefore, the demand curve for each firm appears to be a flat line. When the demand curve is flat, price equals marginal revenue and entrepreneurs will maximize profit by increasing output until the cost of the last unit produced (marginal cost) equals marginal revenue. Such behavior is called "marginal cost pricing" and results in the condition $P = \text{MR} = \text{MC}$ at the profit-maximizing output. This represents the short-run equilibrium of the firm.

The firm continually adjusts output as the equilibrium price changes. The competitive firm's supply is identical to its marginal cost curve. As price rises the firm moves up the supply curve by producing more output and selling at the higher market price. As price falls the firm moves down the supply curve by producing less.

Let's suppose that at the current market price profits are above the normal rates of return earned by similar resources in alternative uses. Owners of those resources will enter the market, start new firms, and produce output. But by doing so they will increase the supply of the product and, *ceteris paribus*, drive down the market price which is each firm's marginal revenue. The entry of firms will continue until the above-normal returns are eliminated. Thus, each firm is forced by the competition (or threat of competition) from other firms to operate efficiently. Thus, the producer is forced to the minimum average total cost (ATC) of producing his profit-maximizing output.

In the competitive market, firms exert persistent pressure on prices and profits. Since there are low barriers to entry, competitive firms respond quickly to consumer demands and the awareness of profit opportunities. When there are long-run positive economic profits to be made, new firms enter the market until prices are lowered enough to eliminate further profit. When there are long-run losses, firms exit from the market until the price rises enough so that normal profits (economic profit of zero) are earned. This dynamic behavior leads to efficient production and efficient allocation of resources.

Competitive forces relentlessly push the market toward key economic goals. First, consumers are willing to pay an amount (p) for the last unit produced that is just equal to the amount required (MC) to get firms to produce it. Furthermore, MC = minimum ATC, because if ATC were any higher, returns would be above average and new firms would enter the market and drive the price down. Consumers get what they want at the lowest possible price. The economy's resources are used most efficiently in perfectly competitive markets. Examples of competitive markets are easy to find. Mining and metals, agricultural products, construction materials, and the stock market are excellent examples.

Learning Objectives

After reading Chapter 6 and doing the following exercises, you should:	True or false	Multiple choice	Problems and applications	Common errors	Pages in the text
1. Know the elements of market structure.	25, 26	1, 3, 6, 7, 24	1		110
2. Be able to classify markets on the basis of the elements of market structure.		3, 6, 7, 27, 28			110
3. Be able to list the characteristics of the competitive market structure.		3, 6, 7, 27, 28			110
4. Be able to tell why the demand curve facing a competitive firm is flat.	1, 2, 3, 4, 5, 15, 25	1, 2, 4			111-113
5. Know the difference between the firm's demand curve and the market demand curve.	1, 2, 3, 4, 5, 6, 17, 26, 27	1, 8, 24, 27	1	1	113
6. Know the rules for making the profit maximizing production decision.	14, 18, 19, 22	5, 15, 18, 23	3	6	114-118

Learning Objectives (con't.)	True or false	Multiple choice	Problems and applications	Common errors	Pages in the text
7. Be able to graph the production decision and show the relevant profit and cost rectangles.	16, 20, 21, 22, 23, 24	17, 21, 22	3	4, 5	118-119
8. Understand why the marginal cost curve is the firm's supply curve.	10	9	2, 4		119-120
9. Know the determinants of competitive market supply and be able to create a market supply curve.		9, 11, 16, 19, 20, 26	2		120-121
10. Be able to demonstrate competitive market equilibrium.	6, 8	10, 13			121-124
11. Understand the role of profits and losses as signals for entry and exit in competitive markets.	6, 8, 13	12, 14, 25		2, 5	121-122
12. Understand the elements of competitive market equilibrium and why it is the standard by which other market structures are judged.	8, 9, 11, 12, 13	12, 13, 25		2, 3	125-127

Key-Term Review

Review the following terms; if you are not sure of the meaning of any term, write out the definition and check it against the Glossary in the text.

barriers to entry
competitive firm
competitive market
competitive profit-maximization rule
efficiency
equilibrium price

marginal cost
marginal cost pricing
market mechanism
market power
market structure
market supply

monopoly
opportunity cost
production decision
profit
supply
total revenue

Fill in the blank following each of the statements below with the appropriate term from the list above.
 1. If a firm has _____ then it views .. 1._____
    its demand curve as downward sloping.

91

2. _____ such as the number of .... 2. _____
   firms in a market, determines how much market
   power a firm has.

3. If there are many firms, then a_____ .... 3. _____
   exists in which each _____ is a .... _____
   "price taker" and faces a flat demand curve.

4. Such firms use_____to ensure that ..... 4. _____
   price covers the _____ of the goods ... _____
   that are supplied.

5. According to the_____, a competitive .. 5. _____
   firm maximizes _____ by producing .. _____
   the output where price just equals marginal cost.

6. These individual_____ decisions can ... 6. _____
   be added together to find _____ for .... _____
   the entire competitive market.

7. In a competitive market, the_____ .... 7. _____
   works through entry and exit to push prices
   toward the_____ at which market .... _____
   supply equals market demand.

8. In a competitive market the_____ .... 8. _____
   given plant and equipment in short-run decisions,
   leads to_____ .... _____
   because the maximum amount of output is
   achieved for the given inputs that are used.

9. In the long run, _____ is likely to be .. 9. _____
   equal to total cost, resulting in zero economic
   profit.

10. In such markets, resources are valued at their
    _____ which is their value in their ...... 10. _____
    next best alternative use.

11. In a _____ market in which there is ...... 11. _____
    only one firm, there are_____ which .... _____
    prevent other firms from entering the market.

True or False: *Circle your choice.*

T   F   1. The demand curve faced by an individual competitive firm is determined by the
           market price and is thus perfectly inelastic.

T   F   2. The demand curve faced by the perfectly competitive market slopes downward and
           to the right.

T   F   3. For the perfectly competitive firm, marginal revenue and price have the same value.

T   F   4. For the perfectly competitive market, marginal revenue and price have the same
           value.

T   F   5. Price and average revenue have the same value.

T   F   6. When perfectly competitive firms earn zero economic profits in the long run, they exit from the market.

T   F   7. If a perfectly competitive firm were to raise its price above the market price, it would lose all of its customers.

T   F   8. A perfectly competitive market achieves the equilibrium price through entry and exit.

T   F   9. The long-run competitive equilibrium price occurs at the output where price equals the minimum average cost.

T   F   10. The marginal cost curve of a competitive producer must be perfectly flat.

T   F   11. Competitive markets are responsive to the desires of consumers.

T   F   12. Perfectly competitive firms are forced to be efficient by government regulations.

T   F   13. In competitive markets, losses are the signal for firms to exit from the market.

T   F   14. A competitive firm should produce until the next unit produced would raise added costs above additional revenues.

T   F   15. If a firm faces a horizontal demand curve, the firm is a price taker.

T   F   16. If demand is elastic, a quantity decrease will more than offset a price increase, causing total revenue to fall.

T   F   17. If the price of a good remains the same but the firm's output is changing, *ceteris paribus,* the demand curve facing the firm is infinitely elastic.

T   F   18. Only at an output where marginal revenue equals marginal cost will profits be maximized.

T   F   19. Since a firm's goal is to maximize profits, it should expand production as long as it is making profits.

T   F   20. The marginal cost curve intersects the average total cost (ATC) curve at the lowest point of the ATC curve.

T   F   21. Fixed costs remain constant at all rates of production.

T   F   22. If the price elasticity of demand is less than 1, a price increase always leads to greater profits.

T   F   23. Maximizing profits and minimizing losses amount to the same thing; the only difference is that in one case profits are greater than zero and in the other they are less than zero.

T   F   24. When the firm makes the production decision some factors are fixed.

T   F   25. Competitive firms face flat demand curves because they have no market power.

T   F   26. The market demand curve slopes downward to the right only in noncompetitive markets.

T   F   27. The perfectly elastic demand curve faced by a competitive firm is consistent with a downward-sloping market demand curve for the firm's product.

Multiple Choice: *Select the correct answer.*

_____ 1. A catfish farmer, as a producer in a competitive market, faces a firm demand curve that:
(a) Is inelastic.
(b) Is unit elastic.
(c) Appears flat (horizontal).
(d) Slopes upward to the right.

2. In the catfish market the demand curve is:
   (a) Flat.
   (b) Perfectly elastic.
   (c) Vertical.
   (d) Downward sloping to the right.

3. A catfish farmer:
   (a) Is able to keep other potential catfish producers out of the market.
   (b) Would like to keep other potential catfish producers out of the market but cannot do so.
   (c) Will not care if more catfish producers enter the market.
   (d) Is powerless to alter his own rate of production.

4. If marginal cost exceeds marginal revenue, a competitive firm can usually increase its profits (or decrease its losses) by:
   (a) Increasing output.
   (b) Raising price.
   (c) Stopping production.
   (d) Decreasing output.

5. Suppose that the discovery of a new production technique reduces the costs of production. In a perfectly competitive market, the short-run effects will be:
   (a) Higher price and greater output.
   (b) Higher price and smaller output.
   (c) Lower price and smaller output.
   (d) Lower price and greater output.

6. Which of the following conditions is not characteristic of a perfectly competitive market?
   (a) Information is perfect.
   (b) Products of all sellers in the market are identical or nearly so.
   (c) Zero economic profit in the long run.
   (d) The market price is determined by an organization of sellers.

7. Which of the following conditions is characteristic of a perfectly competitive market?
   (a) The seller does not lose all customers when the selling price is raised above the market price.
   (b) The seller can produce and sell as much as desired at the established market price without affecting that price.
   (c) High barriers to entry.
   (d) The seller is affected by the actions of any competitors.

8. The market demand curve in a competitive market is downward sloping:
   (a) Because of the law of diminishing returns.
   (b) Because the firms in the market have market power.
   (c) Because of the law of demand.
   (d) All of the above.

9. The marginal cost curve is the same as the firm's supply curve when it is:
   (a) Above minimum average costs and the firm's demand curve is downward sloping.
   (b) Below minimum average costs and the demand curve is flat.
   (c) Above minimum average costs and the firm's demand curve is flat.
   (d) Below minimum average costs and the demand curve is downward sloping.

10. Which of the following conditions always characterizes a firm that is in short-run competitive equilibrium where profits are maximized?
    (a) Price equals minimum average total cost.
    (b) Price equals marginal cost.
    (c) There are no economic profits.
    (d) All of the above characterize such a firm.

11. The market supply curve will shift due to all of the following except:
    (a) Changes in technology.
    (b) Changes in the number of supplying firms.
    (c) Changes in expectations about making profits in a market.
    (d) Changes in the current income of buyers.

12. In a competitive market where firms are incurring losses, which of the following should be expected as the market moves to long-run equilibrium, *ceteris paribus*?
    (a) A higher price and fewer firms.
    (b) A lower price and fewer firms.
    (c) A higher price and more firms.
    (d) A lower price and more firms.

13. In long-run competitive equilibrium, price equals:
    (a) The minimum of the average cost curve.
    (b) The minimum of the marginal cost curve.
    (c) The minimum of the demand curve.
    (d) All of the above.

14. If the market price falls below the long-run equilibrium price in a competitive market, there will be:
    (a) Exit.
    (b) Barriers to entry.
    (c) Zero economic profit.
    (d) All of the above.

15. Which of the following are characteristic of competitive market structure?
    (a) Many buyers and sellers.
    (b) Low barriers to entry.
    (c) Identical products.
    (d) All of the above.

16. A market supply curve of a product shows, *ceteris paribus*:
    (a) The amount of the product that firms are willing to supply for a market at various prices.
    (b) The amount of output that will be supplied by firms at various factor costs.
    (c) The quantities that firms are willing and able to supply at various prices in a given time period, *ceteris paribus*.
    (d) The marginal cost curve of a representative firm.

17. When a competitive firm raises its price, total revenue definitely:
    (a) Increases, thus increasing profits.
    (b) Falls, thus lowering profits.
    (c) Increases, but profits may fall.
    (d) Increases if demand is inelastic.

18. When a competitive firm maximizes profits, it is:
    (a) Minimizing losses.
    (b) Maximizing the difference between total revenue and total cost.
    (c) Finding the production level at which its price equals its marginal cost.
    (d) Doing all of the above.

19. When the wage rate paid to the production workers of a firm is increased, *ceteris paribus:*
    (a) The firm's marginal cost curve shifts upward and supply falls.
    (b) Supply increases, and the supply curve rises.
    (c) The supply curve shifts to the right.
    (d) The firm's marginal cost curve shifts downward and the supply curve shifts rightward.

20. Which of the following is not a determinant of either supply or demand?
    (a) Shortages.
    (b) Technological change.
    (c) Expectations.
    (d) Prices of other goods.

21. When the average cost curve is flat:
    (a) Marginal costs are rising with output.
    (b) Marginal costs are falling with output.
    (c) Marginal costs equal average costs.
    (d) The curve has been drawn incorrectly.

22. When a firm's average revenue curve is flat:
    (a) No matter how much the firm produces in a period of time, price remains constant.
    (b) Its marginal revenue curve is equal to its average revenue curve.
    (c) Its demand curve is flat.
    (d) All of the above are the case.

23. While consumers try to maximize utility, firms generally try to maximize:
    (a) Profits.
    (b) Revenues.
    (c) Sales.
    (d) Production in a given period of time, *ceteris paribus*.

24. The price elasticity of demand measures the percentage change in quantity demanded caused by a 1 percent change in the:
    (a) Price of substitutes, *ceteris paribus.*
    (b) Price of resources, *ceteris paribus.*
    (c) Price of the good itself, *ceteris paribus.*
    (d) Prices of all of the above.

25. A firm that makes an investment decision views all factors of production as:
    (a) Variable over the long run.
    (b) Variable over the short run.
    (c) Fixed over the long run.
    (d) Fixed over the short run.

26. Which of the following groups of determinants includes only supply determinants?
    (a) Technology, price of resources, buyer expectations, and number of buyers.
    (b) Price of other goods, buyer expectations, income, and technology.
    (c) Price of other goods, buyer expectations, technology, and number of sellers.
    (d) Price of resources, technology, buyer expectations, and taxes.

27. A competitive firm faces:
    (a) A downward-sloping marginal revenue curve and a downward-sloping market demand curve.
    (b) A downward-sloping marginal revenue curve but a flat market demand curve.
    (c) A flat demand curve from the point of view of the firm but a downward-sloping market demand curve.
    (d) A downward-sloping demand curve from the point of view of the firm but a flat market demand curve.

28. Which of the following groupings contains a word or phrase that does not belong?
    (a) Long-run competitive equilibrium, minimum long-run average cost, zero economic profit.
    (b) Entry, exit, production decision.
    (c) Long-run, investment decision, all costs are variable.
    (d) Many firms, marginal cost pricing, perfect information.

Problems and Applications

Exercise 1

This exercise provides the link between individual and market demand curves. It shows how the equilibrium in the market determines the demand curve from the seller's point of view. It also shows how the market equilibrium determines the supply curve from the buyer's point of view.

1. Hard-time Charlie needs psychiatric help. He would like to engage a psychiatrist for four hours per week at the current price of $6 per hour. However, at a price of $12 per hour, Charlie would only want two hours per week. In Figure 6.1 draw Charlie's individual demand curve. (Assume the demand curve is a straight line.)

Figure 6.1. Demand curve of the buyer

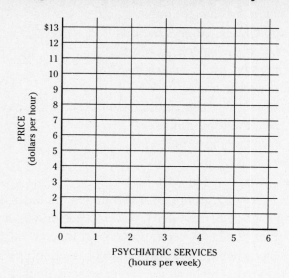

2. Suppose that Charlie is not the only one with a problem. There are 9,999 other hard-time Charlies in the same city who have identical demand curves. In Figure 6.2 graph the market demand curve for all of the hard-time Charlies combined and label it *D*.

Figure 6.2. Market demand and supply curves

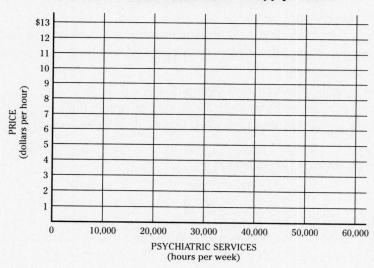

3. Lucy is a psychiatrist who is fond of visits from Charlie, particularly at the $12 per hour rate. At that rate she would be willing and able to schedule 50 hours of couch time per week. But at the lower $6 per hour rate she would be willing to schedule only 10 hours per week. In Figure 6.3 draw Lucy's supply curve. (Assume it is a straight line.)

98

Figure 6.3. Supply curve of the supplier

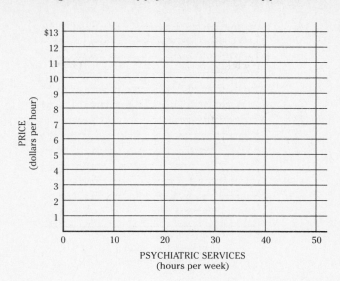

PRICE
(dollars per hour)

PSYCHIATRIC SERVICES
(hours per week)

4. There are 999 other psychiatrists in the city with supply curves like Lucy's. Draw the market supply curve for psychiatrists in Figure 6.2 and label it *S*. (Assume it is a straight line.)

5. The equilibrium price for psychiatric services for hard-time Charlies in this market is:
   (a) $12 per hour.
   (b) $9 per hour.
   (c) $6 per hour.
   (d) $3 per hour.
   (e) $0 per hour.

6. One of the 10,000 hard-time Charlies is suddenly married and needs no more psychiatric services. Is the new market demand curve for psychiatric services significantly different from that in Figure 6.2?

7. Table 6.1 shows how the market equilibrium price changes in response to the quantity demanded by one good-time Charlie before and after his marriage. Fill in the table.

Table 6.1

Psychiatric services (hours per week)	Market equilibrium price (dollars per hour)
0 (after marriage)	$_____
30 (before marriage)	$_____

8. Table 6.1 represents psychiatric services sellers are willing and able to sell to Charlie. In Figure 6.4 diagram the supply curve that Charlie is facing.

99

Figure 6.4. Supply curve from buyer's viewpoint

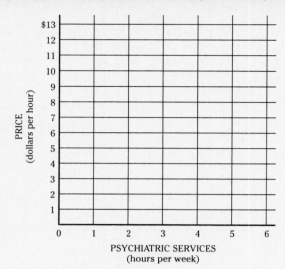

9. When there are many buyers in a market, the quantity bought by any one buyer is likely to have little effect on the market equilibrium price in a given period of time. Each buyer therefore views the supply curve facing him or her as:
   (a) Upward sloping.
   (b) Downward sloping.
   (c) Flat.

10. Our once hard-time Charlie is divorced and single again, so there are again an even 10,000 hard-time Charlies. Now Lucy takes a week-long world tour. Is the resulting new market supply curve for psychiatrists during the week of Lucy's vacation much different from the one you labeled *S* in Figure 6.2? _____

11. Fill in Table 6.2, which shows how the market equilibrium price changes in response to the quantity supplied by Lucy.

Table 6.2

Psychiatric services (hours per week)	Market equilibrium price (dollars per hour)
0 (during vacation)	$_____
30 (before vacation)	$_____

12. Table 6.2 shows what buyers are willing and able to buy of Lucy's services. In Figure 6.5, diagram the demand curve Lucy is facing.

100

Figure 6.5. Demand curve from seller's viewpoint

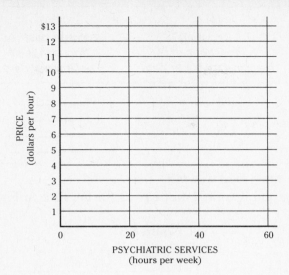

13. When there are many suppliers in a market, the quantity supplied by any one seller is likely to have little effect on market equilibrium price in a given time period. Each supplier therefore views the demand curve facing him or her as:
    (a) Upward sloping.
    (b) Downward sloping.
    (c) Flat.
    (d) Indeterminate

14. Is the demand curve of the buyer (Figure 6.1) the same as the demand curve facing the individual seller (Figure 6.5)? _____

15. Is the supply curve of the seller (Figure 6.3) the same as the supply curve facing the individual buyer (Figure 6.4)? _____

This exercise should alert you to the importance of distinguishing *individual* (or firm) demand or supply curves from market demand and supply curves. You should also be aware that a downward-sloping demand curve for an individual buyer is not necessarily the demand curve seen by a supplier. Also, the upward-sloping supply curve of an individual seller is not necessarily the supply curve perceived by the buyer.

Exercise 2

This exercise gives practice in relating the concepts of supply and marginal cost. It also gives practice in graphing, shifting, and moving along the different curves.

Assume you own a machine tool manufacturing company that produces one standardized type of tool. Your total costs change as shown in Table 6.3. On the basis of Table 6.3, answer the questions below.

Table 6.3. Costs of machine tool manufacturer

(1) Quantity (thousands of machine tools per day)	(2) Total cost (TC) (thousands of machine tools per day)	(3) Average cost (AC) (thousands of dollars per day)	(4) Marginal cost (MC) (dollars per machine tool)
0	$ 0	$_____	$_____
1	5	_____	_____
2	20	_____	_____
3	60	_____	_____

1. Fill in columns 3 and 4 of Table 6.3.
2. Graph the average and marginal cost curves for the firm in Figure 6.6.

Figure 6.6

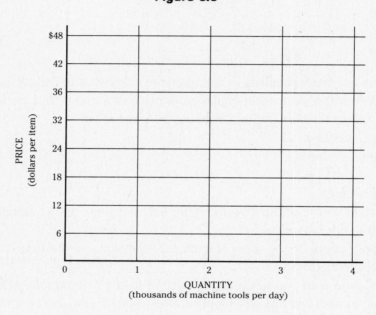

3. Suppose that total cost increases as shown in Table 6.4. Fill in columns 3 and 4 of Table 6.4, then graph the new average and marginal cost curves using dotted lines in Figure 6.6.

Table 6.4. Costs after a cost increase

(1) Quantity (thousands of machine tools per day)	(2) Total cost (TC) (thousands of machine tools per day)	(3) Average cost (AC) (thousands of dollars per day)	(4) Marginal cost (MC) (dollars per machine tool)
0	$ 0	$_____	$_____
1	6	_____	_____
2	24	_____	_____
3	72	_____	_____

102

4. Because of the cost increases:
   - (a) The marginal cost curve has shifted upward, but it is uncertain how the supply curve shifts.
   - (b) The marginal cost curve has shifted downward, but it is uncertain how the supply curve shifts.
   - (c) Since the supply curve and marginal cost curve consist of the same points, both have shifted upward.
   - (d) Since the supply and marginal cost curve consist of the same points, both have shifted downward.

5. T   F   Because the supply curve has shifted upward, there is a greater supply.

6. If you expect prices to fall in the near future because you expect a recession, you might decide to cut back your operations and invest your money in securities. The machine tool supply curve of your firm would:
   - (a) Shift to the left.
   - (b) Shift to the right.
   - (c) Remain unchanged, but you would move to a lower quantity supplied along your supply curve.
   - (d) Remain unchanged, but you would move to a higher quantity supplied along your supply curve.

7. If prices do fall in the market for machine tools, you would lower your prices to remain competitive. The machine tool supply curve of your firm would:
   - (a) Shift to the left.
   - (b) Shift to the right.
   - (c) Remain unchanged, but you would move to a lower quantity supplied along your supply curve.
   - (d) Remain unchanged, but you would move to a higher quantity supplied along your supply curve.

8. Suppose there were a new technology that made production of machine tools more efficient. If you adopted this new technology, your machine tool supply curve would:
   - (a) Shift to the left.
   - (b) Shift to the right.
   - (c) Remain unchanged, but you would move to a lower quantity supplied along your supply curve.
   - (d) Remain unchanged, but you would move to a higher quantity supplied along your supply curve.

Exercise 3

This exercise gives you a chance to sort out all of the different formulas for costs and revenues, to graph them, and then to find the rule that will lead to profit maximization.

1. Several formulas that use symbols with which you should familiarize yourself appear below. Match each formula with the number of one of the columns in Table 6.5. To find what the symbols in the formula mean, look at Table 6.5. (*Note:* FC is a fixed cost, and Δ means "the change in.")

103

	Column			Column
a. TC - FC	_____	e.	TC / q	_____
b. ΔTC / Δq	_____	f.	ΔTR / Δq	_____
c. TR - TC	_____	g.	TR / q	_____
d. $p \times q$	_____	h.	(TR - TC) / q	_____

Table 6.5. Cost and revenue data

Qty. (q) items per week)	Price (p) ($ per item)	(1) Total revenue (TR) ($ per week)	(2) Total cost (TC) ($ per week)	Profit ($ per week)	(3) Avg. profit ($ per item)	(4) Avg. revenue (AR) ($ per item)	(5) Avg. total cost (ATC) ($ per item)	(6) Total variable cost (TVC) ($ per week)	(7) Marginal cost (MC) ($ per item)	(8) Marginal revenue (MR) ($ per item)
0	$4	$_____	$ 400	$_____	$_____	$_____	$_____	$_____	$_____	$_____
100	4	_____	1,000	_____	_____	_____	_____	_____	_____	_____
200	4	_____	1,300	_____	_____	_____	_____	_____	_____	_____
300	4	_____	1,500	_____	_____	_____	_____	_____	_____	_____
400	4	_____	1,600	_____	_____	_____	_____	_____	_____	_____
500	4	_____	1,700	_____	_____	_____	_____	_____	_____	_____
600	4	_____	1,850	_____	_____	_____	_____	_____	_____	_____
700	4	_____	2,100	_____	_____	_____	_____	_____	_____	_____
800	4	_____	2,450	_____	_____	_____	_____	_____	_____	_____
900	4	_____	3,600	_____	_____	_____	_____	_____	_____	_____

2. After checking your answers, complete Table 6.5.
3. In Figure 6.7, diagram the average revenue, average total cost, marginal revenue, and marginal cost curves.

Figure 6.7

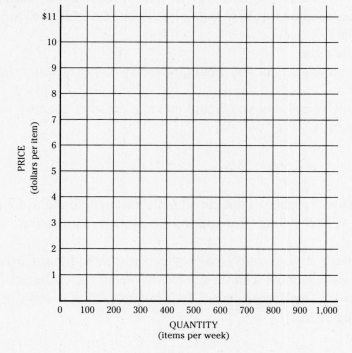

104

Now you can test to see which rules give you the production rate that earns the greatest profit for the firm. Fill in Table 6.6 with the production rate or rates (from the rows of Table 6.5) at which the particular rule is satisfied.

Table 6.6

When this occurs . . .	The production rate is:
4. Maximum profits	_____
5. Maximum average profit	_____
6. Minimum total cost	_____
7. Maximum revenue	_____
8. Minimum average total cost	_____
9. Maximum average revenue	_____
10. Minimum marginal cost	_____
11. Marginal cost = price	_____
12. Marginal cost = marginal revenue	_____
13. Marginal cost = average total cost	_____

Very few rules give the unique profit-maximizing production rate of 800. As a matter of fact, only the MC = MR rule, which applies to all firms, and the MC = p rule, which applies only when the demand curve is flat, yield the production rate at which profits are maximized.

Exercise 4

The media often provide information that suggests shifts in a market supply curve or a movement along such a curve. By using one of the articles in the text, this exercise will show the kind of information to look for. If your professor makes a newspaper assignment for this chapter from the *Instructor's Manual*, this exercise will provide an example of how to do it.

Reread the Headline article on page 39 in Chapter 2 entitled "Surplus Punches Hole in Oil Price." Then answer the following questions, using Figure 6.8 to answer Question 1.

1. Which of the four diagrams in Figure 6.8 best represents the movement or shift in oil supply resulting from the restoration of oil production capability in Iraq?

   a   b   c   d   (circle one)

Figure 6.8

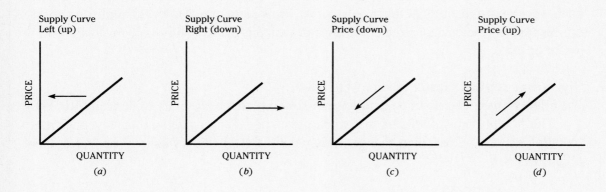

2. What phrase indicates the market in which the supply shift or movement occurred?

3. What sentence indicates the change in the determinant of supply or price that caused the shift or movement you chose in Figure 6.8?

4. What phrase indicates who the seller is?

5. Where does the article mention a change in price or quantity that resulted from the shift in supply or change in quantity supplied?

Common Errors

The first statement in each "common error" below is incorrect. Each incorrect statement is followed by a corrected version and an explanation.

1. The demand curve for a competitive market is flat. WRONG!
   The demand curve for a competitive firm is flat. RIGHT!
   The error above results from failure to distinguish between the market and the firm. Review Exercise 1 if this distinction is not clear.

2. Competitive firms do not make profits. WRONG!
   Competitive firms can make economic profits in the short run. RIGHT!
   In the long run, firms enter a market and compete away economic profits. In the short run, a change in demand or supply may cause price to change and may bestow temporary economic profits on a firm.

3. Since competitive firms make zero profits in the long run, they cannot pay their stockholders and so they should shut down. WRONG!
   Since competitive firms make zero economic profits in the long run, they are able to pay all factors of production, including the skill of entrepreneurs, to keep the firms in existence. RIGHT!
   Be careful! Keep the accounting and economic definitions of such words as "profit" separate and distinct. Keep movements along the supply curve (firms increase production rates) separate from shifts of the supply curve (firms enter or exit). Avoid confusing short-run responses (increasing production rates in existing plants) with long-run responses (entry or exit).

4. Higher prices yield greater profits. WRONG!
   The effect of price increases on total revenue depends on the elasticity of demand. RIGHT!
   The law of demand tells us that when prices rise, quantity falls; total revenues may actually decrease. Costs also change; if they don't fall as quickly as total revenues, then *profits* fall.

5. If a firm is taking a loss, it is not maximizing profits. WRONG!
   A firm may be maximizing profits even if it is making zero profits or even taking a loss. RIGHT!

   Minimizing losses is essentially the same as maximizing profits. A firm is maximizing profits as long as there is nothing it can do to make larger profits. Remember, even if the firm is taking a loss, it will not shut down if it can cover variable costs.

6. A firm should always increase the rate of production as long as it is making a profit. WRONG!
   A profitable firm should increase production rates only as long as additional revenues from the increase in production exceed the additional associated costs. RIGHT!

   If the increase in production rates generates more costs than revenue, the firm will be less profitable. In this case, continued expansion will ultimately result in zero profits.

■ANSWERS ■

Key-Term Review

1. market power
2. market structure
3. competitive market
   competitive firm
4. marginal cost pricing
   marginal cost

5. competitive profit-maximization rule
   profit
6. supply
   market supply
7. market mechanism
   equilibrium price

8. production decision
   efficiency
9. total revenue
10. opportunity cost
11. monopoly
    barriers to entry

True or False

1. F	5. T	9. T	13. T	17. T	21. T	25. T
2. T	6. F	10. F	14. T	18. T	22. T	26. F
3. T	7. T	11. T	15. T	19. F	23. T	27. T
4. F	8. T	12. F	16. T	20. T	24. T	

Multiple Choice

1. c	5. d	9. c	13. d	17. d	21. c	25. a
2. d	6. d	10. b	14. a	18. d	22. d	26. d
3. b	7. b	11. d	15. d	19. a	23. a	27. c
4. d	8. c	12. a	16. c	20. a	24. c	28. b*

*["Production decision" is short run while entry and exit are long-run decisions. Other topics include (a) long-run profit maximization in competitive markets, (c) long-run decisions and (d) characteristics of competitive firms.]

Problems and Applications

Exercise 1

1. Figure 6.1 Answer

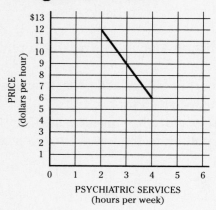

2. Figure 6.2 Answer

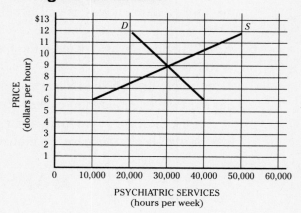

3. Figure 6.3 Answer

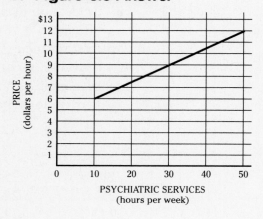

4. See line labeled *S* in Figure 6.2 answer.
5. b
6. No

7. Table 6.1 Answer

Hours per week	Price
0	$9
30	9

8. Figure 6.4 Answer

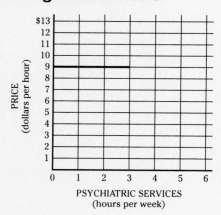

9. c
10. No

11. Table 6.2 Answer

Hours per week	Price
0	$9
30	9

12. Figure 6.5 Answer

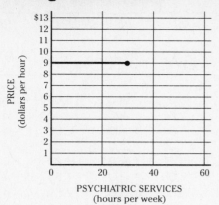

13. c
14. No
15. No

Exercise 2

1. Table 6.3 Answer

Quantity	AC	MC
0	$ --	$ --
1	5	5
2	10	15
3	20	40

2. Figure 6.6 Answer

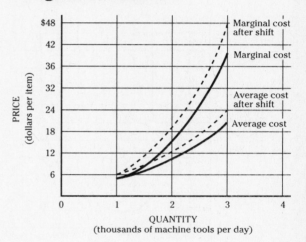

3. Table 6.4 Answer

Quantity	AC	MC
0	$ --	$ --
1	6	6
2	12	18
3	24	48

4. c
5. F
6. a
7. c
8. b

See also the dotted lines in Figure 6.6 answer.

Exercise 3

1.　a. 6　　b. 7　　c. 2　　d. 1　　e. 5　　f. 8　　g. 4　　h. 3

109

2. Table 6.5 Answer

(q)	(p)	(1) (TR)	(TC)	(2) Profit	(3) Avg. profit	(4) (AR)	(5) (ATC)	(6) (TVC)	(7) (MC)	(8) (MR)
0	$4	$ 0	$ 400	$- 400	$ —	$--	$ —	$ —	$ —	$--
100	4	400	1,000	- 600	- 6.00	4	10.00	600	6.00	4
200	4	800	1,300	- 500	- 2.50	4	6.50	900	3.00	4
300	4	1,200	1,500	- 300	- 1.00	4	5.00	1,100	2.00	4
400	4	1,600	1,600	0	0.00	4	4.00	1,200	1.00	4
500	4	2,000	1,700	300	0.60	4	3.40	1,300	1.00	4
600	4	2,400	1,850	550	0.92	4	3.08	1,450	1.50	4
700	4	2,800	2,100	700	1.00	4	3.00	1,700	2.50	4
800	4	3,200	2,450	750	0.94	4	3.06	2,050	3.50	4
900	4	3,600	3,600	0	0.00	4	4.00	3,200	11.50	4

3. Figure 6.7 Answer

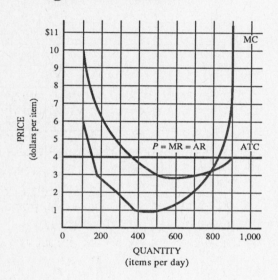

Problems 4-13 (Table 6.5) are expressed in number of items per week.

4. 800
5. 700
6. 0
7. 900
8. 700
9. all output levels
10. 400-500
11. 100-200 when the marginal cost curve falls below price (this is where profits are minimized); 800-900 when the marginal cost curve rises above price (this is where profits are maximized)
12. 100-200 when the marginal cost curve falls below marginal revenue (this is where profits are minimized); 800-900 when the marginal cost curve rises above marginal revenue
13. 700-800

Exercise 4

1. Diagram *b* since there is greater output with Iraq's new production.
2. "World" markets for oil are referred to in the first sentence.
3. "The potential for more oil supply was apparent" indicates that expectations have changed, and the statement "producers sought to reduce their oil supply" further suggests that producer expectations are fueling the surplus as they try to take advantage of the high post-war equilibrium price of $25.00.
4. "Producers sought to reduce their oil supply."
5. The article mentions both the drop in price from $25 to $18 and the 2 million barrel Kuwaiti increase as well as the 1 million barrel potential Iraqi increase.

CHAPTER 7

Monopoly

Quick Review

In this chapter we are concerned with monopoly—a market structure at the opposite end of the spectrum from a competitive market. In monopoly there is a single producer. In a competitive market there are a larger number of producers.

Let's focus on the following questions:
- What price will a monopolist charge for his output?
- How much will he produce?
- Are consumers better or worse off when only one firm controls the entire market?

The key to each of these questions rests with market power. Market power is the ability to influence the market price of goods and services. The extreme case of market power is monopoly. The demand curve faced by the monopolist and the market demand curve are identical. Accordingly, the firm must recognize the effect of increased production on the price at which its output may be sold. To sell larger quantities of output in a given time period, it must lower the price of its product. Such price reductions cause marginal revenue and price to diverge. A firm without market power has no such problem; it may sell as much output as it desires at the prevailing market price.

Like all profit-maximizing firms, a monopolist will produce at that rate of output at which marginal revenue equals marginal cost. The monopolist will attain a higher level of profit than a competitive firm because of its ability to equate industry (its own) marginal revenue and marginal cost. By contrast, a competitive firm ends up equating marginal cost and price, since it has no control over the market supply, market demand, or equilibrium price.

The higher profits by a monopolist attract envious entrepreneurs. A market-power position and its related profits are maintained only if barriers to entry keep other firms out of the market. Monopolists charge a price which is higher than marginal cost. They also fail fully to utilize available resources. Finally, monopolists do not necessarily pick the least-cost technologies for production. Competitive firms do achieve these economic objectives in the long run.

The principal arguments in favor of market power focus on the alleged ability of large firms to pursue long-term research and development, on the incentives implicit in the opportunity to attain market power, and on the greater efficiency that larger firms may attain. The first two arguments are weakened by the fact that competitive firms are under much greater pressure to innovate and *can stay ahead in the profit game only if they do so*. Nevertheless, larger firms may be able to achieve economies of scale—lower minimum average costs brought about by a larger scale of plant—and thus may be considered desirable on the grounds of efficiency. A firm with economies of scale over the entire range of market output is called a natural monopoly. Larger firms are not necessarily more efficient, however, since either constant returns to scale or even diseconomies of scale may arise as firm size increases. Few firms are natural monopolies.

Recently economists have investigated the restraining power of *potential* competition in markets where the barriers to entry are not too high. This idea is included in the concept of "contestable markets." Because monopolies have so many adverse impacts on the economy, governments at all levels have been empowered to prevent or regulate the concentration of market power.

Learning Objectives

After reading Chapter 7 and doing the following exercises, you should:	True or false	Multiple choice	Problems and applications	Common errors	Pages in the text
1. Know the meaning of market power.	1	6, 7, 14, 17, 21	4		131
2. Know why a monopolist has market power and a downward-sloping demand curve and why price and marginal revenue diverge.	2, 10, 11	9, 20		1	132-133
3. Be able to show the relationship between the market demand and individual demand curve for a monopolist.	10, 11			3	132-134
4. Be able to determine a monopolist's most profit-able rate of production.	15	1, 2, 10, 11, 18, 19, 23, 24, 25	1, 2	1, 2, 3	134-135
5. Be able to show why monopoly typically results in higher profits, less output, and higher prices than would occur in a competitive market.	4	12	3	2	135-136
6. Know the difference between marginal cost pricing for a competitive firm and profit maximization for a monopoly.	4, 12				140

Learning Objectives (con't.)	True or false	Multiple choice	Problems and applications	Common errors	Pages in the text
7. Be able to contrast a competitive market's long-run behavior with that of a monopoly.	4, 5, 6, 14, 16, 20	1, 2, 4, 5, 8, 12, 19, 29	3, 4		140
8. Be able to describe the advantages and disadvantages of monopoly and competition.	3	3			141-143
9. Be able to distinguish economies of scale from constant returns to scale and diseconomies of scale.	7, 8, 13	13, 15, 16		4	142-143
10. Be able to explain the differences between the pure monopoly model and that of a natural monopoly.		13, 14, 22			143
11. Understand the idea of "contestable" markets.	1, 9, 17, 18, 19	26, 27, 28	4		143-145

Key-Term Review

Review the following terms; if you are not sure of the meaning of any term, write out the definition and check it against the Glossary in the text.

barriers to entry	marginal cost pricing	market power	patent
contestable market	margin revenue (MR)	monopoly	production decision
economies of scale	market demand	natural monopoly	profit-maximization rule

Fill in the blank following each of the statements below with the appropriate term from the list above.

1. A firm with no competitors is a .... 1. _____
   and, since such firms can control price,
   they have .... _____
2. A one-unit increase in production will change total
   revenue by an amount called the .... 2. _____
3. A competitive firm will increase its production rate
   until price equals marginal cost. Such behavior is
   called .... 3. _____
4. To keep out potential competitors, a monopoly firm
   can erect .... 4. _____

113

5. The government creates a barrier to entry when it protects new inventions with a ....5. _____

6. If average costs are always lower with greater rates of production, there are ....6. _____
and the market is likely to be a .... _____

7. In the short run a firm does not have the option to build a foreign plant, so temporarily its.......................7. _____
is to make the goods for export with existing domestic plant and equipment.

8. When a firm experiences growth in its foreign markets it is experiencing an increase in its ....8. _____

9. While only competitive firms use marginal cost pricing, both competitive firms and monopolists use the ....9. _____

10. A market in which the behavior of even imperfectly competitive firms is constrained by potential competition is called a ....10. _____

True or False: *Circle your choice.*

T   F   1. Since a competitive firm can sell unlimited quantities of output at the prevailing price, it can affect the market price of a good or service.

T   F   2. A monopolist can pick any point on the market supply curve and designate it as a new equilibrium.

T   F   3. Monopolists have a clear advantage over competitive markets in pursuing research and development and receiving the full benefit of research efforts.

T   F   4. Monopolists maximize profits at the output level at which price equals marginal cost.

T   F   5. In competitive markets, firms can make economic profits from innovation in the short run because of the time it takes other competitive firms to catch up.

T   F   6. Barriers to entry prevent the use of an invention in a monopolistic market from accruing to firms other than the monopolist.

T   F   7. A firm may achieve economies of scale by increasing production in a given plant.

T   F   8. The term "constant returns to scale" means that no matter how large a plant is built, the minimum average cost of production will still be the same.

T   F   9. By prosecuting illegal anticompetitive market behavior, the antitrust agencies make monopolists competitive.

T   F   10. The monopolist has a flat demand curve because of high barriers to entry.

T   F   11. The demand curve for the monopolist is exactly the same as the market demand curve.

T   F   12. Since both monopolists and competitive firms maximize profits at the output level at which marginal revenue equals marginal cost, monopolists and competitive markets with the same marginal cost curves and demand curves will produce the same output.

T   F   13. Diseconomies of scale (the opposite of economies) occur as a firm increases input, and its fixed costs are spread over greater production, causing average fixed costs to decrease in the short run.

T F 14. Monopolists redistribute income when they raise prices and profits above competitive levels.

T F 15. Monopolists exit when they are experiencing losses in the long run.

T F 16. Firms have an incentive to enter a market when economic profits are being earned in that market. Increased entry of new firms, however, reduces prices and profits.

T F 17. The theory of contestable markets focuses on market behavior rather than market structure.

T F 18. Barriers to entry are significant in determining how "contestable" a market is.

T F 19. When markets are contestable, firms *must* behave like pure competitors, even though the market structure is imperfectly competitive.

T F 20. Patents are a barrier to entry.

Multiple Choice: *Select the correct answer.*

_____ 1. In monopoly and competition, a firm should expand production when:
(a) Price is below marginal cost.
(b) Price is above marginal cost.
(c) Marginal revenue is below marginal cost.
(d) Marginal revenue is above marginal cost.

_____ 2. A monopolist with many plants produces less than would be produced if all of the plants were competing with one another in a competitive market:
(a) Because the market demand curve slopes downward for the monopolistic firm but not for the competitive firms.
(b) Because the market demand curve slopes downward for the monopolistic market and for the competitive market.
(c) Because the marginal revenue curve is below the demand curve for the monopolistic firm but not for the competitive firms.
(d) None of the above.

_____ 3. Monopoly may be considered more desirable than competition:
(a) Because the monopolist has more incentive to keep costs down.
(b) Because in polluting industries, monopoly is the best way of increasing output above the level of production that would be reached under competition.
(c) Because monopoly—for example, that which comes from the control of patents—is the best way of rewarding inventive efforts.
(d) Because economies of scale can only be fully realized by a single firm in a natural monopoly.

_____ 4. When a monopoly continues to make above-normal profits in the long run, you can be sure that:
(a) It produces more efficiently than a competitive market can.
(b) Barriers to entry prevent other firms from competing away the above-normal profits.
(c) There is a conspiracy between the government and the monopolist to maintain high prices.
(d) It has an inelastic demand curve, which gives it greater revenues.

5. Monopoly is said to be inefficient when:
   (a) Price in the long run is not equal to the lowest point of the long-run average cost curve.
   (b) The monopolist is not forced to choose the optimum size of plant because it can maximize profit with a plant of a different size.
   (c) The monopolist does not produce at an output level at which long-run marginal cost equals the minimum of long-run average cost.
   (d) All of the above are the case.

6. Which of the following is most likely *not* a monopolist?
   (a) The only doctor in a small community.
   (b) A large soft-drink firm such as Coca-Cola.
   (c) The electric power company in your area.
   (d) The water company in your area.

7. A monopolist has market power:
   (a) Because it faces a downward-sloping demand curve.
   (b) Because when it produces an extra unit of output, it must lower its price on all of its production.
   (c) Because its marginal revenue curve is below its demand curve.
   (d) For all of the above reasons.

8. Which of the following is the same for monopoly and competition under the same cost conditions?
   (a) The goal of maximizing profits.
   (b) Production levels.
   (c) Long-run economic profits.
   (d) Efficiency of production.

9. The demand curve and marginal revenue curve are different for a monopoly:
   (a) Because the supply curve is upward sloping for monopoly.
   (b) Because the marginal cost curve is upward sloping for monopoly.
   (c) Because lower revenues due to lower prices must be subtracted from revenue gains due to the greater output.
   (d) For all of the above reasons.

10. Which of the following rules will always be satisfied when a firm has maximized profit?
    (a) p = lowest level of long-run average costs.
    (b) p = MC.
    (c) MR = MC.
    (d) p = AC.

11. The supply curve for a monopolist:
    (a) Slopes upward.
    (b) Is the same as the marginal cost curve.
    (c) Is the same as the marginal revenue curve.
    (d) Doesn't exist.

12. Which of the following is *not* a barrier to entry into a monopoly?
    (a) Profits of the monopolist.
    (b) Advertising.
    (c) Patents.
    (d) Difficulty of obtaining resources.

13. Which of the following types of monopoly always achieves economies of scale?
    (a) A pure monopoly.
    (b) A discriminating monopoly.
    (c) A natural monopoly.
    (d) None of the above.

14. Which of the following types of monopoly has market power?
    (a) Pure monopoly.
    (b) Discriminating monopoly.
    (c) Natural monopoly.
    (d) All of the above.

Choose among the four diagrams presented in Figure 7.1 to answer Questions 15-20.

Figure 7.1

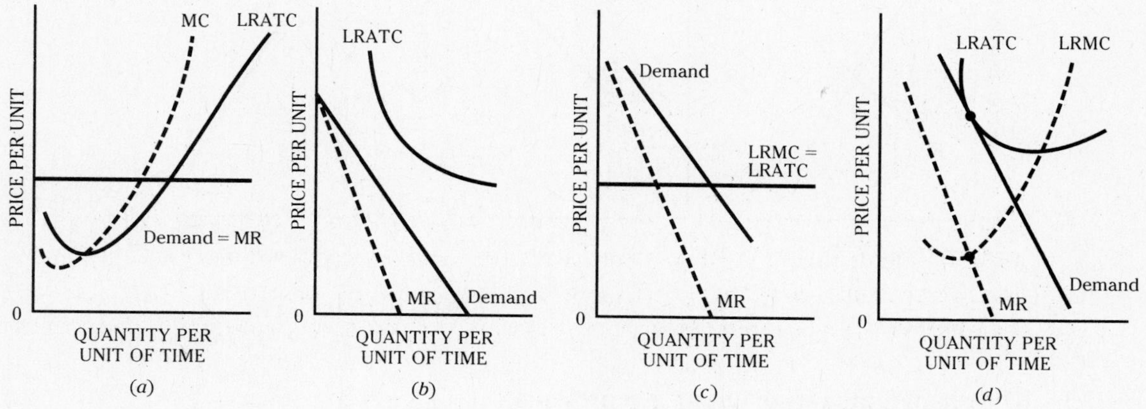

15. In which case are there always economies of scale?
16. In which case are there constant returns to scale?
17. In which case does the firm have no market power?
18. In which case can a monopolist make only negative profits?
19. In which case is the firm making zero economic profit when it maximizes profits?
20. Average profits are computed by:
    (a) (TR - TC)/q.
    (b) AR - MC.
    (c) Demand curve - marginal cost curve.
    (d) MR - AC.

117

In Questions 21-22, decide what type of pricing is being used.

_____ 21. Farmers plant a particular crop long before they know what price they will receive for it.
   (a) Monopoly pricing.
   (b) Competitive pricing.
   (c) Pricing to maximize revenue.
   (d) None of the above.

_____ 22. Cities often provide their own sewer and water services. Rates are often determined by a rate-making board.
   (a) Monopoly pricing.
   (b) Marginal cost pricing.
   (c) Price taking.
   (d) None of the above.

Use the three diagrams in Figure 7.2 to answer Questions 23-25.

Figure 7.2

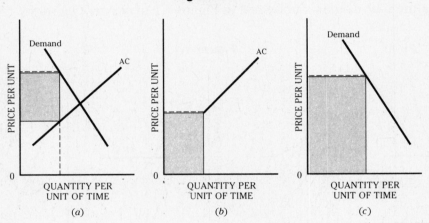

(a)   (b)   (c)

_____ 23. The shaded area in diagram *a* represents:
   (a) Total revenue.
   (b) Total cost.
   (c) Total profit.
   (d) None of the above.

_____ 24. The shaded area in diagram *b* represents:
   (a) Total revenue.
   (b) Total cost.
   (c) Total profit.
   (d) None of the above.

_____ 25. The shaded area in diagram *c* represents:
   (a) Total revenue.
   (b) Total cost.
   (c) Total profit.
   (d) None of the above.

118

26. The U.S. automobile market is thought to be:
    (a) A monopoly.
    (b) Perfectly competitive.
    (c) Contestable.
    (d) None of the above.

27. The theory of contestable markets relies on:
    (a) Market behavior.
    (b) Potential entry.
    (c) Market structure.
    (d) All of the above.

28. In the U.S. automobile market, the major restraint on market power is:
    (a) Antitrust legislation.
    (b) Antitrust enforcement.
    (c) Foreign competition.
    (d) None of the above.

29. Which of the following groupings contains a word or phrase that does not belong?
    (a) Economies of scale, barriers to entry, natural monopoly.
    (b) Market power, marginal cost pricing, long-run profit.
    (c) Marginal profit, marginal revenue, marginal cost.
    (d) Average profit, average revenue, average cost.

Problems and Applications

Exercise 1

This exercise shows graphically how to represent total revenue, total cost, and total profit on the basis of average revenue and average cost curves.

Table 7.1. Revenue and cost from producing and selling cards

Quantity of cards (millions of decks per month)	Revenue		Cost	
	Total (millions of dollars per month)	Average (dollars per month)	Total (millions of dollars per month)	Average (dollars per month)
0	$ 0.0	$_____	$ 0.0	$_____
4	6.4	_____	2.8	$_____
10	10.0	_____	10.0	_____
20	0.0	_____	30.0	_____

1. In Table 7.1, the total revenue and average cost are presented for the Black Jack Playing Card Company, which has a monopoly on the production of playing cards. Fill in the information on average revenue and average costs for the production levels shown in Table 7.1. In Figure 7.3, draw and label the average cost curve and demand (average revenue) curves based on Table 7.1. (Use straight lines for both curves.)

Figure 7.3. Total profit from average revenue and average cost

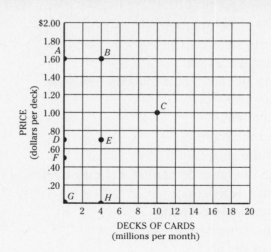

2. In Figure 7.3, shade with vertical lines the total revenue that the Black Jack Playing Card Company would earn by producing and selling 4 million decks of cards per month.

3. Which of the following line segments represents average revenue from selling 4 million decks of cards? _____
   (a) *BE.*　　(c) *BH.*　　(e) None of the above.
   (b) *EH.*　　(d) *AF.*

4. In Figure 7.3, shade with light horizontal lines the total cost that the Black Jack Playing Card Company would incur to produce 4 million decks of cards per month.

5. Which of the following line segments represents the average cost of producing 4 million decks of cards? _____
   (a) *BE.*　　(c) *BH.*　　(e) None of the above.
   (b) *EH.*　　(d) *AF.*

6. Which of the following rectangles in Figure 7.3 represents total profit? _____
   (a) *ABHG* (total shaded area).　　　　　(c) *DEHG* (cross-hatched area).
   (b) *ABED* (non-cross-hatched shaded area).　　(d) None of the above.

7. Which of the following line segments represents the average profit from producing and selling 4 million decks of cards? _____
   (a) *BE.*　　(c) *BH.*　　(e) None of the above.
   (b) *EH.*　　(d) *AF.*

8. Compute each of the following:
   (a) The area of *ABHG* (total shaded area) in Figure 7.3 under the demand curve. _____
   (b) The total revenue from selling 4 million decks of cards. _____
   (c) The length of line segment *BH* multiplied by the length of line segment *GH* in Figure 7.3. _____
   (d) The average revenue multiplied by the quantity sold (4 million decks of cards). _____
   Does each of these methods result in the same total revenue calculation?

120

9. Compute each of the following:
   (a) The area *DEHG* (cross-hatched area) under the average cost curve in Figure 7.3._____
   (b) The total cost from selling 4 million decks of cards._____
   (c) The length of line segment *EH* multiplied by the length of line segment *GH* in Figure 7.3. _____
   (d) The average cost multiplied by the quantity sold (4 million decks of cards)._____
   Does each of these methods result in the same total cost calculation?

10. Compute each of the following:
   (a) The area of *ABED* (non-cross-hatched area) between the demand and average cost curves in Figure 7.3._____
   (b) The total profit from selling 4 million decks of cards._____
   (c) The area *ABHG* (total shaded area) minus area *DEHG* (cross-hatched area) in Figure 7.3._____
   (d) The total revenue minus total cost from producing and selling 4 million decks of cards._____
   (e) The length of line segment *BE* multiplied by the length of line segment *GH* in Figure 7.3._____
   (f) The average profit multiplied by the quantity sold (4 million decks of cards)._____
   Does each of these methods result in the same total profit calculation?

Exercise 2

This exercise is a review of the cost and revenue formulas and gives further experience with profit maximization.

1. Match the algebraic formulas at the right with the equivalent economic terms at the left.

   fixed cost (FC)   a. TR - TC
   variable cost (VC)   b. FC + VC
   total revenue (TR)   c. same as total cost at zero production rate
   total cost (TC)   d. $\Delta TC / \Delta q$
   average total cost (ATC)   e. TC / q
   profit   f. type of cost that is zero at a zero production rate
   price (p)   g. (TR - TC) / q
   marginal cost (MC)   h. $\Delta TR / \Delta q$
   marginal revenue (MR)   i. p x q or TC + profit
   average profit   j. TR / q

2. Table 7.2 shows the cost breakdown from projected income statements of the American Ferris Aluminum Company. It shows what costs would be at four levels of production. Using these data, fill in Table 7.2. (*Note:* If you do not remember how to sort fixed and variable costs, look at their definitions in the text. If you still have trouble, see the problems and applications of Chapter 5 in this study guide.)

Table 7.2. Cost of aluminum production, by category, at four production levels

	Aluminum production (tons per week)			
	0	1,000	2,000	3,000
Price (dollars per unit)	$ 120	$ 100	$ 80	$ 60
Cost (dollars per week):				
Production workers	0	15,000	30,000	90,000
Managers, maintenance, interest, and taxes	26,000	26,000	26,000	26,000
Leased equipment payments	34,000	34,000	34,000	34,000
Electricity and bauxite	0	25,000	60,000	120,000

Table 7.3. Costs and revenues, American Ferris Aluminum Company, at four production levels

	Aluminum production (tons per week)			
	0	1,000	2,000	3,000
Fixed costs dollars per week)	$_____	$_____	$_____	$_____
Total cost (dollars per week)	_____	_____	_____	_____
Marginal cost (dollars per ton)	_____	_____	_____	_____
Average total cost (dollars per ton)	_____	_____	_____	_____
Total revenue (dollars per week)	_____	_____	_____	_____
Marginal revenue (dollars per ton)	_____	_____	_____	_____

3. In order to draw a demand curve, you need to have a demand schedule that relates:
   (a) Total revenue to total cost.
   (b) The production rate to each price.
   (c) The profit to each level of production.
   (d) The marginal cost at each level of production.
4. Using your computations in Table 7.3, graph the demand, marginal revenue, average total cost, average variable cost, and marginal cost in Figure 7.4. In this problem you are dealing with discrete data, *so things don't work out exactly.* Still, you should be able to answer questions based on this graph. In Figure 7.4 your demand curve should pass through point A, your average total cost curve through point B, your marginal revenue curve through point C, and your marginal cost curve through point D.

Figure 7.4. Profit maximization and representation

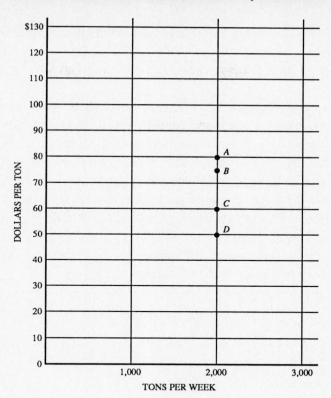

5. Which of the four production rates in Table 7.3 comes nearest to the point at which marginal revenue and marginal cost are equal? _____ This is the profit-maximizing production rate.

6. The profit-maximizing *price* for a monopolist:
    (a) Can be read on the *y*-axis horizontally from the demand curve, *below* the point where MR = MC.
    (b) Is equal to marginal revenue at the point at which MR = MC.
    (c) Can be read from the *y*-axis horizontally to the left of the point where MR = MC.
    (d) Can be read on the *y*-axis horizontally from the demand curve, *above* the point where MR = MC.

7. The profit-maximizing price for the monopolist pictured in Figure 7.4 is:
    (a) $100 per ton.
    (b) $80 per ton.
    (c) $70 per ton.
    (d) $60 per ton.

8. In Figure 7.4, shade in total profit at the profit-maximizing production rate. If you have done so correctly, the *area* that you have shaded equals which of the following?
    (a) Profits at a production rate of 2,000 tons per week in Table 7.3.
    (b) Total revenue minus total cost at all rates of production.
    (c) Average revenue minus average cost at all rates of production.
    (d) All of the above.

123

Exercise 3

This exercise helps to compare monopoly and competition graphically, particularly with respect to output and price.

In *A Soldier's Story* Omar Bradley described his experiences in North Africa during World War II. He observed:

> In Relizane, as elsewhere in North Africa where there were American troops, the Arab bootblack soon upset the economic equilibrium of his community. As the result of lavish GI tipping, shines skyrocketed from one franc to 15 francs each. At 50 francs to an American dollar, an enterprising bootblack could earn more in a day than his parents could make in a month of farm labor. These prices, however, brought on a black market in PX shoe polish and the price for polish soon rose to a dollar a can. A few of the more enterprising bootblacks eventually monopolized the trade by cornering the supply of brown polish.

Fill in each blank in the following questions on the basis of the preceding quotation.

_____ 1. When the Americans came to North Africa, the _____ for shoe-polishing services_____.
   (a) Demand.
   (b) Supply.
   (c) Marginal cost.
   (d) Average cost.

_____ 2. (a) Shifted to the right.
   (b) Shifted to the left.

As a result of this change, the price of a shoeshine rose to 15 francs.

_____ 3. The supply curve of farm labor probably _____ because of the newly profitable service.
   (a) Shifted to the right.
   (b) Shifted to the left.
   (c) Remained unchanged.

_____ 4. The market supply curve of shoe polishers probably _____ as a result of the increased entry into shoe polishing.
   (a) Shifted to the left.
   (b) Shifted to the right.
   (c) Remained unchanged.

_____ 5. Shoeshines rose in price because shoeshiners had to pay higher prices for shoe polish. As a result, the supply curve for shoeshines _____ .
   (a) Shifted upward.
   (b) Shifted downward.
   (c) Remained the same.

6. Figure 7.5 presents the market demand and supply curves for shoeshines. The market supply curve equals the sum of the marginal cost curves of all bootblacks. What letter in Figure 7.5 indicates the number of shoeshines that would be offered if the shoeshine trade were competitive?_____.

124

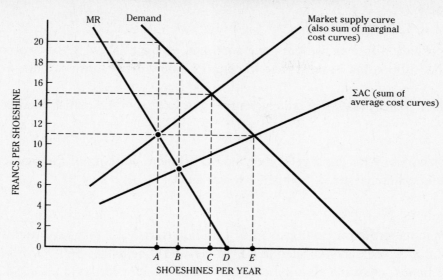

Figure 7.5. The shoeshine market

7. What would the price of a shoeshine be?_____ .
   (a) 20 francs per shoeshine.
   (b) 18 francs per shoeshine.
   (c) 15 francs per shoeshine.
   (d) None of the above.

8. What letter in Figure 7.5 indicates the number of shoeshines that would be offered if the shoeshine trade were monopolized? _____ .

9. Under the monopoly, the price would be _____ .
   (a) 20 francs per shoeshine.
   (b) 15 francs per shoeshine.
   (c) 14 francs per shoeshine.
   (d) None of the above.

10. If General Patton, under whom Bradley was serving, required his men to have polished shoes each day and they had no time to do it themselves, the demand for shoeshines would become more _____ , even at very high prices.
    (a) Elastic.
    (b) Inelastic.
    (c) Unit elastic.

Exercise 4

Many newspapers provide information from competitive markets, such as the want ads, market prices, and advertising. If your professor makes a newspaper assignment for this chapter from the *Instructor's Manual*, this exercise will provide an example of how to do it.

Reread the Headline article on page 112 in Chapter 6 entitled "Southern Farmers Hooked on New Cash Crop" from *USA Today*. Then quote the words that give an example of each of the following types of information which can help verify that a market is really competitive.

1. *Structural characteristics.* What phrases indicate that large numbers of farmers are involved?

   Supppose each farmer had only one pond and each catfish weighed two pounds Use the information in the article to determine how many farmers there would be.

2. *Conduct.* What passage(s) indicate entry to or exit from the catfish market?

3. *Performance.* What passage(s) indicate the efficient working of the market mechanism which is characteristic of competitive markets?

4. Compute the profit on Hollingsworth's 1 million catfish if it takes 10 weeks to feed them at $18,000 a week, as indicated in the article, and if he makes $60,000 from each one of his 10 ponds. Assume all other economic costs besides feed add up to $420,000.

5. *Market boundaries.* Based on information in the article only, which of the following best characterizes the market boundaries of the catfish market? It appears to be strictly:
   (a) A local market.
   (b) A regional market.
   (c) A national market.
   (d) An international market.

6. What information in the article provides a clue about the extent of the market boundaries?

Common Errors

The first statement in each "common error" below is incorrect. Each incorrect statement is followed by a corrected version and an explanation.

1. The shaded area in Figure 7.6*a* shows total profits.

Figure 7.6*a*

WRONG!

The shaded area in Figure 7.6 *b* shows total profits.

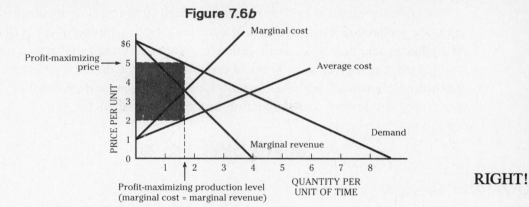

Figure 7.6*b*

RIGHT!

Notice that profit-maximizing production is found at the point where the MR curve intersects the MC curve. But *after* finding the profit-maximizing output level, forget about MR = MC. When you're finding profits, don't use marginal curves; use the *average* curves. Simply find the difference between the demand curve (which is also the average revenue curve) and the average cost curve. This procedure gives you average profit. Then shade in everything to the left of the average profit until the *y*-axis is reached.

Here's a little rule to keep things straight:
- Use marginal curves to find profit-maximizing production.
- Use average curves to find profits.

2. Monopolists have supply curves. WRONG!
Monopolists have marginal cost curves, but not supply curves. RIGHT!

The marginal cost indicates the quantity that a competitive firm will supply at a given price. (*Remember:* Price equals marginal cost for the competitive firm.) But we cannot tell what a monopolist will supply at a given price by looking at the marginal cost curve. We need to know marginal revenue and therefore the demand curve before we can tell what quantity the firm will supply. (*Remember:* Marginal cost equals marginal revenue when profits are maximized.)

Be careful! Do not label the marginal cost curve of a monopolist (or any noncompetitive firm) as a "supply" curve in your diagrams.

3. A monopolist wishes to be on the inelastic part of the demand curve. WRONG!
A monopolist will operate on the elastic part of the demand curve. RIGHT!

If demand is inelastic, then the monopoly can usually decrease costs and increase revenues by cutting back production. This procedure means more profits. Remember the total-revenue test for the elasticity of demand. If demand is inelastic, then a firm can raise prices and get more revenues. Of course, with lower production rates, the firm also experiences lower costs. There is no doubt about it, if any firm is on the inelastic portion of its demand curve, it can make greater profits by raising prices!

4. When there are economies of scale, a firm can simply increase production rates in the short run and unit costs will decline. WRONG!

127

When there are economies of scale, a firm can choose a plant size designed for increased production rates at lower unit costs. RIGHT!

Economies of scale are not realized through production decisions in the short run. They are realized through investment decisions, by the choice of an optimal-sized plant for higher production rates. Scale refers to plant size or capacity, not to production rates within a plant of a given size. Think of economies of scale in terms of investment decisions concerning choices of optimal capacity for the long run, *not* production decisions concerning the lowest cost production in the short run.

■ ANSWERS ■

Key-Term Review

1. monopoly
    market power
2. marginal revenue (MR)
3. marginal cost pricing

4. barriers to entry
5. patent
6. economies of scale
   natural monopoly

7. production decision
8. market demand
9. profit-maximization rule
10. contestable market

True or False

1. F	4. F	7. F	10. F	13. F	16. T	19. F
2. F	5. T	8. T	11. T	14. T	17. T	20. T
3. T	6. T	9. F	12. F	15. T	18. T	

Multiple Choice

1. d	5. d	9. c	13. c	17. a	21. b	25. a
2. c	6. b	10. c	14. d	18. b	22. a	26. c
3. d	7. d	11. d	15. b	19. d	23. c	27. d
4. b	8. a	12. a	16. c	20. a	24. b	28. c

29. b Market power and marginal cost pricing are not consistent. Other topics include (a) barriers to entry, (c) marginal measures used in profit maximization, and (d) average measures of economic quantities.

Problems and Applications

Exercise 1

1. Table 7.1 Answer

Quantity	Average revenue	Average cost
0	$ __	$ __
4	1.60	0.70
10	1	1.00
20	0	1.50

Figure 7.3 Answer

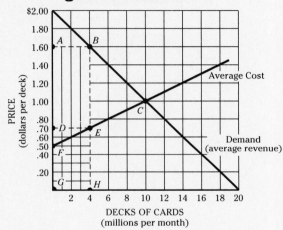

2. See area with vertical lines in Figure 7.3 answer.
3. c
4. See cross-hatched shaded area in Figure 7.3 answer.
5. b
6. b
7. a
8. Each results in same estimate: $6.4 million per month. (4 million decks per month x $1.60 per deck)
9. Each results in same estimate: $2.8 million per month. (4 million decks per month x $0.70 per deck)
10. Each results in same estimate: $3.6 million per month. (4 million decks per month x $0.90 per deck)

Exercise 2

1. FC c   TR i   ATC e   *p* j   MR h
    VC f   TC b   profit a   MC d   average profit g

2. Table 7.3 Answer

	Aluminum production			
	0	1,000	2,000	3,000
Fixed costs	$60,000	$ 60,000	$ 60,000	$ 60,000
Total cost	60,000	100,000	150,000	270,000
Marginal cost	—	40	50	120
Average total cost	—	100	75	90
Total revenue	0	100,000	160,000	180,000
Marginal revenue	—	100	60	20

3. b

4. Figure 7.4 Answer

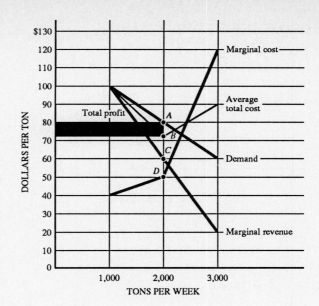

5. 2,000 tons per week
6. d
7. b
8. See Figure 7.4 answer; a

Exercise 3

1. a	3. b	5. a	7. c	9. a
2. a	4. b	6. c	8. a	10. b

Exercise 4

1. The title indicates many "southern farmers." The article indicates 340 million pounds of catfish. Dividing this by 2 pounds per catfish gives the number of catfish (170 million). Since there are 100,000 fish in each pond according to the article, there would be 1,700 farmers.

2. "Catfish are replacing crops," "business is growing among farmers," and the title, "Southern Farmers Hooked on New Cash Crop," suggest entry.

3. "But you can't take a poor row-crop farmer and make him a good catfish farmer" introduces a discussion that indicates that inefficient farmers will not survive the market. Also, the phrase "You get about 60 cents per fish" suggests that a farmer is a price taker, not a price maker.

4. Feed costs would be $180,000 ($18,000 per week x 10 weeks). Adding this to other economic costs of $420,000 results in total economic costs of $600,000. There would be zero economic profit.

5. c

6. The article indicates the Mississippi Delta is where 80 percent of the farm-bred catfish are grown. This would suggest a regional market from the supply perspective. However, data are given for the total United States. On the basis of the article, the entire United States is the effective market being served.

130

CHAPTER 8

The Labor Market

Quick Review

Most of us do not think of ourselves in the abstract as "inputs," or factors of production, but in the language of the circular flow of economic activity, that's what we are. In the circular flow model there are markets for products and markets for factors. People are demanders in the product market but suppliers in the factor market. This chapter discusses the supply side of that market first and then looks at the demand side. Here are some important questions we discuss.

- How do people decide how much time to spend working?
- What determines the wage rate an employer is willing to pay?
- Why are some workers paid so much and others so little?

Let's begin with the first question. People choose between leisure and the satisfaction of material needs. Given the institutional structure of our economy, material needs are satisfied mainly by working for income. When we work, however, we sacrifice leisure. Hence, the opportunity cost of goods and services obtained by working is the number of hours of leisure that must be sacrificed to earn the required income. Conversely, the opportunity cost of leisure is the amount of goods and services that cannot be bought because of the time not spent working. Psychological and social needs may also motivate people to work. These needs affect the utility of both leisure and the income gained from work.

The marginal utility of labor reflects the satisfaction to be gained from added income as well as any direct pleasure a job may provide. A worker compares the marginal utility of work with that of leisure and chooses either more work or more leisure, depending on which offers greater marginal utility.

Now let's look at the demand side of the market. The demand for labor depends on the demand for the goods or services that labor produces. The demand for labor is thus a derived demand, and the marginal revenue product curve is a derived demand curve. It shows the additional revenue generated by an additional unit of labor. An employer will not want to pay a worker more than the extra revenue that the worker creates. Hence, the marginal revenue product curve sets an upper limit to wages.

The more labor a business employs, the less revenue each additional unit of labor brings to the firm. This reflects the law of diminishing returns: employing more workers in a given firm implies that each worker has less plant and equipment with which to work. As a result, each worker's marginal product declines as more workers are hired.

The demand for other factors is similarly derived. Their demand curves also slope downward and to the right as a result of the workings of the law of diminishing returns.

The interaction of the market-demand and market-supply curves determines the equilibrium market wage. When either the market-supply or market-demand curve shifts due to changes in its nonprice determinants, surpluses or shortages may result. The labor market adjusts just as a product market does. Shortages lead to wage increases, surpluses to wage decreases.

The marginal revenue product is not the only means by which wage rates are determined, however. Wage rates also reflect market power, custom, discrimination, and the opportunity wage. Women's rights advocates have developed a doctrine called "comparable worth" to reinforce the Equal Pay Act of 1963. They argue that jobs may be comparable even though they are not identical (that is, a typist = a truck driver). If comparable, they should get equal pay. Adopting this idea would require a subjective ranking of all occupations. The U.S. Commission on Civil Rights has rejected it.

Learning Objectives

After reading Chapter 8 and doing the following exercises, you should:	True or false	Multiple choice	Problems and applications	Common errors	Pages in the text
1. Understand the labor-supply curve and its nonprice determinants.	1, 2	1, 2, 6, 7, 9		1, 2	149-152
2. Be able to apply the law of diminishing marginal utility to the labor market.	2	1, 2, 6, 7, 9		1, 2	149-152
3. Know how many people determine the number of hours they want to work.	1	1, 2, 6, 7, 9		1, 2	149-152
4. Be able to explain the shape of the individual labor-supply curve and the market labor-supply curve.	4, 5	5	1, 2, 3	2	152
5. Understand that the demand for factors of production is derived from the demand for goods and services.	7, 12	13, 16, 23, 26	1, 2, 3	3, 6	153
6. Be able to derive the marginal revenue product curve and know why it slopes downward.	7, 9, 10, 11	13, 15, 16, 19, 22, 23, 24, 25, 26, 27	1, 2, 3	5	153-158
7. Understand how the firm uses the wage rate and the marginal revenue product of a factor to make the hiring decision.	7	8, 17, 18, 20	2, 3	4	158-161

Learning Objectives _(cont'd.)_	True or false	Multiple choice	Problems and applications	Common errors	Pages in the text
8. Be able to use changes in productivity and market prices to predict changes in the demand for a factor.	7, 8, 10		2	5	160-161
9. Understand how market supply and market demand interact to determine market wage rates when their nonprice determinants change.		5, 7, 10, 12, 17, 18, 19, 20	2	7	161-162
10. Know how to analyze the impact of policies and institutions that influence the labor market.	3, 6	3, 4, 11, 28, 29	4		162-164
11. Understand the implications of the "comparable worth" doctrine.	13, 14	21			167
12. Know that the "opportunity wage" reflects a worker's productivity in his or her best alternative employment, _ceteris paribus._		21, 30, 31			165-166

Key-Term Review

Review the following terms; if you are not sure of the meaning of any term, write out the definition and check it against the Glossary in the text.

demand for labor
derived demand
equilibrium wage
labor supply

law of diminishing returns
marginal physical product (MPP)
marginal revenue product (MRP)

market supply of labor
opportunity cost
opportunity wage

Fill in the blank following each of the statements below with the appropriate term from the list above.

1. By summing the individual _____ curves, .. 1. _____
   we can obtain the _____. .... _____

2. Since the marginal revenue product is computed on the basis of the demand for the product produced, it is referred to as a .... 2. _____

3. In order to make this choice, a firm must know, in addition to the input cost, the amount of output each additional unit of a factor provides, which is the .... 3. _____

4. As more of a factor is used, its marginal productivity will probably fall, in accordance with the .... 4. _____

5. As the marginal productivity of labor declines, the curve that represents the .... 5. _____
develops a downward slope.

6. If you know the marginal physical product and the price of the product, then for any factor you can compute the .... 6. _____

7. The highest pay that an individual can earn in alternative jobs is his or her............................. 7. _____

8. The value of the next best alternative use of resources is the .... 8. _____

9. Because the minimum wage exceeds the_____, 9. _____
unemployment is the obvious result.

True or False: *Circle your choice.*

T   F   1. The fact that you are willing to have leisure time and are able to pay for it by working means that you have a supply curve for labor.

T   F   2. The chief reason people work is that work itself has utility.

T   F   3. If a union achieves above-equilibrium wages for its membership, the wages of nonunion workers will suffer.

T   F   4. The market supply of labor curve is the horizontal summation of the individual labor-supply curves of laborers in the labor market.

T   F   5. If the market supply of labor were to bend backward, employers would have to reduce wages to obtain larger quantities of labor.

T   F   6. When a firm is taxed by the government, employees do not feel the effects of the tax; only a firm's profits are affected.

T   F   7. A firm's upper limit of willingness to pay labor is determined by the marginal revenue product curve.

T   F   8. When the demand for a firm's product changes, the firm's demand for factors of production changes as well.

T   F   9. The law of diminishing returns suggests that the fewer the workers employed, the more total output they can produce together in a given time period, *ceteris paribus.*

T   F   10. If a firm's marginal physical product curve slopes downward, its marginal revenue product curve must also slope downward.

T   F   11. Because of the law of diminishing returns, the demand curve for a product slopes downward.

T   F   12. Unlike most demand curves, derived demand curves may not be governed by the law of demand.

T   F   13. Advocates of comparable worth use supply and demand to establish pay scales.

T   F   14. The U.S. Commission on Civil Rights has rejected the comparable worth doctrine.

Multiple Choice: *Select the correct answer.*

1. The main reason that people work is:
   (a) The work ethic.
   (b) Materialistic wants.
   (c) That too much leisure is not good.
   (d) None of the above.

2. The constraint that is *most* important in determining the tradeoff between leisure and work is:
   (a) Income.
   (b) Time.
   (c) Available goods and services.
   (d) Satisfaction from working.

3. To maintain above-equilibrium wages, unions use which of the following forms of exclusion:
   (a) Union membership.
   (b) Required apprenticeship programs.
   (c) Employment agreements negotiated with employers.
   (d) All of the above.

4. The effect of union exclusion on nonunion workers is to:
   (a) Increase the shortages of nonunion workers.
   (b) Lower the wages of nonunion workers.
   (c) Increase the number of jobs for nonunion workers.
   (d) All of the above.

5. Because of the work ethic, the *supply curve* for labor is:
   (a) Higher than it would be if people had only materialistic needs.
   (b) Lower than it would be if people had only materialistic needs.
   (c) Higher than it would be if the United States were a slaveholding society, as ancient Greece was.
   (d) None of the above.

6. Which of the following examples *best* suggests that the marginal utility of work is higher than the marginal utility of leisure?
   (a) At the end of the 1960s, many college students did not bother to get jobs.
   (b) During the Vietnam War, many young men were drafted into the army in order to provide the necessary military personnel.
   (c) During 1972-73, union representatives pushed for optional overtime in contracts with several major companies that previously had required involuntary overtime.
   (d) During the recession of 1974-75, some unions had to accept lower pay in order to maintain jobs.

_____ 7. Shifts of the labor-supply curve are caused by:
  (a) Changes in tastes for jobs.
  (b) Wage increases.
  (c) Changes in the number of job vacancies.
  (d) All of the above.

Figure 8.1 shows possible movements along or shifts of the market labor-supply curve.

Figure 8.1

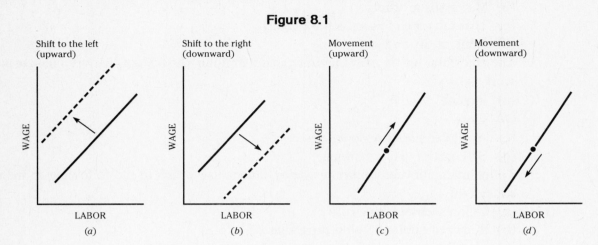

Choose the letter of the diagram that best represents what would happen to the private labor market in Questions 8-12, _ceteris paribus._

_____ 8. The wage rate rises.
_____ 9. Job status increases.
_____ 10. There is a reduction in the size of the labor force.
_____ 11. Wage controls push wages below market levels.
_____ 12. Women are legally permitted to serve in combat functions in the armed forces for the first time.
_____ 13. The differences between demand in the product market and demand in the factor market include:
  (a) The fact that the demand curve for the product is governed by the law of demand and the derived demand curve is not.
  (b) The fact that the demand curve for a product is the same as the marginal revenue curve, but the derived demand is not the same as the marginal revenue product.
  (c) The fact that the axes of the two demand curves are labeled differently.
  (d) All of the above.
_____ 14. In order to calculate marginal revenue product, we need to know:
  (a) The marginal physical product and the marginal revenue of the product.
  (b) The marginal physical product and the unit price of the factor.
  (c) The marginal revenue and the amount of the product produced.
  (d) The marginal revenue and the cost of the factor.

136

15. The diminishing returns to a factor may be due to:
    (a) The declining utility of a good as we consume more of it.
    (b) Crowding or overuse of other factors as production is increased.
    (c) The decline in the demand curve for a product.
    (d) The decline in the marginal revenue curve for a product.

16. The marginal revenue product curve and marginal physical product curve have similar shapes:
    (a) Because marginal revenue product depends on marginal physical product.
    (b) Because the product demand curve slopes downward in accordance with the law of diminishing returns.
    (c) Because the law of demand and the law of diminishing returns are due to the same economic behavior.
    (d) For all of the above reasons.

17. Employment will definitely rise when:
    (a) Productivity and wages rise.
    (b) Productivity rises and wages fall.
    (c) Productivity falls and wages rise.
    (d) Productivity and wages fall.

18. A change in wages causes a shift in:
    (a) The marginal revenue product curve for labor
    (b) The marginal physical product curve for labor.
    (c) The derived demand curve for labor.
    (d) None of the above.

19. A change in productivity causes a change in:
    (a) The marginal revenue product of labor.
    (b) The marginal physical product of labor.
    (c) The derived demand for labor.
    (d) All of the above.

20. A change in the demand for a product usually causes, *ceteris paribus*:
    (a) A shift in the marginal revenue product curve for labor.
    (b) A change in the price of the product.
    (c) A shift in the demand curve for labor.
    (d) All of the above.

21. Which of the following help to explain why the wages received by two workers with different jobs are not the same?
    (a) Differences in marginal revenue products at their respective jobs.
    (b) Wages that they would receive in alternative jobs.
    (c) The prices of the products they produce.
    (d) All of the above.

Figure 8.2 presents four diagrams. For Questions 22-27, pick the diagram that best illustrates: (Pay attention to the units in which each axis is measured.)

Figure 8.2

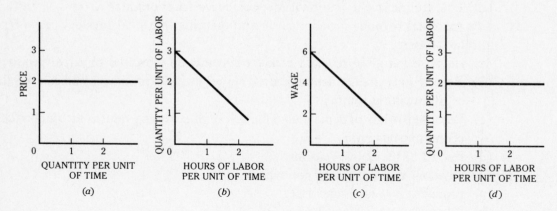

22. The law of diminishing returns.
23. The demand curve in a factor market.
24. The derived demand curve.
25. The marginal revenue product curve.
26. The curve that one can always find by multiplying the marginal physical product by marginal revenue.
27. The demand curve for a product.
28. Which of the following policies is consistent with *shortages* of labor in the labor market?
    (a) Wage controls (ceilings).
    (b) Price controls (ceilings).
    (c) Minimum-wage legislation.
    (d) None of the above.
29. Which of the following policies is consistent with surpluses of labor in the labor market?
    (a) Price supports in the product market.
    (b) Minimum-wage legislation.
    (c) Wage controls (ceilings).
    (d) All of the above.
30. The economic theory of wage determination and the comparable worth doctrine:
    (a) Can be reconciled since both depend on supply and demand.
    (b) Cannot be reconciled because the former depends on demand and supply and the latter depends on subjective evaluations.
    (c) Cannot be reconciled because one depends on free markets and the other depends on market intervention.
    (d) Have been reconciled by the city of Los Angeles.

_____ 31. If the comparable worth doctrine was widely adopted, economic theory would predict:
  (a) Surpluses in those occupations where the wage was raised.
  (b) Shortages in those occupations where the wage was not raised.
  (c) That a new mechanism would be required to eliminate the shortages and surpluses.
  (d) All of the above.

_____ 32. Which of the following groupings contains a word or phrase which does not belong?
  (a) Union membership, required apprenticeship programs, marginal revenue.
  (b) Wage rate, interest rate, rent.
  (c) Labor, capital, land.
  (d) Tastes, income, expectations.

Problems and Applications

Exercise 1

This exercise gives practice in using the formulas for derived demand and graphing of derived demand; it will help you with Exercise 3 as well.

1. Match the formulas on the right with the appropriate economic term on the left. (*Note: q* refers to the quantity of a product, and *L* refers to the amount of labor services during a given time period. Assume labor is the only cost. Remember that the symbol Δ refers to a small change in a variable.)

_____ total cost (TC)	a. $p \times q$
_____ marginal cost (MC)	b. $\Delta TR / \Delta L$
_____ total revenue (TR)	c. Wage $\times L$
_____ marginal revenue (MR)	d. $\Delta TC / \Delta q$
_____ marginal revenue product (MRP)	e. $\Delta TR / \Delta q$

Refer to the diagrams in Figure 8.3 in answering Questions 2-6.

Figure 8.3

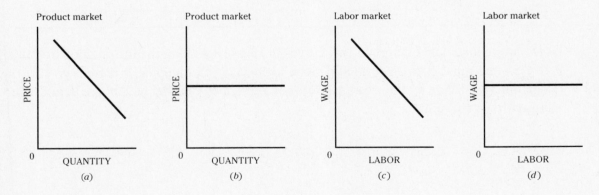

139

2. Which curve might represent a firm's marginal revenue in a competitive market?_____
3. Which curve represents marginal revenue product when marginal physical productivity is declining?_____
4. Which curve represents the supply curve of labor (wage rate) when a firm does not have the market power to influence the wage rate? _____
5. Which curve might represent the demand curve for labor in a perfectly competitive labor market? _____
6. Which curve might represent the demand curve for a product of a competitive firm?_____

Exercise 2

This exercise provides experience in computing and graphing derived demand as well as determining the profit-maximizing wage. It shows that a solution in the product market is the same as the solution in the labor market.

Profit Maximization in the Product Market: Review

1. You are a producer of Rotgut Ripple, which sells for $1 per gallon. In its desire to lend some local color to your country, the government permits you to produce it in the hills, where the ingredients cost nothing. It is hard to get people to work for you. You have to pay $3 an hour for labor, which is your only cost. Table 8.1 shows your costs and revenues according to the amount of labor you hire. Complete Table 8.1.

Table 8.1. Cost and revenue of Rotgut Ripple production, by labor hours

(1) Wage (dollars per hour)	(2) Labor (workers per hour)	(3) Quantity produced (gallons per hour)	(4) Total cost (dollars per hour)	(5) Marginal cost (dollars per gallon)	(6) Price (dollars per gallon)	(7) Total revenue (dollars per hour)	(8) Marginal revenue product (dollars per worker)
$3	0	0	$_____	$_____	$1	$_____	$_____
3	1	15	_____	_____	1	_____	_____
3	2	27	_____	_____	1	_____	_____
3	3	36	_____	_____	1	_____	_____
3	4	42	_____	_____	1	_____	_____
3	5	45	_____	_____	1	_____	_____
3	6	46	_____	_____	1	_____	_____

2. Draw your demand and marginal cost curves in Figure 8.4 using the information in Table 8.1. Your marginal cost curve should slope upward if you compute it correctly. (Remember to divide by the *change* in *q*—not *L*!) Label your demand curve *D* and your marginal cost curve MC.

140

Figure 8.4

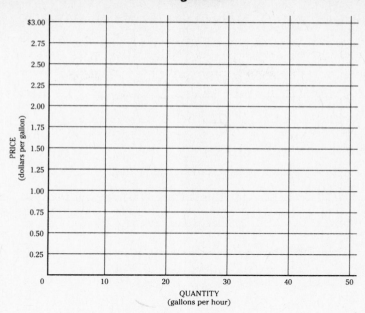

PRICE (dollars per gallon) [y-axis: $3.00, 2.75, 2.50, 2.25, 2.00, 1.75, 1.50, 1.25, 1.00, 0.75, 0.50, 0.25]

QUANTITY
(gallons per hour) [x-axis: 0, 10, 20, 30, 40, 50]

3. You would maximize profits at the production level at which:
   (a) Demand equals average cost.
   (b) Demand equals marginal revenue.
   (c) MR equals MC.
   (d) AC equals MC.
4. How many gallons of Ripple would you produce each hour to maximize profits?
   (a) 0.
   (b) 15.
   (c) 27.
   (d) 36.
   (e) 42.
   (f) 45.
   (g) 46.
5. That means you will hire how many workers per hour?
   (a) 0.
   (b) 1.
   (c) 2.
   (d) 3.
   (e) 4.
   (f) 5.
   (g) 6.

Profit Maximization in the Labor Market
   6. T F The demand curve for Ripple workers is found by plotting the marginal revenue product curve.
   7. T F The supply curve for Ripple workers is the marginal cost curve.
   8. In Figure 8.5 draw the demand curve for labor. Label it DL.

141

Figure 8.5

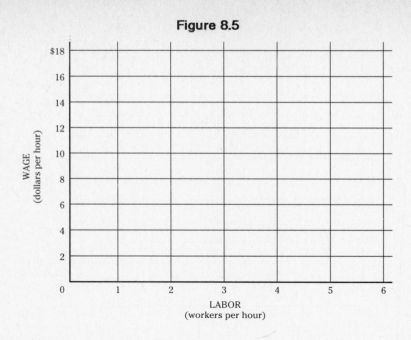

LABOR
(workers per hour)

9. Draw the supply curve for Ripple workers at the wage of $3 in Figure 8.5 and label it LS.
10. How many workers will be hired if you are to maximize profits?
    (a) 0.
    (b) 1.
    (c) 2.
    (d) 3.
    (e) 4.
    (f) 5.
    (g) 6.
11. How much Ripple will be produced per hour? _____
12. T F By using either the labor or product market, it is possible to find how much product will be produced and how much labor will be used by a profit-maximizing firm.

Exercise 3

This exercise illustrates the relationship between marginal productivity, marginal revenue, and marginal revenue product by letting you compute each from the same data.

1. T F The marginal physical product (MPP) measures the change in total output that occurs when one additional worker is hired.
2. Which of the following formulas would provide a correct calculation of the marginal physical product? (Remember that the symbol Δ refers to a small change in a variable.)
    (a) q/L
    (b) $\Delta q/L$
    (c) $\Delta q/\Delta L$
    (d) $\Delta TR/\Delta L$
3. In column 3 of Table 8.2 compute marginal physical product associated with each unit of labor that is used.

Table 8.2. Marginal physical product and marginal revenue product

(1) Labor (workers per hour)	(2) Quantity produced (gallons per hour)	(3) Marginal physical product (gallons per worker)	(4) Price (dollars per gallon)	(5) Total revenue (dollars per hour) (2) x (4)	(6) Marginal revenue (dollars per gallon)	(7) Marginal revenue product (dollars per worker) (3) x (6)
0	0	———	$ 1	———	———	———
1	15	———	1	———	———	———
2	27	———	1	———	———	———
3	36	———	1	———	———	———
4	42	———	1	———	———	———
5	45	———	1	———	———	———
6	46	———	1	———	———	———

4. The law of diminishing returns states that:
   (a) The marginal revenue declines as additional labor is employed in a given production process.
   (b) The marginal revenue product declines as additional labor is employed in a given production process.
   (c) The marginal physical product of labor declines as additional labor is employed in a given production process.
5. T   F   There are diminishing returns to labor with increased production in this example.
6. Marginal revenue product can be computed by multiplying marginal physical product by the marginal revenue. Complete Table 8.2.
7. The reason the demand curve for labor in Figure 8.5 slopes downward is:
   (a) Diminishing returns to labor.
   (b) The market power of labor in labor markets.
   (c) The market power of the Ripple firm in labor markets.
   (d) Declining demand for Ripple.
8. T   F   The derived demand in this example is downward sloping because of diminishing returns to labor.

Exercise 4

The media often report shifts in the supply and demand for labor that affect workers' jobs, their livelihood, and even their mental health. By using one of the articles in the text, this exercise will show the kind of information to look for to identify such shifts. If your professor makes a newspaper assignment for this chapter from the *Instructors Manual,* this exercise will provide an example of how to do it.

Reread the Headline article on page 176 in Chapter 9 of the text entitled "Passive Smoke Deadly" from *USA Today.* Then answer the following questions:

1. If consumers change their behavior because of the information in the report, which of the diagrams in Figure 8.6 would best represent the change in the market for cigarettes?

    a   b   c   d   e   f   g   h   (circle your choice)

Figure 8.6

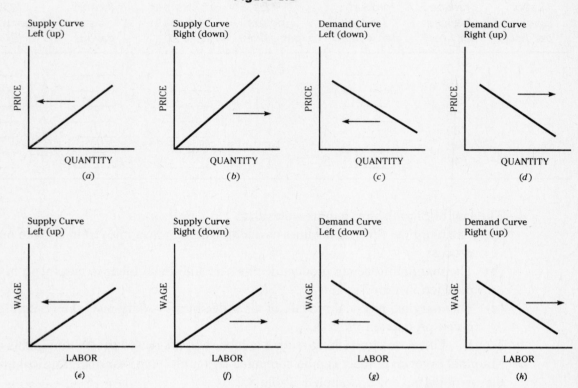

2. Consistent with the shift you chose in Question 1, decide which diagram (now used to represent the labor market), would best represent what whould happen in the market for labor which is used to produce cigarettes if buyers change their behavior because of the report.

    a   b   c   d   e   f   g   h   (circle your choice)

3. If the government levied an additonal tax on cigarette producers, which diagram would represent the effect of the tax in the product market?

    a   b   c   d   e   f   g   h   (circle your choice)

4. Consistent with the shift in Question 3, decide which diagram (now used to represent the labor market), would best represent what would happen in the market for labor which is used to produce cigarettes if the government imposed a tax on cigarettes.

    a   b   c   d   e   f   g   h   (circle your choice)

Common Errors

The first statement in each "common error" below is incorrect. Each incorrect statement is followed by a corrected version and an explanation.

1. People work because they have to. WRONG!
   Generally people work in order to buy the goods and services they want. RIGHT!
   People have flexibility in choosing the conditions under which they will work. What they *choose* to do reflects their utility of leisure compared to their utility of the goods and services they can buy with their income from work. If their needs for goods were satisfied, they might not work at all.

2. The labor-supply curve is the same as the supply curve of the products that labor produces. WRONG!
   The labor-supply curve is a supply curve of a factor market, whereas a product-supply curve applies to a product market. RIGHT!

   Supply curves in different markets are not the same curves, although they may look the same. The chief difference is found on the axes, as shown in Table 8.3.

Table 8.3. **Axes of labor-supply and product-supply curves**

Axis	Labor-supply curve	Product-supply curve
x-axis	Labor services in a given time period	Output in a given time period
y-axis	Wage for labor	Price of product

3. Workers demand jobs. WRONG!
   Employers demand labor services and workers (employees) supply them. RIGHT!
   Demand refers to what a buyer is willing and able to buy. Certainly workers are not seeking to pay their employers. Rather, the workers are trying to find someone who is willing and able to pay them for their labor.

4. Employers employ those factors that are least expensive. WRONG!
   Employers want to employ those factors that are most cost-effective. RIGHT!
   If a factor is cheap, there may be a reason. It may not last long, may not work correctly, or may require heavier use of other factors of production—for example, maintenance workers. The marginal productivity of the cheap factor may therefore be low. An apparently more expensive factor might perform its proper function well and even save on the costs of other factors. The marginal productivity of the more expensive input would more than make up for its higher cost. Businesses would choose the more expensive factor of production.

5. Marginal revenue product is the same as marginal revenue. WRONG!
   The marginal revenue product curve applies to the factor market while the marginal revenue curve applies to the product market. RIGHT!
   The formula for marginal revenue product is

$$\frac{\text{Change in total revenue}}{\text{Change in quantity of input}}$$

145

while that for marginal revenue is

$$\frac{\text{Change in total revenue}}{\text{Change in quantity of output}}$$

Marginal revenue shows changes in total revenue due to increased output and therefore is appropriate in analyzing what happens in the product market.

Marginal revenue product shows changes in total revenue due to the increased use of a factor and therefore is appropriate in analyzing what happens in the factor market. Both curves are derived from the demand curve in the product market. However, in order to find marginal revenue product, it is necessary also to know the relationship between the quantity of input and quantity of output. That is why the marginal physical product becomes important.

6. The law of diminishing returns means that average total costs will rise as a firm expands. WRONG!
The law of diminishing returns applies only to changes in the use of one factor while all others remain constant. RIGHT!

If a firm could expand all factors of production proportionately, there might be no decline in productivity at all, and thus no increase in average total cost. If the firm could do so without affecting factor prices, there would then be no change in unit costs either. The law of diminishing returns applies to changes of only one factor or group of factors, *ceteris paribus* (all other factors being held constant).

7. No one is hurt when companies are taxed except the companies themselves. WRONG!
Part of the burden of taxes on a company may fall on the factors of production that a company employs. RIGHT!

Remember that the demand for factors is derived from the product market. If the sales tax, for example, alters the demand curve for a product, it will alter the demand curve for the factors used to produce the product.

■ ANSWERS ■

Key-Term Review

1. labor supply
   market supply of labor
2. derived demand
3. marginal physical product (MPP)
4. law of diminishing returns

5. demand for labor
6. marginal revenue product (MRP)
7. opportunity wage
8. opportunity cost
9. equilibrium wage

True or False

| 1. T | 3. T | 5. T | 7. T | 9. F | 11. F | 13. F |
| 2. F | 4. T | 6. F | 8. T | 10. T | 12. F | 14. T |

146

Multiple Choice

1. b	6. d	11. d	16. a	20. d	24. c	28. a
2. b	7. a	12. b	17. b	21. d	25. c	29. b
3. d	8. c	13. c	18. d	22. b	26. c	30. b
4. b	9. b	14. a	19. d	23. c	27. a	31. d
5. b	10. a	15. b				

32. a While some categories reflect union restrictions on the amount of labor, employment agreements do not. Other topics include (b) factor payments, (c) factors, and (d) determinants of demand.

Problems and Applications

Exercise 1

1. TC c   MC d   TR a   MR e   MRP b
2. b
3. c
4. d
5. d
6. b

Exercise 2

1. **Table 8.1 Answer**

(2) Labor	(4) Total cost	(5) Marginal cost	(7) Total revenue	(8) Marginal revenue product
0	$ 0	$--	$ 0	$--
1	3	1/5	15	15
2	6	1/4	27	12
3	9	1/3	36	9
4	12	1/2	42	6
5	15	1	45	3
6	18	3	46	1

3. c
4. f
5. f
6. T
7. F

2. Figure 8.4 Answer

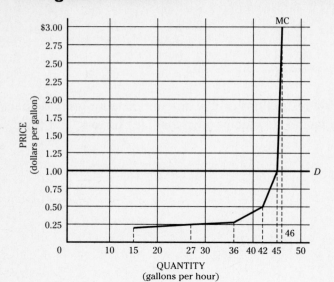

8. Figure 8.5 Answer

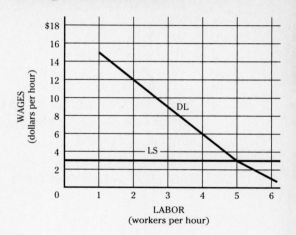

9. See line LS in Figure 8.5 answer.
10. f
11. 45 gallons per hour
12. T

Exercise 3

1. T
2. c
3. **Table 8.2 Answer**

(1) Labor	(3) Marginal physical product	(5) Total revenue	(6) Marginal revenue	(7) Marginal revenue product
0	--	--	--	--
1	15	$15	$1	$15
2	12	27	1	12
3	9	36	1	9
4	6	42	1	6
5	3	45	1	3
6	1	46	1	1

4. c
5. T
6. See columns 6 and 7 in Table 8.2 answer.
7. a
8. T

Exercise 4

1. c
2. g
3. a
4. g

CHAPTER 9

Government Intervention

Quick Review

Sometimes government intervention can improve the way the economy answers the questions WHAT, HOW, and FOR WHOM. Markets do not always result in the best and most efficient outcomes for society. This means that we must study the conditions under which markets fail and the conditions under which government intervention can correct market failure. Specifically we will investigate:

- Under what circumstances do markets fail?
- How can government intervention help?
- How much government intervention is desirable?

There are several ways to justify government intervention. One justification is market failure, the failure of the market mechanism when left on its own to produce an "optimal mix" of output. This first justification for government intervention resides in the concept of "public goods." These goods and services are consumed jointly, both by those who pay and by those who don't. Those who don't pay are termed "free riders." National defense is a good example, because the consumption of national defense is communal. Consumption by one person does not preclude consumption by another. Public goods are different from private goods, for consumption of a private good by one person generally does preclude consumption by another.

The existence of externalities—costs or benefits of a market activity that are borne by a third party—is often cited in justifying public-sector activity, too. Externalities can be negative (such as the pollution from a steel mill) or positive (such as the enrichment of the surrounding community when education is produced and consumed). Because the market has no way of accounting for all costs and all benefits of some forms of economic activity, it tends to underproduce those that generate external benefits and overproduce those that generate external costs.

One wonders why producers pollute (although we all contribute to the problem in one way or another). The answer lies in market incentives. In making production decisions, producers will choose the profit-maximizing rate of output and, of course, produce it at the lowest possible cost—even if by doing so they push some real costs onto society as a whole. When they are successful in pushing these costs onto third parties, we say that an "externality" has been created. It represents a divergence between social cost (the full resource cost of an economic activity) and private costs (those borne directly by the producer or consumer of a good).

The solutions to the pollution problem lie in two basic areas: (1) using market incentives and (2) bypassing the market and using direct controls. We shouldn't lose sight of the fact that a pollution-free economy would be very difficult and expensive to achieve. Resources would have to be reallocated to fight pollution and would have to be taken away from the production of other goods and services that we also desire. Prices and patterns of employment would change.

The existence of market power—the ability of a single firm to alter the market price of a specific product—also justifies public-sector intervention. Market power—whether bestowed by a legal sanction (copyrights, patents, etc.), efficiencies of large-scale production, or some other factor—can be used to restrict output and raise prices. The public sector usually counters market power by antitrust activity. Finally, equity in the answer to the FOR WHOM question is the basis for a large measure of public-sector activity. The market mechanism, left on its own, would provide too little for some (the aged, the infirm, some of the very young) than is thought fair. Since the public at large is thought to benefit from expenditures made to address this problem, income redistribution—for example, through transfer payments—is considered a public good.

Although the examples above focus on micro failures (i.e., when the economy is on the production-possibilities curve), macro failure can occur too, as when we fail to reach the production-possibilities curve or suffer from inflation. Thus, government is expected to intervene at the macro level to alleviate the problem of unemployment and monitor the behavior of the price level.

Learning Objectives

After reading Chapter 9 and doing the following exercises, you should:	True or false	Multiple choice	Problems and applications	Common errors	Pages in the text
1. Understand the nature and causes of market failure.		2, 3, 9, 12, 23	1	1	171-180 183-186
2. Be able to describe the communal nature of public goods and the free-rider dilemma.	1, 3, 4	4, 5, 6, 8	1	1	173-176
3. Know the nature of externalities and how they influence decision making on the part of producers and consumers.	3, 5, 6, 7, 8, 10, 11, 14, 15, 16, 18	5, 6, 10, 15, 18			176-181
4. Use the concepts of social cost and private cost to explain the problems associated with externalities.	6, 7, 9, 10, 11, 12, 13, 17, 20	16, 17			179-180
5. Understand the basic policy options which can be used to address the problems associated with externalities.	18	11, 13, 14, 19, 20, 21			181-183

Learning Objectives (cont'd.)	True or false	Multiple choice	Problems and applications	Common errors	Pages in the text
6. Understand how antitrust activity attempts to combat monopoly power.		26, 27, 28, 32			184-185
7. Be familiar with some fundamental antitrust laws.		24, 26, 27, 28, 29, 30			184-185
8. Understand that inequity in income distribution is an example of market failure with respect to the FOR WHOM question.		23			185-186
9. Be able to distinguish macro failure and government failure from market failure.		2, 7, 25			186
10. Recognize that every government activity has an opportunity cost associated with it.	19	1, 19, 22, 31	1		186-189

Key-Term Review

Review the following terms; if you are not sure of the meaning of any term, write out the definition and check it against the Glossary in the text.

antitrust	market failure	private costs
emission charge	market mechanism	private good
externalities	market power	public good
free rider	opportunity cost	social costs
government failure	optimal mix of output	transfer payments

Fill in the blank following each of the statements below with the appropriate term from the list above.

1. The existence of public goods represents, in a way, our inability to produce the best mix of outputs using only the .... 1. _____

2. Social security checks, benefit checks, and welfare payments provided by the government are all examples of .... 2. _____

3. The private goods forgone when resources are used to produce public goods is a measure of their .... 3. _____

151

4. When one person cannot be prevented from receiving benefits from another person's purchase, the first person is said to be a .... 4._____

5. A good or service that cannot be provided efficiently or in the right amount by the private sector is called a .... 5._____

6. When consumption of a good by one person precludes consumption by someone else, such a good is called a .... 6._____

7. The_____ which are incurred by a ...... 7._____
producer, plus any external costs imposed on others, add up to .... _____

8. Immunization clinics not only prevent a person from getting a disease but reduce the incidence of the disease generally; that is, they have effects on third parties. Such effects are called .... 8._____

9. _____ enforcement is used to............. 9._____
counter the problem of monopoly power.

10. One way to force firms to internalize the costs of pollution would be to levy an .... 10._____

11. _____ occurs when public-sector .... 11._____
intervention fails to move the economy closer to its goals.

12. _____ means that the market .... 12._____
mechanism has not led to production of the ..... _____

13. _____ is the ability to alter market ..... 13._____
outcomes.

True or False: *Circle your choice.*

T   F   1. The term "public sector" refers only to federal government purchases of goods and services.

T   F   2. Income transfers are payments to individuals for which nothing is currently rendered in return.

T   F   3. A public good is a good or service for which consumption by one person excludes consumption by others.

T   F   4. Police protection is an example of a service that involves the free-rider problem.

T   F   5. If public goods were produced and marketed like private goods, the market would fail to provide them in the quantity society is willing and able to pay for.

T   F   6. If you burn garbage in your backyard and the smoke damages a neighbor's house, the damage is considered an externality.

T   F   7. If your neighbors spray the weeds in their yards and this activity prevents weed seeds from blowing into your yard, the benefit you receive is an externality.

T　F　8. Externalities come into existence only when the social costs of a market activity exceed the social benefits of a market activity.

T　F　9. For any given market activity, if the social cost is less than the private cost, that activity should be curtailed from what it would be using the market mechanism.

T　F　10. Pollution results from the rational response of producers to market incentives.

T　F　11. Firms that are able to push part of their costs onto society by polluting produce less output of their product than society desires.

T　F　12. Externalities are a measure of the divergence between social costs and private costs.

T　F　13. The key to pollution abatement lies in forcing polluters to externalize their internal costs.

T　F　14. When a firm pollutes, its marginal cost curve no longer intersects the average cost curve at its lowest point.

T　F　15. Pollution-abatement programs lead to increases in the prices charged for the products of the polluting industry.

T　F　16. Pollution-abatement programs eliminate jobs in the polluting industries.

T　F　17. Social costs of an economic activity do not include the activity's private costs.

T　F　18. If the cost of cleaning up the air should be borne by those who pollute it, then automobile prices should be increased to cover the costs of including antipollution devices.

T　F　19. Pollution abatement imposes opportunity costs on society.

T　F　20. Social costs are the sum of private costs and external costs.

Multiple Choice: *Select the correct answer.*

_____ 1. The opportunity costs of government activity:
(a) Can be measured in terms of the private-market activity forgone.
(b) Are represented as the slope of a production-possibilities curve showing public versus private goods.
(c) Reflect the limited resources available for public and private activity.
(d) All of the above statements are true.

_____ 2. Which of the following groups best represents macroeconomic goals:
(a) Full employment, price stability, economic growth.
(b) Rate of production, choice of factors of production, and the pricing of specific goods.
(c) Welfare of individual consumers and business firms.
(d) Land, labor, and capital.

_____ 3. The optimal mix of output is identical to:
(a) The equilibrium of aggregate supply and aggregate demand.
(b) The most desired point on a production-possibilities curve.
(c) The output at which costs just equal benefits in cost-benefit analysis.
(d) All of the above.

_____ 4. Governments usually build highways because it is difficult to exclude people who don't pay for the highways from using those highways. What type of market failure is most likely involved?
(a) Inequity.
(b) Public goods.
(c) Government failure.
(d) Market power.

_____ 5. The social security tax is:
(a) A progressive tax at all income levels.
(b) A regressive tax above a certain income level.
(c) A proportional tax at all income levels.
(d) None of the above.

_____ 6. If the economy relies entirely on the market mechanism to answer the WHAT, HOW, and FOR WHOM questions, it tends to:
(a) Overproduce goods that yield external benefits and overproduce goods that yield external costs.
(b) Overproduce goods that yield external benefits and underproduce goods that yield external costs.
(c) Underproduce goods that yield external benefits and overproduce goods that yield external costs.
(d) Underproduce goods that yield external benefits and underproduce goods that yield external costs.

_____ 7. A source of government failure that is not generally an example of market failure includes:
(a) Monopoly.
(b) Externalities.
(c) Inequity.
(d) Waste.

_____ 8. The free-rider dilemma is:
(a) Exemplified by thrill seekers who follow fire trucks.
(b) A distinguishing characteristic of public goods.
(c) An issue with every good produced in the public sector.
(d) An argument for a laissez-faire policy.

_____ 9. In economics, a public good:
(a) Is any good produced by the government.
(b) Generates government failure.
(c) Is provided in an optimal amount by the market.
(d) Is not subject to the exclusion principle.

_____ 10. When external costs result from the production of a good, the output level of that good tends to be:
(a) Larger than is desirable.
(b) Smaller than is desirable.
(c) Neither too small nor too large.
(d) Too small if the private costs exceed the external costs.

_____ 11. It has been suggested that owners of private automobiles should be taxed in proportion to the amount of their exhaust emissions. If this policy were implemented:
   (a) Consumers would insist on truly effective smog-control devices, no matter what the cost.
   (b) The demand for public transportation would probably rise.
   (c) The efficiency of automobiles as measured by gallons per mile would fall.
   (d) None of the above would be the case.

_____ 12. A monopolist has market power:
   (a) Because it faces a downward-sloping demand curve.
   (b) Because when it produces an extra unit of output, it must lower its price on all of its production.
   (c) Because its marginal revenue curve is below its demand curve.
   (d) For all of the above reasons.

_____ 13. If emission charges were applied to all production and consumption activities:
   (a) The relative price of highly polluting activities would increase.
   (b) People would stop producing and consuming.
   (c) Pollution would be eliminated.
   (d) There would be no redistribution of income.

_____ 14. Pollution levels can be reduced by:
   (a) Transforming waste materials for which the environment has little assimilative capacity into forms for which the environment has a greater assimilative capacity.
   (b) Reducing the levels of production and consumption.
   (c) Stricter enforcement of clean-air laws.
   (d) All of the above.

_____ 15. A firm that can dump its unfiltered waste products into our waterways will be:
   (a) Paying the full cost of production.
   (b) Paying more than the full cost of production.
   (c) Enabled to sell its product at a lower price than if it filtered its wastes.
   (d) Doing none of the above.

_____ 16. Social costs:
   (a) Are less than private costs.
   (b) Include private costs.
   (c) Are unrelated to private costs.
   (d) None of the above.

_____ 17. When social costs and private costs of consumption and production diverge, then inevitably:
   (a) Producers have an incentive to produce too little.
   (b) Consumers have an incentive to consume too much.
   (c) Both producers and consumers have an incentive to produce and consume too much.
   (d) None of the above.

_____ 18. Internalizing external pollution costs can result in an:
   (a) Upward shift in the polluting firm's MC curve.
   (b) Upward shift in the polluting firm's ATC curve.
   (c) Upward shift in the polluting firm's TFC curve.
   (d) All of the above.

155

_____ 19. A required deposit on beverage containers purchased by consumers will:
  (a) Increase beverage consumption.
  (b) Increase beverage production.
  (c) Raise the opportunity cost of polluting.
  (d) Eliminate container waste pollution.

_____ 20. An emission charge:
  (a) Increases social marginal cost and thus induces lower output.
  (b) Increases private marginal cost and thus induces higher output.
  (c) Increases private maginal cost and thus induces lower output.
  (d) Increases the difference between private and social costs.

_____ 21. The purpose of an emission charge is to:
  (a) Decrease the difference between social and private costs.
  (b) Induce firms to internalize pollution externalities.
  (c) Induce a socially optimal rate of output.
  (d) All of the above.

_____ 22. The costs of environmental protection can be measured by:
  (a) The difference between social benefits and social costs.
  (b) The difference between marginal social benefits and marginal social costs.
  (c) The materials balance problem.
  (d) The opportunity cost of resources used to protect the environment.

_____ 23. The distribution of income is basically the answer to:
  (a) The WHAT question of society.
  (b) The HOW question for society.
  (c) The FOR WHOM question for society.
  (d) None of the above.

_____ 24. Antitrust activity addresses:
  (a) Market power.
  (b) Inequity.
  (c) Government failure.
  (d) Externalities.

_____ 25. If government production forces the economy inside the production-possibilities curve, then there is:
  (a) Government failure.
  (b) Waste.
  (c) Inefficiency.
  (d) All of the above.

_____ 26. The first antitrust act to prohibit "conspiracies in restraint of trade" was:
  (a) The Sherman Act.
  (b) The Clayton Act.
  (c) The Federal Trade Commission Act.
  (d) Case decisions such as those for AT&T and IBM.

_____ 27. Exclusive dealing is prohibited by:
  (a) The Sherman Act.
  (b) The Clayton Act.
  (c) The Federal Trade Commission Act.
  (d) Case decisions such as those for AT&T and IBM.

28. The creation of another antitrust agency besides the Justice Department was accomplished through:
    (a) The Sherman Act.
    (b) The Clayton Act.
    (c) The Federal Trade Commission Act.
    (d) Case decisions such as those for AT&T and IBM.

29. In 1982 two major antitrust cases against major companies ended with the following results:
    (a) AT&T and IBM were both broken up.
    (b) AT&T was broken up, but IBM was not.
    (c) IBM was broken up, but AT&T was not.
    (d) Neither IBM nor AT&T was broken up.

30. The federal government's antitrust suit against IBM was dropped because:
    (a) The Justice Department successfully argued there was no "natural" basis for the dominance of IBM.
    (b) IBM was shown to be a natural monopoly.
    (c) Big was not necessarily bad.
    (d) The Justice Department showed the computer market was a contestable market.

31. When a regulatory agency hires personnel to enforce regulations, the cost of government involvement is:
    (a) An administrative cost.
    (b) A compliance cost.
    (c) An efficiency cost.
    (d) None of the above.

32. What type of market failure provided the justification for breaking up AT&T?
    (a) Inequity.
    (b) Public goods.
    (c) Externalities.
    (d) Market power.

Problems and Applications

Exercise 1

This exercise examines a form of public good and provides practice in the kind of cost-benefit analysis that government analysts use when evaluating projects.

The Army Corps of Engineers lists the benefits and costs of a water project as shown in Table 9.1. The project is a dam in Brown's Valley which is located in Brown County.

Table 9.1. Benefits and costs of a dam in Brown's Valley

Cost items	Cost (millions of dollars)	Benefit items	Benefit (millions of dollars)
Purchase of land	$2.0	Irrigation	$4.0
Land preparation	4.0	City water supply	4.0
Fill material	2.0	Flood control	1.0
Construction company services	1.0	Future recreation	5.0
Future maintenance cost	1.0		
Total	$_____	Total	$_____

1. Fill in the totals in Table 9.1. What is the benefit-cost ratio for the Brown's Valley dam?_____
2. If the resources were available, would the project be worth doing?_____
3. Suppose the people in Brown's Valley object to the new dam. They commission their own study, which shows that the value of future recreation will be only $3 million rather than $5 million. They also find that putting in recreation facilities will cost an additional $4 million. Compute the new benefit-cost ratio._____
4. Is the project worth doing if these new estimates are correct?_____
5. Because there is such a controversy over the figures, one of the civic leaders, Mr. Collins, initiates a study to examine a new Brown's Valley Project and alternative sites for a dam that would be more acceptable to the majority of people. The engineers return with the three recommended project sites shown in Table 9.2. Compute the benefit-cost ratios of each project and complete Table 9.2.

Table 9.2. Benefit-cost ratios (millions of dollars)

	Virginia Ranch	Yuba	New Brown's Valley
Benefits	$15.0	$18.0	$10.0
Costs	7.5	10.0	6.0
Benefit-cost ratio	_____	_____	_____

_____6. If only one project can be done, which site should be chosen for construction?
   (a) Virginia Ranch.
   (b) Yuba.
   (c) New Brown's Valley.
_____7. Which of the following reasons *best* explains why the other projects might not be undertaken?
   (a) Their benefit-cost ratios are less than 1.
   (b) Brown County cannot afford more than one project and must select the one with the highest benefit-cost ratio.
   (c) Brown County can earn a 10 percent return for investing in the stock or money markets.

158

_____8. The reason that people in Brown's Valley would not be able to raise the money privately and would have to do it through taxes is:
(a) The free-rider problem.
(b) The dam is a public good.
(c) Charges cannot be levied on a project that does not yet exist.
(d) All of the above.

_____9. Communities downriver from the dam want to bid for the water. However, because these new demands would raise the price of water, the farmers prevent sale of the water to those communities. This suggests that the dam:
(a) Should have been provided by private enterprise through the market mechanism instead of big government.
(b) Has externalities that have not been included in the cost part of the benefit-cost ratio.
(c) Has externalities that have not been included in the benefit part of the benefit-cost ratio.

_____10. What type of government is *best* suited to manage water projects, considering the existence of significant externalities that affect residents in multiple government jurisdictions?
(a) City government.
(b) County government.
(c) State government.
(d) Federal government.

Exercise 2

This exercise shows how externalities affect third parties.

A chemical plant and a plastics factory are located adjacent to the same stream. The chemical plant is located upstream. The downstream plastics factory requires pure water for its production process. Its basic supply is the stream that runs past both firms.

Figure 9.1

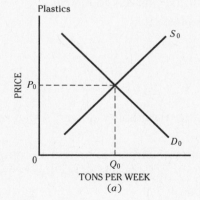 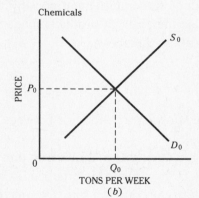

In Figure 9.1 a and b, S_0 and D_0 represent the supply and demand for plastics and chemicals, respectively. Assume that the economy is initially competitive and resources are allocated efficiently. Equilibrium price and quantity are P_0 and Q_0 in each case. But then the chemical producer

159

decides to dump waste products into the stream rather than dispose of them with the costly process that had been used.

1. In Figure 9.1 *b* draw in a new private supply curve for chemicals after the dumping in the stream begins. Label it S_1. (There are many ways to draw the curve.)
2. The pollution from the chemical plant forces the plastics manufacturer to use a costly water-purifying system. Draw a new private long-run supply curve for plastics in Figure 9.1 *a*. Label it S_1. (There are many ways to draw this curve correctly.)
3. The effect of pollution on the quantity of chemicals sold is as if:
   (a) A new, improved technology were discovered.
   (b) Wages to its labor force were reduced.
   (c) The social security tax had been abolished.
   (d) All of the above were the case.
4. As a result of the chemical plant's polluting activities:
   (a) The price of chemicals has risen.
   (b) The price of chemicals has fallen.
   (c) The price of plastics has not changed.
   (d) None of the above is the case.
5. As a result of the chemical plant's activities:
   (a) More chemicals are produced and sold than society desires.
   (b) More labor is used to produce chemicals than society desires.
   (c) More capital inputs are used to produce chemicals than society desires.
   (d) All of the above are the case.
6. The effect of the chemical firm's pollution is to:
   (a) Raise the price of plastics and reduce the quantity sold.
   (b) Lower the price of plastics and increase the quantity sold.
   (c) Raise the price of plastics and increase the quantity sold.
   (d) Do none of the above.
7. The impact of the pollution on the plastics industry in this example is to:
   (a) Reduce the output of plastics below the level that society desires.
   (b) Reduce the employment possibilities in the plastics industry.
   (c) Raise the price of products made with plastics.
   (d) Do all of the above.

Exercise 3

This exercise shows the difference between private marginal costs and social marginal costs.

1. An iron-producing firm mines iron ore. Assume the iron ore market is competitive. Table 9.3 depicts the private (internalized) costs and social costs of the firm's iron production at each daily production rate. Complete Table 9.3.

160

Table 9.3. Costs of producing iron

Production rate (tons per day)	Total private cost (dollars per day)	Private marginal cost (dollars per ton)	Total social cost (dollars per day)	Social marginal cost (dollars per ton)
0	$ 0	$ --	$ 0	$ --
1	40	_____	80	_____
2	90	_____	170	_____
3	150	_____	270	_____
4	220	_____	380	_____
5	300	_____	500	_____
6	390	_____	630	_____
7	490	_____	770	_____
8	600	_____	920	_____
9	720	_____	1,080	_____
10	850	_____	1,250	_____
11	990	_____	1,430	_____
12	1,140	_____	1,620	_____

2. In Figure 9.2 graph the demand and marginal cost curves facing the firm for its iron if the price of the iron in the market is $140 per ton. Label the private marginal cost curve PMC. Label the social marginal cost curve SMC. Label the demand curve "Demand."

Figure 9.2

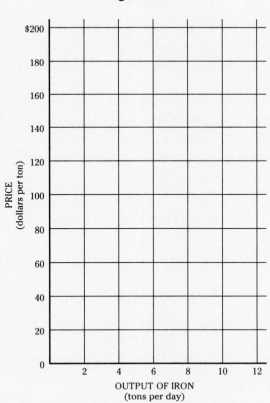

3. What is the profit-maximizing production rate for the firm if it considers only its private costs?
   (a) 5 tons per day.
   (b) 7 tons per day.
   (c) 9 tons per day.
   (d) 11 tons per day.
4. What is the profit-maximizing production rate if the firm is required to pay all social costs?
   (a) 5 tons per day.
   (b) 7 tons per day.
   (c) 9 tons per day.
   (d) 11 tons per day.
5. What tax should be charged per ton of iron produced in order to induce the iron-producing firm to pay the true social costs of its production?
   (a) $4 per ton.
   (b) $40 per ton.
   (c) $100 per ton.
   (d) $50 per ton.

Common Errors

The first statement in each "common error" below is incorrect. Each incorrect statement is followed by a corrected version and an explanation.

1. Fire protection, police protection, education, and other services can be produced more efficiently by the private sector than by the public sector. WRONG!
   The public sector can produce many services more efficiently than the private sector. RIGHT!
   You should recognize now that the existence of externalities and the free-rider problem force society to produce some goods and services through public-sector expenditures. Many of the goods and services we take for granted (such as education) would not be produced in sufficient quantities if left to the private sector. And can you imagine trying to provide for your own defense against foreign countries?

■ ANSWERS ■

Key-Term Review

1. market mechanism
2. transfer payments
3. opportunity cost
4. free rider
5. public good

6. private good
7. private costs
   social costs
8. externalities
9. antitrust

10. emission charge
11. government failure
12. market failure
    optimal mix of output
13. market power

True or False

1. F	4. T	7. T	10. T	13. F	16. T	19. T
2. T	5. T	8. F	11. F	14. F	17. F	20. T
3. F	6. T	9. F	12. T	15. T	18. T	

Multiple Choice

1. d	6. c	11. b	16. b	21. d	25. d	29. b
2. a	7. d	12. d	17. c	22. d	26. a	30. c
3. b	8. b	13. a	18. d	23. c	27. b	31. a
4. b	9. d	14. d	19. c	24. a	28. c	32. d
5. b	10. a	15. c	20. c			

Problems and Applications

Exercise 1

1. See Table 9.1 answer.
2. yes
3. $\dfrac{\$12,000,000}{\$14,000,000} = 0.86$
4. no
5. See Table 9.2 answer.

6. a
7. b
8. d
9. c
10. d

Table 9.1 Answer

Cost	Benefit	Benefit-cost ratio
$10,000,000	$14,000,000	1.4 = ($14,000,000 / $10,000,000)

Table 9.2 Answer

	Virginia Ranch	Yuba	New Brown's Valley
Benefit-cost ratio	2.0	1.8	1.67

Exercise 2

1. **Figure 9.1 Answer**

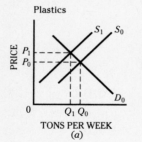

Plastics

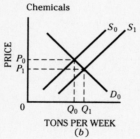

Chemicals

2. See Figure 9.1 answer (*a*), line S_1.
3. d
4. b
5. d
6. a
7. d

Exercise 3

1. **Table 9.3 Answer**

Production rate	Private marginal cost	Social marginal cost
0	$ --	$ --
1	40	80
2	50	90
3	60	100
4	70	110
5	80	120
6	90	130
7	100	140
8	110	150
9	120	160
10	130	170
11	140	180
12	150	190

2. **Figure 9.2 Answer**

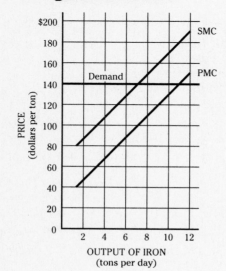

3. d
4. b
5. b

164

CHAPTER 10

The Business Cycle

Quick Review

The Great Depression of the 1930s threw thousands out of work. No market economy seemed to avoid the drastic unemployment and reduction in prices that accompanied the prolonged slump. At the other extreme, during the seventies the United States experienced inflation in which prices rose rapidly. Today many countries experience much more dramatic price increases, and policy makers are pulled in many different directions to avoid the miseries that attend high unemployment, low production, and inflation. The fear of these economic problems influences politics and economic decision making all over the world. To address these problems, we need to answer the following questions:

- What are business cycles?
- What damage does unemployment cause?
- Who is hurt by inflation?

Macroeconomics tries to answer these questions.

The goal of macroeconomic policy is to achieve full employment with price stability. Economists have recognized that the ability of policy makers to reach these goals changes cyclically. The cycles are measured by examining the fluctuations in real GDP. Two consecutive quarters of decline in real GDP defines a recession. The statistics presented in this chapter show that cycles vary greatly in length, frequency, and intensity.

The unemployment that accompanies a recession reduces income and creates social unrest. The unemployment rate is measured by counting those people in the labor force who have no job but are actively seeking employment. If you're a civilian under 16 or you're not looking for work, then you're not in the labor force and you cannot be counted among the unemployed. This criterion eliminates children, mothers at home, and those serving in the armed forces. The number of unemployed is determined through surveys of households across the country. To find the unemployment rate, the number unemployed is divided by the number in the labor force.

Economists typically distinguish four kinds of unemployment: frictional (short-term unemployment between jobs), seasonal (unemployment that varies with the seasons), structural (caused by a mismatch of available labor with skill requirements or job locations), and cyclical (caused by deficient aggregate demand for goods and services). For these reasons, several million people can be unemployed in the United States during any period of time. In the 1960s the President's Council of Economic Advisers thought that an unemployment rate of 4 percent provided the optimal balance between employment and price-level goals, but in the 1970s and 1980s this figure was revised upward to 6 percent to reflect the increased difficulty of reducing structural unemployment. Changes in the age-sex composition of the labor force, more liberal transfer payments, and so on, all contribute to the acceptance of a higher unemployment rate as the best we can do without causing inflation.

Inflation, which is an increase in the average price level of goods and services, is another cyclical problem. The Consumer Price Index (CPI), which reflects cost increases at the consumer level, is published by the Bureau of Labor Statistics and is one of the key measures of inflation. In the Full Employment and Balanced Growth Act of 1978 the goal of price stability was defined by the U.S. government as a 3 percent rate of increase in the price level.

Policy makers have found it difficult to control inflation and unemployment simultaneously. A zero inflation rate would inflict heavy costs on the economy in the form of high unemployment. As the economy expands unemployment can be reduced, but as the economy approaches full employment, the price level begins to rise quickly. Some prices rise faster than the inflation rate; others rise more slowly. At the microeconomic level, inflation causes a redistribution of real income among individuals and firms; it is not an equal-opportunity phenomenon. At the macroeconomic level, inflation leads to some flawed production and consumption decisions, often promotes wasteful buying, and encourages unproductive speculation.

Learning Objectives

After reading Chapter 10 and doing the following exercises, you should:	True or false	Multiple choice	Problems and applications	Common errors	Pages in the text
1. Understand how the business cycle is measured.	1, 2, 3, 4	3			192-198
2. Have in mind a historical perspective on the business cycle from the Great Depression to the present.	2, 3	1, 2, 3	1, 5		195-200
3. Know the relationship between the labor force and the population and be able to calculate the unemployment rate.	5, 6, 7, 8, 9	4, 5	1, 2	2	200-202
4. Be able to categorize the unemployed into seasonal, frictional, cyclical, and structural categories.	10, 11, 12, 13, 14	6, 7, 8, 9, 10, 11, 12, 13	1, 3		202-204
5. Be able to explain the "full-employment" rate of unemployment.	5, 8			1	203-204
6. Know the difference between average prices and relative prices; inflation and deflation.	15, 16, 20	14			205

Learning Objectives (cont'd.)	True or false	Multiple choice	Problems and applications	Common errors	Pages in the text
7. Be able to distinguish between the price, income, and wealth effects associated with the inflationary process.	21, 22, 25, 26, 27	16, 17, 21		3	205-210
8. Understand how inflation creates an uncertain decision-making environment for both firms and households.	17, 18, 19	15, 18		4	211
9. Know that the CPI is a measure of weighted average prices and how to calculate the rate of inflation.	23, 24, 25	19, 20	4	5	212
10. Understand why the full-employment goal may conflict with the price stability goal in the economy.		18	1, 5	1	213

Key-Term Review

Review the following terms; if you are not sure of the meaning of any term, write out the definition and check it against the Glossary in the text.

business cycle	inflation	nominal income	recession
consumer price index	inflation rate	price stability	relative price
deflation	labor force	real GDP	unemployment
full employment	macroeconomics	real income	unemployment rate

Fill in the blank following each of the statements below with the appropriate term from the list above.

1. A _____ is said to occur when .... 1. _____
   real GDP declines for two consecutive
   quarters.
2. The observed pattern of economic growth and
   contraction is known as the .... 2. _____
3. The branch of economics that focuses on the
   behavior of the entire economy is .... 3. _____

167

4. When nominal GDP is adjusted for changes in the price level the resulting figure is called..... 4. _____

5. When the average price level increases continuously, the process is known as .... 5. _____

6. Dividing the number of unemployed people by the number in the labor force yields the .... 6. _____

7. The Council of Economic Advisers has revised upward its estimate of what constitutes_____ 7. _____ to between 5 and 6 percent unemployment.

8. Every person 16 years of age or older who is either employed for pay or actively seeking employment is considered a part of the .... 8. _____

9. Adding together structural, frictional, seasonal, and cyclical unemployment gives a gross estimate of the amount of total .... 9. _____

10. One measure of the_____ is the .... 10. _____ _____ which measures the average .... _____ price increases at the consumer level.

11. When the average price level is falling, there is .... 11. _____

12. When the inflation rate is low and does not vary much, we say there is .... 12. _____

13. When inflation occurs, _____ grows .... 13. _____ at a greater rate than .... _____

14. The measures of inflation do not provide information on how the_____ of a .... 14. _____ single good changes with respect to other prices.

True or False: *Circle your choice.*

T   F   1. During the business cycle, unemployment and production typically move in the same direction.

T   F   2. Business cycles are measured using real GDP.

T   F   3. Unemployment and inflation tend to rise and fall together.

T   F   4. To have a recession, real output must actually fall.

T   F   5. Full employment means everyone in the labor force has a job.

T   F   6. To be counted as part of the labor force, one must be at least 16 years old.

T   F   7. A homemaker with part-time paid employment is part of the labor force; one without paid employment (and who is not looking for employment) is not part of the labor force.

T   F   8. To obtain the unemployment rate, divide the number counted as unemployed by the population.

T   F   9. Everyone who is willing to work and seeking work but cannot find a job is considered unemployed.

T F 10. There is a direct relationship between educational level attained and the unemployment rate.

T F 11. Those who make their livings by driving snowplows are likely to suffer from seasonal unemployment.

T F 12. Someone who quits one job to take another after a short vacation experiences frictional unemployment.

T F 13. When long-distance telephone operators were replaced by direct dialing, one could predict the development of structural unemployment.

T F 14. Cyclical unemployment stems from insufficient demand for goods and services.

T F 15. Inflation is said to occur when an index of weighted average prices rises.

T F 16. Relative price changes are essential in order for the market mechanism to function efficiently.

T F 17. Some buyers respond to inflation by cutting back on purchases of goods and services, whereas others respond by making greater purchases of goods and services.

T F 18. Inflation may cause the economy to produce inside the production-possibilities curve.

T F 19. Sudden speculative hoarding of commodities during an inflationary period ties up resources, causing real income to fall.

T F 20. Some price increases do not contribute to inflation because they are below the inflation rate.

T F 21. If all individuals were able to anticipate inflation correctly and make appropriate adjustments in their market behavior, there would be no redistribution of real income or real wealth due to inflation.

T F 22. The microeconomic effect of inflation is the redistribution of income.

T F 23. The base year for a price index is the year against which price levels of other years are compared.

T F 24. An index of 1.05 for a particular year means that prices are 5 percent higher than in the base year.

T F 25. When doctors' fees rise faster than aspirin prices, real income falls for people who visit a doctor relative to those who prescribe aspirin for themselves.

T F 26. If the prices of things you buy do not increase, but the inflation rate is 10 percent, then your real income falls, *ceteris paribus*.

T F 27. If all prices and wages in the economy rose by the same percentage at the same time, there would be no redistribution of income.

Multiple Choice: *Select the correct answer.*

_____ 1. The Great Depression:
(a) Followed a period of apparent prosperity.
(b) Led to an unemployment rate that reached 25 percent.
(c) Caused President Roosevelt to declare a "bank holiday" in 1933.
(d) Did all of the above.

2. Business cycles in the United States:
   (a) Are remarkably similar in length but vary greatly in intensity.
   (b) Vary greatly in length, frequency, and intensity.
   (c) Are similar in frequency and intensity.
   (d) Are similar in length, frequency, and intensity.
3. The peak of a business cycle should be accompanied by:
   (a) The lowest unemployment rate over the cycle.
   (b) The highest rate of increase in the price level over the cycle.
   (c) The greatest level of real GDP over the cycle.
   (d) All of the above.
4. Who among the following would be counted among the unemployed?
   (a) Someone who is on vacation but will return to a job.
   (b) Someone who is on strike.
   (c) An unpaid employee of a family enterprise such as a farm.
   (d) None of the above.
5. Which of the following would be counted as a member of the labor force?
   (a) The president of General Motors
   (b) A man serving ten years for armed robbery.
   (c) A retired commander of a U.S. Navy nuclear submarine.
   (d) A hard-working homemaker who is not employed outside the home.
6. Which of the following groups typically has the highest unemployment rate?
   (a) White teenagers.
   (b) Black adults.
   (c) Black teenagers.
   (d) White adult females.
7. Which of the following typically have unemployment rates above the national average?
   (a) Black teenagers.
   (b) White teenagers.
   (c) Black adult males.
   (d) All of the above.
8. Which of the following statements *best* describes the relationship between educational level and the unemployment rate?
   (a) An inverse relationship.
   (b) A positive relationship.
   (c) No relationship.
   (d) Not enough information is given to answer.
9. When migrant workers seek employment after the crops have been picked, the unemployment rate goes up. This situation is an example of:
   (a) Frictional unemployment.
   (b) Seasonal unemployment.
   (c) Structural unemployment.
   (d) Cyclical unemployment.

_____ 10. Which of the following situations characterizes frictional unemployment when other forms of unemployment are low?
(a) There are not enough jobs for those experiencing frictional unemployment.
(b) Those who experience frictional unemployment cannot perform the jobs available.
(c) The period of job search will be relatively short.
(d) All of the above.

_____ 11. Cyclical unemployment is inversely related to:
(a) Growth in the real GDP.
(b) Business cycles.
(c) The inflation rate.
(d) All of the above.

_____ 12. Automobile workers in Detroit who are unemployed because of foreign automobile imports at the same time that job vacancies exist for coal miners in West Virginia would most likely be classified as:
(a) Structurally unemployed.
(b) Cyclically unemployed.
(c) Frictionally unemployed.
(d) Seasonally unemployed.

_____ 13. Which of the following is a cause of cyclical unemployment?
(a) Bad weather prevents the employment of migrant workers.
(b) Workers do not possess the appropriate skills for the vacancies that exist.
(c) Unemployment benefits are too high and given for too long a period.
(d) There is simply not sufficient demand for workers at the current wage rate.

_____ 14. Comparing relative prices is more useful than examining absolute prices in:
(a) Determining the redistribution of income due to inflation.
(b) Determining the inflation rate.
(c) Deflating nominal income.
(d) All of the above.

_____ 15. Inflation may cause the economy to operate inside the production-possibilities curve because:
(a) People waste resources when they hoard in anticipation of inflation.
(b) Firms withhold resources anticipating that the relative price of resources will be higher than the inflation rate.
(c) The government takes strong counter-inflationary measures that result in less than real full-employment output.
(d) All of the above can cause the economy to operate inside the production-possibilities frontier.

_____ 16. Nominal income always falls when real income:
(a) Falls and there is inflation.
(b) Falls and there is deflation.
(c) Rises and there is inflation.
(d) Rises and there is deflation.

17. Which of the following must always occur when the price of a product rises faster than the inflation rate?
    (a) The nominal incomes of the users of that product fall.
    (b) The users of that product have higher real incomes than people who do not use it.
    (c) The nominal incomes of the users of that product rise.
    (d) None of the above is true.

18. Which of the following occurrences is *not* an effect of a sudden burst of inflation?
    (a) The economy is pushed inside the production-possibilities curve.
    (b) Confidence in the economy is lowered.
    (c) Government receives lower taxes because of lower real incomes.
    (d) Production and consumption incentives are distorted.

19. The base year used in computing a price index is:
    (a) The year in which prices were at their lowest level.
    (b) The year in which prices were at their average level.
    (c) A recent year from which meaningful comparisons can be made.
    (d) The earliest year for which data are available.

20. A Consumer Price Index that has the value 105 means that:
    (a) Average prices that the typical consumer pays have risen 105 percent over base-year average prices.
    (b) Average prices at which producers sell goods have risen 105 percent over base-year average prices.
    (c) Average prices that the typical consumer pays have risen 5 percent over base-year average prices.
    (d) Average prices at which producers sell goods have risen 105 percent over the average prices of the previous year.

21. Income redistribution occurs during inflation because:
    (a) Not all prices rise by the same amount as average prices.
    (b) Some taxes cause inflation to hit certain income groups harder than others.
    (c) Not all groups can protect their incomes against inflation.
    (d) All of the above are the case.

Problems and Applications

Exercise 1

This exercise shows how to calculate the unemployment rate and indicates the relationship between the unemployment rate and GDP.

1. Compute the unemployment rate based on the information in Table 10.1, and insert it in column 4.

Table 10.1. Unemployment and real GDP, 1970-89

Year	(1) Noninstitutional population	(2) Civilian labor force (thousands of persons 16 and over)	(3) Unemployment (thousands of persons 16 and over)	(4) Unemployment rate (percent)	(5) Percent change in real GDP
1970	140,273	82,771	4,093	_____ %	-0.2%
1971	143,032	84,382	5,016	_____	3.4
1972	146,575	87,034	4,882	_____	5.7
1973	149,422	89,429	4,365	_____	5.8
1974	152,349	91,949	5,156	_____	-0.6
1975	153,333	93,775	7,929	_____	-1.2
1976	158,294	96,158	7,406	_____	5.4
1977	161,166	99,009	6,991	_____	5.5
1978	164,027	102,251	6,202	_____	5.0
1979	166,951	104,962	6,137	_____	2.8
1980	167,745	106,940	7,637	_____	-0.3
1981	170,130	108,670	8,273	_____	2.5
1982	172,271	110,204	10,678	_____	-2.1
1983	174,215	111,550	10,717	_____	3.7
1984	176,383	113,544	8,539	_____	6.8
1985	178,206	115,461	8,312	_____	3.4
1986	180,587	117,834	8,237	_____	2.7
1987	182,753	119,865	7,425	_____	3.7
1988	164,613	121,669	6,701	_____	4.4
1989	186,393	123,869	6,528	_____	2.9

2. In Figure 10.1 graph both the unemployment rate (column 4 of Table 10.1) and the percentage change in the real GDP (column 5).

Figure 10.1

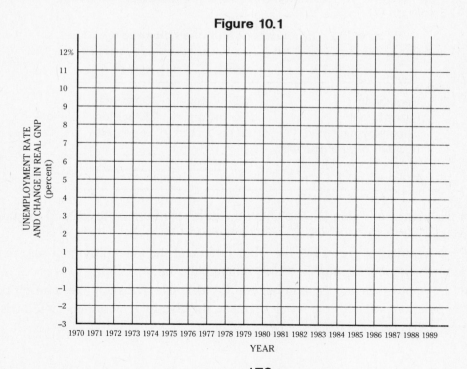

173

3. The relationship between the unemployment rate and the percentage change in the real GDP is best characterized as:
   (a) A direct relationship (the two indicators go up and down together).
   (b) An inverse relationship (the two indicators move in opposite directions).
4. Which indicator seems to change direction first as time passes?
   (a) Percentage change in real GDP.
   (b) The unemployment rate.
5. Which of the following kinds of unemployment is reflected in the fluctuations in Figure 10.1?
   (a) Structural unemployment.
   (b) Seasonal unemployment.
   (c) Cyclical unemployment.
   (d) Frictional unemployment.
6. Which of the following government programs would be *most* appropriate to counteract the kind of unemployment?
   (a) Increase job-placement services.
   (b) Stimulate economic growth.
   (c) Make school last all year long.
   (d) Provide more job training.
7. In what years was full employment, as defined by the Reagan administration, achieved between 1970 and 1989? _____

Exercise 2

This exercise shows the relationship between unemployment and the level of GDP. It is similar to the problem at the end of Chapter 10 in the text.

Suppose the data in Table 10.2 describe a nation's population.

Table 10.2. Employment and unemployment

	Year 1	Year 2
Population	400 million	460 million
Labor force	250 million	250 million
Unemployment rate	8 percent	8 percent
Number of unemployed	_____	_____
Number of employed	_____	_____

1. Fill in the blanks in Table 10.2 to show the number of unemployed and the number of employed.
2. When the population grows but the labor force and the unemployment rate remain constant, the number employed (rises, remains the same, falls).
3. If both the population and the number employed remain constant, but a larger percentage of the population passes through to retirement, the unemployment rate should (rise, remain the same, fall), *ceteris paribus.*

4. The people who immigrate to the United States are generally young and of working age compared to the existing population of the United States. As greater immigration rates are permitted and if the unemployment rate stays constant, the number employed would (rise, remain the same, fall), *ceteris paribus.*

5. Suppose each employee contributes $30,000 worth of goods and services to the GDP. If the unemployment rate rises from 5 percent to 8 percent, by how much would GDP decline? _____

Exercise 3

The following exercise provides practice in categorizing the various kinds of unemployment. Identify each of the following cases as an example of seasonal unemployment, frictional unemployment, structural unemployment, or cyclical unemployment.

1. The immigration service faces its greatest problem during the summer when illegal immigrants cross the border to pick crops. _____

2. People who are fired from jobs with high salaries take longer to find new jobs than those with low salaries. _____

3. At the worst point of the Great Depression nearly one-fourth of the labor force in the United States was unemployed. _____

4. In some cities there are extreme shortages of labor at the same time that there is substantial unemployment. The problem is that the shortages occur in high-tech industries while the unemployment occurs for unskilled workers. _____

Exercise 4

This exercise shows how to compute changes in real income. It is similar to the problem at the end of Chapter 10 in the text.

Suppose that between 1980 and 2000, the average consumer's nominal income increases from $18,000 to $36,000. Table 10.3 lists the prices of a small market basket of goods and services purchased in both of those years. Assuming that this basket of goods is representative of all goods and services purchased, compute the percentage change in real income between 1980 and 2000. _____%

Table 10.3. Price of a small market basket in 1980 and 2000

Item	Quantity (units per year)	Price in 1980	Price in 2000
		(dollars per unit)	
Coffee	20 pounds	$ 3	$ 8
Tuition	1 year	4,000	20,000
Pizza	100 pizzas	8	6
VCR rental	75 days	15	4
Vacation	2 weeks	300	1,000

Exercise 5

Articles on inflation are as politically sensitive as those reporting unemployment numbers. The former often provide selected information on average price increases throughout the economy. By using one of the articles in the text, this exercise will show the kind of information to look for. If your professor makes a newspaper assignment from the *Instructor's Manual,* this exercise will provide an example of how to do it.

Reread the article on page 204 in Chapter 10 entitled "Inflation and the Weimar Republic" from *The Wall Street Journal.* Then answer the following questions:

1. What sentence provides the inflation data for the worst period of inflation?

   To what group or community do these data apply?

2. What sentences indicate the trend in the inflation rate prior to the hyperinflation?

3. What statement indicates the government's interpretation of the numbers?

Common Errors

The first statement in each "common error" below is incorrect. Each incorrect statement is followed by a corrected version and an explanation.

1. The government should eliminate unemployment. WRONG!
   The government must lower unemployment at the same time that it accomplishes other goals. RIGHT!

   Under the Full Employment and Balanced Growth Act of 1978, the government sets an unemployment goal for itself, but this goal is well short of a zero unemployment rate. As we shall see in subsequent chapters, the government may have to sacrifice such goals as price stability if it lowers unemployment too much. In this chapter we have seen that it would be very difficult and even undesirable to eliminate frictional or seasonal unemployment.

2. A rise in the unemployment rate of 0.1 or 0.2 percent for a month is bad. WRONG!
   Monthly changes in the unemployment rate may not have any significant economic implications. RIGHT!

   Small changes in the unemployment rate tell us nothing about what is happening to disguised unemployment (people who seem to be working but are not), discouraged workers (people who are no longer looking), or changes in the labor force; and large changes in seasonal or frictional unemployment are not necessarily bad, and could not be easily remedied even if they were. Be careful in interpreting short-run changes in the unemployment rate.

176

3. When the price of a product rises, there is inflation. WRONG!
   When an average of prices rises, there is inflation. RIGHT!

   The price of a single product may rise while an average of prices of all products falls. Such adjustment in relative prices is essential to the most *efficient* distribution of goods and services through the market. When the average of all prices is rising, however, distribution may not be efficient and capricious redistributions of income may occur.

4. As long as price increases do not exceed the inflation rate, they do not contribute to inflation. WRONG!
   Every price increase contributes to a rise in the inflation rate. RIGHT!

   Since the inflation rate is an average of all price increases, the increase in any price by any amount raises the average. Firms that buy commodities from other firms that raise prices will in turn pass the increase on to their own customers; an increased price may have indirect effects in raising the inflation rate.

■ ANSWERS ■

Key-Term Review

1. recession	5. inflation	9. unemployment	12. price stability
2. business cycle	6. unemployment rate	10. inflation rate	13. nominal income
3. macroeconomics	7. full employment	consumer price index	real income
4. real GDP	8. labor force	11. deflation	14. relative price

True or False

1. F	5. F	9. F	13. T	17. T	21. T	25. T
2. T	6. T	10. F	14. T	18. T	22. T	26. F
3. F	7. T	11. T	15. T	19. T	23. T	27. T
4. T	8. F	12. T	16. T	20. F	24. T	

Multiple Choice

1. d	4. d	7. d	10. c	13. d	16. b	19. c
2. b	5. a	8. a	11. d	14. a	17. d	20. c
3. d	6. c	9. b	12. a	15. d	18. c	21. d

Problems and Applications

Exercise 1

1. Table 10.1 Answer

Year	(4) Unemployment rate (percent)
1970	4.9%
1971	5.9
1972	5.6
1973	4.9
1974	5.6
1975	8.5
1976	7.7
1977	7.1
1978	6.1
1979	5.9
1980	7.1
1981	7.6
1982	9.7
1983	9.6
1984	7.5
1985	7.2
1986	7.0
1987	6.2
1988	5.5
1989	5.3

2. Figure 10.1 Answer

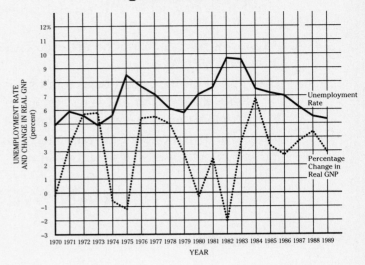

3. b
4. a After a dramatic rise in real GDP, it takes several years for the unemployment rate to reach the lowest level.
5. c
6. b
7. 1970-74, 1978, 1979, 1987, 1988, 1989

Exercise 2

1. **Table 10.2 answer**

	Year 1	Year 2
Population	400 million	460 million
Labor force	250 million	250 million
Unemployment rate	8 percent	8 percent
Number of unemployed	20 million (= 250 x 0.08)	20 million
Number of employed	230 million (= 250 - 20)	230 million

2. remains the same
3. fall
4. rise
5. With 3 percent (8 percent - 5 percent) of the labor force newly unemployed, there are 7.5 million unemployed (= 3 percent x 250 million in the labor force). They could have produced an average of $30,000 a year for a total of $225 billion (= 7.5 million x $30,000) in GDP.

Exercise 3

1. seasonal
2. frictional
3. cyclical
4. structural

Exercise 4

The first step is to find the total expenditure on the items for each year.

In 1980 it is:

20 pounds	x	$3 per pound	=	$ 60
1 year	x	$4,000 per year	=	4,000
100 pizzas	x	$8 per pizza	=	800
75 days	x	$15 per day	=	1,125
2 weeks	x	$300 per week	=	600
		Total	=	$6,585

In 2000 it is:

20 pounds	x	$8 per pound	=	$ 160
1 year	x	$20,000 per year	=	20,000
100 pizzas	x	$6 per pizza	=	600
75 days	x	$4 per day	=	300
2 weeks	x	$1,000 per week	=	2,000
		Total	=	$23,060

179

The percentage change in real income is

$$\frac{36,000 \, / \, 18,000}{23,060 \, / \, 6,585} - 1 = -42.9\%$$

Exercise 5

1. The last sentence of the second paragraph describes the worst period of the hyperinflation. The data are from the German experience.
2. The first two paragraphs describe the trend of inflation before and after World War I.
3. The government is mentioned only at the end of the article in an understatement: "57 years later government policy is still colored by this experience with hyperinflation."

CHAPTER 11

Aggregate Supply and Demand

Quick Review

The basic purpose of macroeconomics is to explain the alternating periods of expansion and contraction known as the business cycle. Specifically, economists have asked:

- What are the major elements of a macro model?
- How do the forces of supply and demand fit into such a model?
- How does the model reflect major debates in macro theory and policy?

This chapter will focus on these overall questions by using the macroeconomic tools of aggregate supply and demand.

The answers to the macroeconomic questions have led to several different schools of thought. The Classical school, which was largely in vogue prior to the 1930s, stressed the self-adjusting nature of the economy. Adjustment mechanisms—such as flexible wages and prices, falling interest rates, and the like—were thought to ensure that any downswing would be short if the economy was left alone.

The Great Depression lasted a long time, and economists and politicians everywhere began to question Classical theory. The great British economist John Maynard Keynes developed an alternative theory that took issue with the self-adjusting view of the Classical school. Keynes asserted that the economy was, in fact, inherently *unstable.* To leave the economy alone was poor policy. Instead, he prescribed increased government spending, income transfers, and lower interest rates to get the economy moving again. The arguments about business cycles are still not settled, but we have learned a great deal, The cycle is measured from peak to trough by the fluctuation in real GDP.

The aggregate demand-supply framework provides a convenient way to compare various theories about how the economy works. While market supply and demand are the tools of microeconomics, aggregate demand and supply are the tools of macroeconomics. For both sets of tools, price (or a price index) is shown along the Y-axis and some measure of quantity is shown along the X-axis. In both cases the law of demand guarantees that the demand curve is downward sloping. The aggregate supply curve slopes upward to the right in the short run but is likely to be vertical in the long run. As with market demand and supply curves, the intersection of the aggregate demand and aggregate supply curves indicates an equilibrium. In both cases, setting prices above the equilibrium results in surpluses, while setting prices below the equilibrium results in shortages.

The chief difference between the microeconomic and macroeconomic use of demand and supply tools is the aggregation of goods that are measured. While market demand and supply curves can be used to analyze what happens in specific markets, aggregate demand and supply are used to illustrate what happens to the aggregate of all goods and services within the economy. We can use GDP as the measure of output with aggregate demand and supply curves. The macro equilibrium that is defined by their intersection may or may not be the employment level desired by society; and even if the macro equilibrium is at the output, employment, and price levels that are desired, it may not last for long. The forces lying behind the equilibrium can change. Shifts in aggregate demand and/ or aggregate supply can lead to unemployment, inflation, or, worse yet, a combination of the two.

Today economists focus on aggregate demand and aggregate supply to explain how the economy works. Their theories can be classified as demand side, supply side, or eclectic, which draws on the other two. The three policy levers used to discuss and demonstrate the several theories are:

1. Fiscal policy—changes in taxes and government spending to alter economic outcomes
2. Monetary policy—the use of money and credit to control economic outcomes
3. Supply-side policies—those that favor tax cuts to increase incentives for producers

Much of what follows in the next several chapters is devoted to explaining the theory of macroeconomic behavior introduced in this chapter.

Learning Objectives

After reading Chapter 11 and doing the following exercises, you should:	True or false	Multiple choice	Problems and applications	Common errors	Pages in the text
1. Know the determinants of macro performance.			1, 2, 3, 4		218-219
2. Be able to contrast the Classical and Keynesian views of how the economy works.	1, 16	2, 5, 9, 12			219-221
3. Be able to explain the downward slope of the aggregate demand curve.	4	3, 8, 13, 14		2	221-223
4. Understand why the aggregate supply curve has an upward slope.	5	3, 10, 15		2	223-224
5. Be able to demonstrate macro-equilibrium using aggregate supply and demand.	2, 6, 7, 8, 9, 15, 18	3, 4, 6, 9, 10, 11	1, 3	1	225-227
6. Understand inflation and instability as macro problems.	3, 9, 10, 13, 14, 17	1, 6, 16	1, 3		227-229

Learning Objectives (cont'd.)	True or false	Multiple choice	Problems and applications	Common errors	Pages in the text
7. Be able to distinguish demand-side, supply-side, and eclectic approaches to stabilization.	11, 12	5, 7, 16	3, 4		229-231
8. Understand how fiscal, monetary, and supply-side policies shift the aggregate supply and demand curves.	16		3, 4		229-231
9. Know the history of economic policy of the 1960s, 1970s, and 1980s.	13, 14	16	3		231-233

Key-Term Review

Review the following terms; if you are not sure of the meaning of any term, write out the definition and check it against the Glossary in the text.

aggregate demand	equilibrium (macro)	macroeconomics	Say's Law
aggregate supply	fiscal policy	monetary policy	supply-side policy
business cycle	inflation	real GDP	unemployment

Fill in the blank following each of the statements below with the appropriate term from the list above.

1. Business cycles are studied in an area of economics called .... 1. _____

2. The price level at which _____ and .... 2. _____
   _____ are equal determines .... _____
   _____. .... _____

3. The idea that "supply creates its own demand" is known as .... 3. _____

4. The fluctuations in real GDP because of changes in aggregate demand are called the .... 4. _____

5. When the _____ declines for two .... 5. _____
   consecutive quarters there is likely to be an increase in .... _____

6. When the average level of prices increases continuously, the process is known as .... 6. _____

7. _____ is the use of money and .... 7. _____
   credit controls to influence macroeconomic activity.

183

8. _____ is the use of taxes and .... 8. _____
   government spending to influence
   macroeconomic activity.

9. The first Reagan administration's economic
   program emphasized tax cuts and was
   known as .... 9. _____

True or False: *Circle your choice.*

T   F   1. In the Classical view of the economy, the product market is brought into equilibrium by flexible wages, the factor market by flexible prices.

T   F   2. If, at the prevailing price level, the aggregate quantity demanded exceeds the aggregate quantity supplied, the price level will tend to fall.

T   F   3. A recession is said to occur when the unemployment rate increases for two consecutive quarters.

T   F   4. The quantity of real output demanded rises as the price level increases, *ceteris paribus.*

T   F   5. The quantity of real output supplied rises with the price level, *ceteris paribus.*

T   F   6. For macroeconomic equilibrium to occur, market demand must equal market supply.

T   F   7. A stable equilibrium means that there is no tendency for price or output to change.

T   F   8. If, at the prevailing price level, the aggregate quantity supplied exceeds the aggregate quantity demanded, the price level will tend to fall.

T   F   9. A stable equilibrium means that the economy is at full employment.

T   F   10. During the business cycle, the change in the unemployment rate is inversely related to the change in income, *ceteris paribus.*

T   F   11. Both Keynesian and monetarist theories of the business cycle are demand-side theories.

T   F   12. Supply-side theories of the business cycle describe fluctuations in the willingness of producers to supply more goods and services, *ceteris paribus.*

T   F   13. The intensity of business cycles is measured using the consumer price index.

T   F   14. Unemployment and inflation tend to be inversely related over the business cycle.

T   F   15. A disequilibrium occurs at the price level where aggregate demand equals aggregate supply.

T   F   16. The Classical approach to the business cycle was for government to do nothing.

T   F   17. A recession occurs when real output falls for two consecutive years.

T   F   18. A surplus exists when, at the prevailing price level, aggregate quantity demanded exceeds the aggregate quantity supplied.

Multiple Choice: *Select the correct answer.*

_____ 1. Which of the following is said to occur when real GDP declines for two consecutive quarters?
   (a) Hyperinflation.
   (b) A recession.
   (c) Low unemployment.
   (d) All of the above.

2. Which of the following characterizes the Classical view of the economy?
   (a) Wages are flexible and prices are not.
   (b) The economy is inherently unstable.
   (c) The economy will "self-adjust" if we let it alone.
   (d) Government can stabilize the economy.

3. In the aggregate demand-aggregate supply diagram:
   (a) The vertical axis measures the average price level.
   (b) The horizontal axis measures real output.
   (c) The horizontal axis measures real income.
   (d) All of the above are correct.

4. Macro equilibrium always occurs:
   (a) When aggregate supply is greater than aggregate demand.
   (b) When the labor force is fully employed.
   (c) When aggregate demand equals aggregate supply at the average price level of the economy.
   (d) Under none of the above conditions.

5. Keynes argued that deficient aggregate demand might originate with:
   (a) Increased consumer savings.
   (b) Inadequate business investment.
   (c) Insufficient government spending.
   (d) All of the above.

6. Starting from an equilibrium at less than full employment:
   (a) If aggregate demand increases, *ceteris paribus,* the economy will experience inflation, or no price level increase.
   (b) If aggregate supply increases, *ceteris paribus,* the economy will be unlikely to experience inflation.
   (c) If both aggregate demand and aggregate supply increase, output and employment should increase, but the price level movement would be uncertain.
   (d) All of the above are the case.

7. The eclectic approach to economic policy suggests that the business cycle can be altered by:
   (a) The money supply.
   (b) Taxes and government spending.
   (c) Incentives for producers.
   (d) All of the above.

8. An aggregate demand curve most likely shifts to the left when:
   (a) Taxes fall.
   (b) Savings fall.
   (c) Government spending falls.
   (d) All of the above occur.

9. Which of the following are inherent in the Classical view of a self-adjusting economy?
   (a) Flexible wages.
   (b) Flexible prices.
   (c) Say's Law.
   (d) All of the above.

10. Which of the following causes the aggregate supply curve to shift?
    (a) Changes in consumer income.
    (b) Changes in consumer savings.
    (c) Changes in costs experienced by American businesses.
    (d) None of the above.

11. With respect to aggregate supply and aggregate demand, what will be most likely to happen when quantity supplied exceeds the quantity demanded?
    (a) Hyperinflation.
    (b) Recession.
    (c) Lower unemployment rates.
    (d) Full employment.

12. Keynes viewed the economy as inherently unstable and suggested that during a downturn policy makers should:
    (a) Cut taxes, increase government spending, and increase transfers.
    (b) Cut taxes, reduce government spending, and increase transfers.
    (c) Raise taxes, increase government spending, and increase transfers.
    (d) Cut taxes, increase government spending, and reduce transfers.

13. The "real balance" effect relies on the idea that as the price level falls:
    (a) Each dollar you own will purchase more goods and services.
    (b) Each bond you own will increase in value, thus increasing your wealth.
    (c) You will begin to save less because your wealth has increased.
    (d) All of the above are the case.

14. When the price level falls in our economy relative to the price level in foreign economies, consumers tend to:
    (a) Buy more imported goods and fewer domestically produced goods, *ceteris paribus.*
    (b) Buy more imported goods and more domestic goods, *ceteris paribus.*
    (c) Buy fewer imported goods and more domestic goods, *ceteris paribus.*
    (d) Buy fewer imported goods and fewer domestic goods, *ceteris paribus.*

15. The upward slope of the aggregate supply curve can best be explained by:
    (a) The "real balance" effect.
    (b) The interest-rate effect.
    (c) The higher costs associated with higher capacity utilization rates.
    (d) None of the above.

16. The reason that policy makers are reluctant to force the economy to an inflation rate of zero is that:
    (a) There would be unacceptable levels of unemployment if the economy were controlled by fiscal policy.
    (b) Wasteful quality changes and new products would be designed to escape price controls if controls were used.
    (c) Shortages of some products would be likely if there were wage-price controls.
    (d) All of the above are true.

_____ 17. Which of the following groupings contains a word which does not belong?
   (a) Internal market forces, external shocks, policy levers.
   (b) Keynesian theory, monetary theory, supply-side theory.
   (c) Macro equilibrium, instability, undesirability.
   (d) Real balance effect, foreign trade effect, interest rate effect.

Problems and Applications

Exercise 1

This exercise examines the effects of tax policy using aggregate supply and demand curves.
   Assume the aggregate demand and supply curves are those shown in Figure 11.1. Then suppose the government reduces taxes, which causes the quantity of output demanded in the economy to rise by $1 trillion per year at every price level. Decide whether the tax change shifts aggregate demand or aggregate supply from its initial position.

Figure 11.1

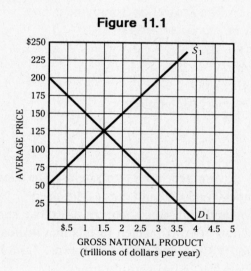

GROSS NATIONAL PRODUCT
(trillions of dollars per year)

1. Draw the new aggregate demand curve (label it D_2) or aggregate supply curve (label it S_2) in Figure 11.1 that results from the tax change.
2. Compute the percentage change in equilibrium GDP caused by the shift._____%
3. Suppose that the unemployment rate drops by one percentage point for every 5 percent increase in GDP. If the unemployment rate was 15 percent before the shift occurred, what would it be after the shift?_____%
4. What is the percentage change in the equilibrium price level as a result of the tax change?
   _____%
5. The shift that occurred in Question 1 (above) is consistent with:
   (a) Stagflation (inflation and a higher unemployment rate).
   (b) Inflation and a lower unemployment rate.
   (c) Deflation and a higher unemployment rate.
   (d) Lower inflation and a lower unemployment rate.

187

Now suppose the lower taxes also induce productivity changes and generate incentives that cause firms (sellers) to lower prices by $50 per unit of output per year after the tax change. In Questions 6-11, compare the new equilibrium to that you established above in Question 1.

6. Draw the new aggregate demand curve (label it D_3) or aggregate supply curve (label it S_3) in Figure 11.1. Compare the new equilibrium to that used in Questions 1-5.

7. Compute the percentage change (on curve S_2 or D_2) in equilibrium GDP caused by the shift. _____%

8. Suppose that the unemployment rate drops by one percentage point for every 5 percent increase in GDP. If the unemployment rate was 8.4 percent before the shift occurred, what would it be after the shift?_____%

9. What would be the percentage change in the equilibrium price level associated with the new level of output?_____%.

10. This shift is consistent with:
    (a) Stagflation (inflation and a higher unemployment rate).
    (b) Inflation and a lower unemployment rate.
    (c) Deflation and a higher unemployment rate.
    (d) A lower price level and lower unemployment rate.

11. The tax cut can best be characterized as:
    (a) Monetary policy only.
    (b) Fiscal policy only.
    (c) Supply-side policy only.
    (d) Both fiscal and supply-side policy.

Exercise 2

This exercise shows how government policy can be used to alleviate problems brought on by natural disasters. Aggregate supply and demand curves are used.

Assume the aggregate demand and supply curves are those shown in Figure 11.2. Suppose drought causes massive destruction of crops, which results in a decrease of $1 trillion of goods and services (GDP) that sellers are willing and able to provide. Decide whether the change shifts aggregate demand or supply from the initial equilibrium.

Figure 11.2

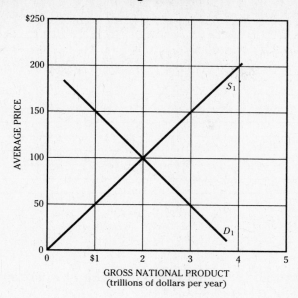

GROSS NATIONAL PRODUCT
(trillions of dollars per year)

1. Draw the new aggregate demand (label it D_2) or aggregate supply curve (label it S_2) in Figure 11.2 that results from the drought.
2. With which of the following is the move to the new equilibrium in Question 1 consistent?
   (a) Stagflation (inflation and a higher unemployment rate).
   (b) Inflation and a lower unemployment rate.
   (c) Deflation and a higher unemployment rate.
   (d) Deflation and a lower unemployment rate.
3. If the price level was held down to 100 by government price controls, would there be a shortage or a surplus after the drought? _____
4. Which curve would shift if the government released some of its inventories to push the equilibrium to a GDP of $2 trillion at a price level of 100? _____
5. Draw the new aggregate demand (label it D_3) or supply curve (label it S_3) in Figure 11.2 that would result from the government's inventory release program.

Exercise 3

This exercise will help to show how aggregate demand and supply can be used to analyze the effects of government policy. Suppose the aggregate demand curve and aggregate supply curve for all of the goods in an economy are presented in Figure 11.3. The economy is assumed to be on aggregate demand curve B in the current fiscal year.

189

Figure 11.3

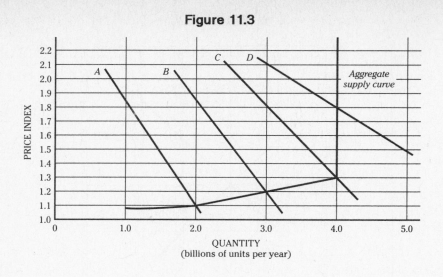

QUANTITY
(billions of units per year)

1. Four aggregate demand curves are shown in Figure 11.3 corresponding to four alternative government policies for the coming fiscal year.

   For the following four government policies, choose the aggregate demand curve in Figure 11.3 that best portrays the expected impact of each policy. Place the letter of your choice in each blank provided.

   _____ Money supply is expanded, taxes are cut, government increases its expenditures.

   _____ Government does nothing.

   _____ Government decides to balance the budget by reducing government spending and by raising taxes.

   _____ Government increases expenditures and cuts taxes.

2. Indicate the equilibrium price index for each policy in Table 11.1.

Table 11.1. Equilibrium prices for four government policies

Aggregate demand curve	A	B	C	D
Equilibrium price index	_____	_____	_____	_____

3. Suppose the price index is currently 1.2 as shown by demand curve *B* in Figure 11.3. Compute the inflation rate under each of the four policies assuming the supply curve remains the same. The formula is

$$100 \times \left(\frac{\text{equilibrium price index - 1.2}}{1.2} \right)$$

Enter your answers for each policy in the appropriate blank of column 1 in Table 11.2.

190

Table 11.2. Inflation rates, equilibrium output, and unemployment rates under four government policies

Aggregate demand curve	(1) Equilibrium price change	(2) Equilibrium output (billions of units per year)	(3) Unemployment rate
A	_____%	_____	_____%
B	_____	_____	_____
C	_____	_____	_____
D	_____	_____	_____

4. In Table 11.2 (column 2) indicate the equilibrium output associated with each of the policies. Use Figure 11.3 to find this information.

5. Which of the following *best* represents the U.S. unemployment rate?
   (a) The number of people divided by the U.S. labor force.
   (b) The number of people employed divided by the U.S. population.
   (c) The number of people counted as unemployed divided by the U.S. labor force.
   (d) The number of people unemployed divided by the U.S. population.

6. Table 11.3 shows a *hypothetical* U.S. population, the labor force, the number of people who are employed, and the number of people who are unemployed at each production rate for the economy. Compute the unemployment rate at each production rate in the table.

Table 11.3. Computation of the unemployment rate

Production rate (billions of units per year)	2	3	4
U.S. population (millions)	200	200	200
Labor force (millions)	100	100	100
Number of people unemployed (millions)	15	8	5
Number of people employed (millions)	85	92	95
Unemployment rate (percent)	_____	_____	_____

7. Using the information in Table 11.3, complete column 3 in Table 11.2, which shows the unemployment rate corresponding to each government policy.

8. The government's dilemma is:
   (a) That it cannot reach an unemployment level of 5 percent without experiencing inflation of at least 8 percent.
   (b) That it cannot reach stable prices (0 percent increase) without experiencing an unemployment rate of 8 percent or more.
   (c) That when it makes gains in holding inflation below 8 percent, unemployment increases.
   (d) Expressed by all of the above statements.

191

9. Which of the four aggregate demand curves places the economy closest to full-employment output and moderate inflation?
    (a) Aggregate demand curve *A*.
    (b) Aggregate demand curve *B*.
    (c) Aggregate demand curve *C*.
    (d) Aggregate demand curve *D*.

Exercise 4

The media often provide information about changes in government policies and the effects of such changes. By using one of the articles in the text, this exercise will show the kind of information to look for. If your professor makes a newspaper assignment from the *Instructor's Manual,* this exercise will provide an example of how to do it.

Reread the article in Chapter 11 on page 231 entitled "Regulation of Business May Ease" from the *Washington Post.* Then answer the following questions.

Figure 11.4. Possible shifts of aggregate demand or supply

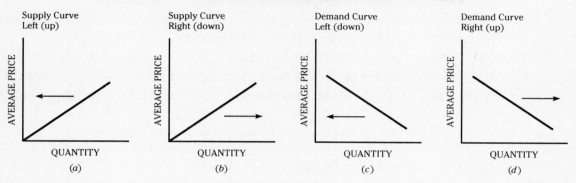

1. Quote the part of the article which indicates a policy change.

2. In what way does the article indicate the government agency or representative responsible for making or enforcing the policy?

3. Quote evidence of an actual or expected change in quantity or price due to the policy change.

4. What prices will be affected by the change?

5. Who is first affected by the change in the market?
    (a) The buyer.
    (b) The seller.
6. What determinants of demand and supply are changing?

7. Examine the diagrams in Figure 11.4. Which one best represents the expected shift?
            a   b   c   d   (circle one)

192

Common Errors

The first statement in each "common error" below is incorrect. Each incorrect statement is followed by a corrected version and an explanation.

1. Full employment is achieved at the equilibrium GDP. WRONG!
   Full employment is not necessarily achieved at the equilibrium GDP. RIGHT!
   At full employment, the economy fully utilizes resources without producing high inflation rates. When resources are fully employed, no additional goods and services can be produced. However, the equilibrium GDP refers to the equality between the aggregate demand for goods and services, not to any particular level of resource employment.

2. Aggregate demand (supply) and market demand (supply) are the same. WRONG!
   Aggregate demand (supply) and market demand (supply) involve very different levels of aggregation. RIGHT!
   Market demand can be found for specific markets only. Products in each market must be homogeneous. The firms in that market are competitors. The market demand is used for microeconomic applications. Aggregate demand applies to all markets within the economy and involves their average prices. It is not even possible to sum the market demand curves to find the aggregate demand curve because the prices of different commodities cannot be measured in the same units; an average price must be computed. Aggregate demand is used for macroeconomic applications, not microeconomic ones. The distinction between aggregate supply and market supply is similar to that between aggregate demand and market demand.

■ ANSWERS ■

Key-Term Review

1. macroeconomics
2. aggregate demand
   aggregate supply
   equilibrium (macro)
3. Say's Law
4. business cycle
5. real GDP
   unemployment
6. inflation
7. monetary policy
8. fiscal policy
9. supply-side policy

True or False

1. F	4. F	7. T	10. T	13. F	15. F	17. F
2. F	5. T	8. T	11. T	14. T	16. T	18. F
3. F	6. F	9. F	12. F			

Multiple Choice

1. b	4. c	7. d	9. d	11. b	13. d	15. c
2. c	5. d	8. c	10. c	12. a	14. c	16. d
3. d	6. d					

17. c   Macro equilibrium is not a macro failure. Other topics include (a) determinants of macro performance, (b) macroeconomic theories, and (d) reasons for a downward-sloping aggregate demand curve.

Problems and Applications

Exercise 1

1. See Figure 11.1 answer, D_2.

Figure 11.1 Answer

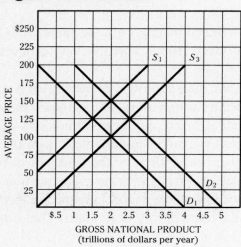

GROSS NATIONAL PRODUCT
(trillions of dollars per year)

2. Equilibrium GDP before the shift is $1.5 trillion each year.
   Equilibrium GDP after the shift is $2.00 trillion each year.
   Percentage change = (2.0 - 1.5) / 1.5 = 33%

3. $\dfrac{33\% \text{ change in output}}{5\%}$ = 6.6% drop in the unemployment rate.

   The new unemployment rate is 8.4% (= 15% - 6.6%).

4. Equilibrium price before the shift is 125.
   Equilibrium price after the shift is 150.
   Percentage change = (150 - 125) / 125 = 20%.

5. b

6. See Figure 11.1 answer, S_3.

7. Equilibrium GDP before the shift is $2.0 trillion
   Equilibrium GDP after the shift is $2.5 trillion.
   Percentage change = (2.5 - 2.0) / 2.0 = 25%.

8. $\dfrac{25\% \text{ change in output}}{5\%}$ = 5% drop in the unemployment rate.

   The new unemployment rate is 3.4% (= 8.4% - 5%).

194

9. Equilibrium price before the shift is 150.
   Equilibrium price after the shift is 125.
   Percentage change = (125 - 150) / 150 = -17%.
10. d
11. d

Exercise 2

1. See Figure 11.2 answer, S_2.

   Figure 11.2 Answer

   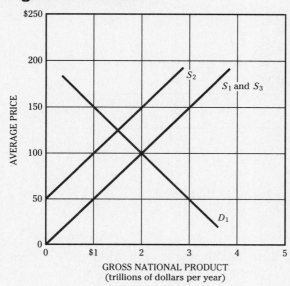

   GROSS NATIONAL PRODUCT
   (trillions of dollars per year)

2. a Since the drought causes prices to rise and the GDP to fall, its effects on the economy are consistent with stagflation.
3. Shortage. The price ($100) is below the new equilibrium price of $125.
4. The supply curve would have been shifted back to its original position.
5. See Figure 11.2 answer, S_3.

Exercise 3

1. D, B, A, C
2. **Table 11.1 Answer**

Aggregate demand curve	A	B	C	D
Equilibrium price index	1.1	1.2	1.3	1.8

3. See Table 11.2 answer, column 1.

Table 11.2 Answer

Aggregate demand curve	(1) Equilibrium price change	(2) Equilibrium output (billions of units per year)	(3) Unemployment rate
A	- 8.3%	2.0	15%
B	0.0	3.0	8
C	8.3	4.0	5
D	50.0	4.0	5

4. See Table 11.2 answer, column 2.
5. c
6. **Table 11.3 Answer**

Production rate (billions of units per year)	2	3	4
Unemployment rate (percent)	15	8	5

7. See Table 11.2 answer, column 3.
8. d
9. c

Exercise 4

1. "President Bush... is considering a three-month freeze on a wide array of new federal regulations..."
2. By reporting the President's address in State of the Union message the article indicates who is responsible for the change.
3. "whether their goals could be met in a less budensome or costly way"
4. Prices of the firms that are regulated should go down as their costs go down.
5. b
6. Seller expectations
7. b

CHAPTER 12

Fiscal Policy

Quick Review

The amended Employment Act of 1946 has made full employment, price stability, and continued economic growth the basic goals of macroeconomic policy. John Maynard Keynes developed the theory that showed how the government can use fiscal policy to pursue these goals. In studying his contribution we will examine the following questions:
- Why did Keynes think the economy was inherently unstable?
- How can fiscal policy help stabilize the economy?
- How will the use of fiscal policy affect the government's budget deficit?

The analytical tools for exploring these issues are aggregate demand and supply.

Aggregate demand is a schedule of possible output-price level combinations that may be achieved by the economy. The shape and position of an aggregate demand curve are determined by the sum of four basic components: consumption expenditures by households *(C)*, investment expenditures by businesses *(I)*, government expenditures *(G),* and net exports *(X - M).* These components of aggregate demand behave in very different ways and with different degrees of volatility. While consumption is the largest component, investment spending is the most volatile. It is difficult to expect that aggregate demand, which is the sum of these components, will always be appropriate to achieve the goals set for the economy.

Specifically, Keynes showed that aggregate demand may not fully utilize the capacity of the economy to produce goods and services; in other words, it may not achieve full employment. The capacity of the economy to produce goods and services is determined by the shape of the aggregate supply curve. Keynes viewed the aggregate supply curve as horizontal when the economy fails to completely utilize its capacity. In other words, when the economy is below full employment, increased aggregate demand does not raise prices. However, when full employment is achieved, the aggregate supply curve becomes vertical. This means that additional aggregate demand leads to inflation. Keynes believed that government should use fiscal policy to achieve full employment and to avoid the extremes of recession and inflation.

Fiscal policy is designed to stabilize the economy by adjusting government expenditures *(G)* and taxes *(T).* Government changes fiscal policy by changing its spending or tax rates. Government can move aggregate demand toward full employment and price stability if it cuts taxes or raises expenditures (expansionary fiscal policy) when there is recession, or if it raises taxes or cuts spending (contractionary fiscal policy) when there is inflation. The multiplier assures that even modest changes in government spending or taxes will have a significant impact on total spending.

The economy is potentially unstable for the same reason that fiscal policy can be so effective. Small changes in aggregate demand are multiplied into large changes in income.   When any of the components of aggregate demand, such as government spending, increases someone receives higher income. After saving part of this income, the recipient turns around and spends most of it, while leaving a small part for saving. The increased spending becomes someone else's income. The original change in aggregate demand is multiplied in size as it churns through the economy. The size of the multiplier depends on the marginal propensity to consume (MPC), which measures how much of each extra dollar of income consumers will spend on consumption. The key formula for computing the multiplier is

$$\text{Multiplier} = \frac{1}{1 - \text{MPC}}$$

The multiplier occurs in the economy because of successive rounds of spending. However, with each round of spending, people save part of their additional income. What fraction they save is determined by the marginal propensity to save (MPS).

Because of the multiplier effect, any change in government spending creates a much larger change in GDP. The government frequently pursues its stabilization function through deficit spending. To eliminate recession the government may have to increase government expenditure while simultaneously lowering taxes. The stabilization function of government therefore often makes it difficult to balance the budget.

Learning Objectives

After reading Chapter 12 and doing the following exercises, you should:	True or false	Multiple choice	Problems and applications	Common errors	Pages in the text
1. Know the components of aggregate demand.	3, 16	5, 22		1, 2, 3	238-240
2. Be able to contrast the Keynesian and Classical views of how the economy works.	2, 8, 9, 10, 11, 15	7, 9, 10, 13, 14, 15		4	238-240
3. Be able to graph the aggregate supply-demand model.	7, 8, 9, 10, 12, 13	1		4	240
4. Know what fiscal policy is and who makes it.		2	2		238, 241-242
5. Be able to demonstrate how fiscal policy and supply-side policy affect the economy.	17		2		245-246
6. Know how the multiplier process works and be able to calculate it.	4, 5, 6, 19, 20, 22	6, 11, 12, 17, 23	1, 2	2	242-245

Learning Objectives (cont'd.)	True or false	Multiple choice	Problems and applications	Common errors	Pages in the text
7. Be able to devise stabilization policies for differing economic circumstances.	14, 15	2, 3, 4, 16, 18, 19	2		248-249
8. Be able to calculate the multiplier effects of a change in taxes or transfers.	22, 23, 24	6, 11, 12	1		245-246
9. Understand why the stabilization goal may conflict with the budget balancing goal.	1, 2, 18, 21	20, 21	2	1	250-252

Key-Term Review

Review the following terms; if you are not sure of the meaning of any term, write out the definition and check it against the Glossary in the text.

aggregate demand   deficit spending   marginal propensity to consume (MPC)
aggregate supply   disposable income (DI)   marginal propensity to save (MPS)
budget deficit   equilibrium (macro)   multiplier
budget surplus   fiscal policy   net exports
consumption   investment   saving

Fill in the blank following each of the statements below with the appropriate term from the list above.

1. In the equation for aggregate demand, I represents .... 1. _____

2. C in the equation represents .... 2. _____

3. The X-M in the equation represents .... 3. _____

4. The _____ is found by dividing the .... 4. _____
change in C by the change in .... _____

5. The excess of disposable income over consumption is.. 5. _____

6. The ratio of the change in saving to a change in disposable income is known as the .... 6. _____

7. _____ is established at the price- .... 7. _____
-output combination at which _____ .... _____
equals .... _____

8. Congress may initiate new spending programs to counteract the effects of recession; this is referred to as the use of .... 8. _____

199

9. However, such programs are likely to increase the_____ which means the .... 9. _____
government is engaging in .... _____

10. Many people disapprove of such spending and urge the government to bring expenditures below government revenues for a .... 10. _____

11. When the government reduces its spending, the .... 11. _____
causes household after-tax disposable income to fall by more than the reduction in government expenditure.

True or False: *Circle your choice.*

T   F   1. Full employment is achieved only when prices are stable.

T   F   2. According to Keynes, inflation occurs when aggregate demand increases beyond the full employment level.

T   F   3. The largest component of aggregate demand is government spending.

T   F   4. If consumers are optimistic, the marginal propensity to save rises.

T   F   5. The marginal propensity to consume (MPC) is related to the marginal propensity to save (MPS) by the formula MPC = 1 - MPS.

T   F   6. Increased saving necessarily results in a lower macro equilibrium income for society, *ceteris paribus.*

T   F   7. Keynes felt that if the economy was at less than full employment, it would automatically adjust to full employment.

T   F   8. Keynes viewed the aggregate supply curve as being horizontal in a recession.

T   F   9. Keynes viewed the aggregate demand curve as being vertical in a recession.

T   F   10. Classical economists believed that flexible wages and prices would allow the economy to self-adjust to macro equilibrium at full employment.

T   F   11. Say's Law says that demand creates its own supply.

T   F   12. By definition, equilibrium GDP occurs when there is full employment in an economy.

T   F   13. Equilibrium GDP is the most desired level of GDP for an economy.

T   F   14. When there is inflation, too much money chases too few goods and there are not enough resources available, which means wages are bid up by employers to prevent their employees from seeking work elsewhere.

T   F   15. According to Keynes, government can curb inflation by increasing government expenditures.

T   F   16. Private expenditures include *C, I, G,* and imports.

T   F   17. Fiscal policy involves changes in government spending and/or taxes but not regulation of prices or production.

T   F   18. By attempting to balance the budget during a recession, the government is likely to worsen the recession.

T   F   19. If the macro equilibrium is $400 million below full employment, then the government should increase expenditures by $400 million to raise equilibrium income to the full-employment level.

T F 20. When government spending increases, saving also increases through the multiplier process.

T F 21. The government deficit is simply the difference between government expenditures and tax revenues.

T F 22. An increase in transfer payments of $10 million would have the same impact as a $10 million increase in government spending.

T F 23. Income transfers are payments to individuals for which no current goods or services are exchanged.

Multiple Choice: *Select the correct answer.*

_____ 1. Full employment is first achieved at the GDP level at which:
(a) The lowest possible rate of unemployment is obtained.
(b) The lowest rate of unemployment possible occurs with stable economic growth.
(c) The lowest rate of unemployment possible occurs with price stability.
(d) None of the above is the case.

_____ 2. Which of the following is eliminated at full employment?
(a) Cyclical unemployment.
(b) Frictional unemployment.
(c) Structural unemployment.
(d) All of the above.

_____ 3. What results when the aggregate demand exceeds full-employment income?
(a) Inventory accumulation.
(b) Unemployment.
(c) Inflation.
(d) All of the above.

_____ 4. What results when the aggregate demand is not sufficient to generate full employment?
(a) Lower inventories
(b) Inflation.
(c) Entry of new firms as a result of increased profits.
(d) Recession.

_____ 5. The only items needed to compute disposable income are:
(a) Consumption and saving.
(b) Consumption, saving, imports, and exports.
(c) Consumption, saving, imports, exports, and taxes.
(d) Consumption, government expenditures, investment, and saving.

_____ 6. The MPC can be found by dividing:
(a) The change in consumption by the change in saving.
(b) The change in consumption by the number of people consuming.
(c) The change in consumption by the change in disposable income.
(d) Consumption by total disposable income.

_____ 7. Classical economists believed that there would be a quick adjustment of aggregate demand to full-employment output as a result of changes in:
(a) Interest rates.
(b) Prices.
(c) Wages.
(d) All of the above.

_____ 8. Producers respond to excessive inventories by:
(a) Increasing production.
(b) Increasing prices.
(c) Investing less.
(d) Increasing employment.

_____ 9. Say's Law is a tenet of:
(a) The Classical position.
(b) The Keynesian position.
(c) Supply side policy.
(d) None of the above.

_____ 10. Unlike Keynes, the Classical economists believed that wages, prices, and interest rates would:
(a) Cause cyclical unemployment if they were determined through the market mechanism.
(b) Adjust so that unemployment would be eliminated through the market mechanism.
(c) Lower aggregate demand instead of raising it when there is a recession.
(d) All of the above.

_____ 11. The multiplier is:
(a) MPC.
(b) MPS.
(c) $\dfrac{1}{1 - MPC}$.
(d) $\dfrac{1}{1 - MPS}$.

_____ 12. The impact of the multiplier depends upon:
(a) The time period over which the multiplier works.
(b) The size of the marginal propensity to consume.
(c) The size of the initial change in expenditure.
(d) All of the above.

_____ 13. When average prices for the economy are above those that would achieve macro equilibrium, then inventories are likely to be:
(a) Too large and there will be inflationary price pressures.
(b) Too large and the unemployment rate should being to rise.
(c) Too small and there will be inflationary price pressures.
(d) Too small and the unemployment rate should begin to rise.

_____ 14. If the economy is below full-employment income:
   (a) The economy is inside its production-possibilities curve.
   (b) Unemployment is unnecessarily high.
   (c) The opportunity cost of additional output is zero.
   (d) All of the above are the case.

_____ 15. Suppose the economy is at full employment and prices are reasonably stable. If the government wants to increase spending for interstate highway repair, which of the following actions will have the _least_ inflationary impact?
   (a) Using deficit financing.
   (b) Lowering some other government expenditure by the amount of the increase in highway repairs.
   (c) Raising taxes by the amount of the new expenditure.
   (d) All of the above have the same inflationary impact.

_____ 16. The government can best eliminate a recession by:
   (a) Increasing government spending and raising taxes.
   (b) Increasing government spending and lowering taxes.
   (c) Decreasing government spending and raising taxes.
   (d) Decreasing government spending and lowering taxes.

_____ 17. The amount of additional income generated by increased government spending depends on:
   (a) The marginal propensity to consume.
   (b) The number of spending cycles that occur in a given period of time.
   (c) The size of the initial increase in government spending.
   (d) All of the above.

_____ 18. According to Keynes, it is inflationary for government to increase spending if:
   (a) It will have to raise taxes to pay for the increased spending.
   (b) Increased government spending will result in deficits.
   (c) The economy is at full employment.
   (d) Equilibrium income is thereby lowered.

_____ 19. During an inflationary period it is appropriate for the government to pursue policies which:
   (a) Make budget surpluses smaller.
   (b) Make budget deficits smaller.
   (c) Make budget deficits larger.
   (d) Eliminate the public debt.

_____ 20. Which of the following presidents presided over the largest tax cuts in U.S. history?
   (a) President Kennedy.
   (b) President Nixon.
   (c) President Johnson.
   (d) President Reagan.

_____ 21. The government is pursuing an expansionary policy if, whatever the value of the budget balance, it:
   (a) Increases its spending and reduces taxes.
   (b) Increases its spending and increases taxes.
   (c) Decreases its spending and reduces taxes.
   (d) Decreases its spending and increases taxes.

22. Personal saving is:
    (a) That part of current disposable income not spent on goods and services in a given time period.
    (b) Disposable income less consumption.
    (c) Greater when income rises.
    (d) All of the above.
23. The marginal propensity to consume is:
    (a) That part of the average consumer dollar that goes to the purchase of final goods.
    (b) The change in consumption divided by the change in disposable income.
    (c) The fraction of each additional (marginal) dollar of consumption spent on disposable income.
    (d) All of above.

Problems and Applications

Exercise 1

The following exercise shows how the multiplier works and two ways to calculate it—an easy way and a hard way.

1. Suppose the economy were at full employment but suddenly experienced a $216 billion drop in business expenditures due to abrupt cancellation of investment plans. Follow the impact of this sudden change through the economy by completing Table 12.1, as in Table 12.1 in your text (p. 244). Assume the marginal propensity to consume is 5/6.

Table 12.1

Spending cycles	Drop in investment expenditure	Amount (billions of dollars per year)	Cumulative decrease in aggregate spending (billions of dollars per year)
First cycle:	recessionary gap emerges	$216	$216
Second cycle:	consumption drops by MPC x 216	_____	_____
Third cycle:	consumption drops by MPC^2 x 216	_____	_____
Fourth cycle:	consumption drops by MPC^3 x 216	_____	_____
Fifth cycle:	consumption drops by MPC^4 x 216	_____	_____
Sixth cycle:	consumption drops by MPC^5 x 216	_____	_____
Seventh cycle:	consumption drops by MPC^6 x 216	_____	_____

2. What will be the final cumulative impact on aggregate demand? (*Hint:* The eighth cycle is $[5/6]^7$ x $216 billion = $60 billion, which brings the cumulative change in aggregate demand to $994. Continue the cycles.)_____
3. Compute the multiplier. _____
4. Multiply the $216 billion by the multiplier._____

Macro equilibrium occurs where aggregate demand and aggregate supply intersect. Full employment occurs at the GDP level where the aggregate supply curve begins to rise sharply, which means that increased aggregate demand will result in increased inflation rather than increased aggregate output.

■ ANSWERS ■

Key-Term Review

1. investment
2. consumption
3. net exports
4. marginal propensity to consume (MPC) disposable income (DI)

5. saving
6. marginal propensity to save (MPS)
7. equilibrium (macro) aggregate demand aggregate supply

8. fiscal policy
9. budget deficit deficit spending
10. budget surplus
11. multiplier

True or False

1. F	5. T	9. F	13. F	16. F	19. F	22. F
2. T	6. T	10. T	14. T	17. T	20. T	23. T
3. F	7. F	11. F	15. F	18. T	21. T	
4. F	8. T	12. F				

Multiple Choice

1. c	5. a	9. a	12. d	15. b	18. c	21. a
2. a	6. c	10. b	13. b	16. b	19. b	22. d
3. c	7. d	11. c	14. d	17. d	20. d	23. b
4. d	8. c					

Problems and Applications

Exercise 1

1. **Table 12.1 Answer**

Spending cycles	Amount	Cumulative decrease in aggregate spending
First cycle:	$216	$216
Second cycle:	180	396
Third cycle:	150	546
Fourth cycle:	125	671
Fifth cycle:	104	775
Sixth cycle:	87	862
Seventh cycle:	72	934

2. $1,296 billion per year.

3. Multiplier = $\dfrac{1}{1 - \text{MPC}} = \dfrac{1}{1 - (5/6)} = 6$

4. 6 x $216 billion per year = $1,296 billion per year

Exercise 2

1. b, d
2. The program is aimed at the household sector, real estate, and business investment—a wide group in an election year.
3. c
4. ". . . expanded tax free-savings plans, . . ."
5. Mostly tax cuts are involved as indicated by the quotation: ". . . changing the Internal Revenue Service withholding tables. . ."

CHAPTER 13

Money and Banks

Quick Review

Money is clearly very important to the operation of the U.S. economy. The study of money begins with some very basic questions:
- What is money?
- How is money created?
- What role does money creation play in the macroeconomy?

Let's begin by examining what money does for us. Money has three functions; it serves as a
1. Medium of exchange, permitting goods and services to be exchanged without the complications of barter
2. Store of value, permitting people to hold it in order to buy goods and services in the future
3. Standard of value, permitting the prices of disparate goods and services to be compared

Money consists of all of those things that are generally acceptable as a medium of exchange. The most often used definition of the "money supply" is M1, the sum of currency held by the public and balances held in transactions accounts. Other money-supply concepts include "near money," such as savings deposits.

Most of the basic money supply, M1, is in the form of transactions accounts, such as checking accounts (NOW accounts, credit union share drafts, debit accounts). Transactions accounts permit payments to third parties without making a trip to the bank to withdraw money. The third parties can receive the money through transfers by checks, debit cards, or automatic transfers. Most transfer account balances come into existence when banks make loans. When you borrow from a bank, you receive an increase in your checking account. You have more money, and no other member of the public has less. The money supply expands.

Our banking system is based on the fractional-reserve principle. The Federal Reserve System (the "Fed") requires banks to maintain reserves equal to some fraction of their transactions-account liabilities. As a result of this reserve requirement and the fact that banks may lose reserves to other banks via the check-clearing process, a single bank can safely make loans only to the extent of its excess reserves. The banking system, however, can make loans equal to a multiple (1/reserve requirement) of any existing reserves.

Banks and other depository institutions control the money supply by making loans and creating deposits. Banks also hold savings accounts and thus assist in the transfer of purchasing power from

209

savers (those who choose not to spend all of their incomes) to borrowers (those who wish to spend more than their disposable incomes).

Financial institutions which serve as banks include a wide variety of forms. Increasingly banks, savings and loans (S&Ls), and credit unions are being allowed to compete with each other on an equal footing in deposit creation. While the Federal Reserve system controls the deposit-creating capacity of the banks, there are several constraints which may prevent the full capacity from being used. Consumers and businesses must continue using and accepting checks rather than cash. Consumers, businesses, and governments must be willing to borrow money. Finally, banks must be willing to lend it. As consumers retrench from heavy debt loads and banks retrench from bad loans as they have in the early 1990s, deposit creation falls short of the potential that the Fed makes available.

Learning Objectives

After reading Chapter 13 and doing the following exercises, you should:	True or false	Multiple choice	Problems and applications	Common errors	Pages in the text
1. Know the basic characteristics and functions of money.	1, 2, 3	24, 25			255-256
2. Know the difference between a transactions account and other accounts.	4, 5, 6, 21				257-258
3. Be familiar with the composition and various definitions of the money supply.	7, 10, 22	4, 6, 7, 8, 9, 10, 11, 23			257-260
4. Know how banks create money with new loans.	8, 12, 13	4, 12, 14, 15, 18, 19, 20	1, 2	1, 2	260-266
5. Know why the reserve requirement is necessary.	14	1, 5, 22	1, 2	2	
6. Know the difference between required and excess reserves.	16, 17, 18, 20	3, 16, 17, 18, 19	1, 2		263-265
7. Be able to work through the steps of deposit creation using balance sheets (T-accounts).		17, 18, 19, 20	1, 2		264-265
8. Be able to calculate the money multiplier.	15, 19	2, 21	1, 2		266-269
9. Understand the connection between the banking system and the circular flow of economic activity.	9, 11	26			

Key-Term Review

Review the following terms; if you are not sure of the meaning of any term, write out the definition and check it against the Glossary in the text.

aggregate demand
bank reserves
barter
deposit creation

excess reserves
money
money multiplier
money supply (M1)

required reserves
reserve ratio
transactions account

Fill in the blank following each of the statements below with the appropriate term from the list above.

1. To exchange goods and services, an economy without a monetary system must use .... 1. _____

2. When banks make loans, they expand the money supply by balancing loan creation with .... 2. _____

3. A bank account that permits direct payment to a third party is called a .... 3. _____

4. The reserves that a bank must have on its books are its .... 4. _____

5. Something that is generally accepted in exchange for goods and services and that can be used as a standard and store of value is .... 5. _____

6. The ratio of reserves to deposits is the .... 6. _____

7. Bank reserves beyond those required by government regulation are known as .... 7. _____

8. Currency held by the public plus balances in transactions accounts define the .... 8. _____

9. The inverse of the reserve ratio is sometimes called the .... 9. _____

10. _____ are assets held back by a .... 10.._____ bank to fulfill its deposit obligations.

11. Changes in the supply of money can be used to influence .... 11. _____

True or False: *Circle your choice.*

T F 1. Money eliminates the need to exchange goods directly through barter.

T F 2. When you purchase $5 worth of gasoline, money is serving as a medium of exchange.

T F 3. In times of rising prices, money serves well the function of a store of value.

T F 4. Checking accounts are transactions accounts.

T F 5. Savings accounts are a kind of transactions account.

T F 6. NOW accounts are a kind of transactions account.

T F 7. M1 is made up of the dollar value of all coin, currency, and transactions accounts in existence, whether held by the public or by banks.

T F 8. When you get a loan at a bank, the bank creates money.

T F 9. Banks transfer money from savers to spenders by lending funds held on deposit.

T F 10. Savings accounts at commercial banks are part of M1.

T F 11. A commercial bank is one that accepts deposits only from commercial establishments.

T F 12. When you withdraw money from your checking account, the money supply gets smaller.

T F 13. When you deposit $100 of coins in your checking account, M1 gets larger.

T F 14. The minimum-reserve ratio is established by the Federal Reserve System.

T F 15. The higher the legal minimum-reserve ratio, the greater the lending power of the banks.

T F 16. To calculate required reserves, multiply the minimum-reserve ratio by the amount of transactions account balances on the bank's balance sheet.

T F 17. If the minimum-reserve ratio is 20 percent, then $1 of reserves can support $5 more in transaction account balances.

T F 18. Total reserves minus required reserves equal excess reserves.

T F 19. Each bank in a multibank system is free to expand its loans by an amount equal to the money multiplier times its excess reserves.

T F 20. The amount any bank in a multibank system can lend is equal to its excess reserves.

T F 21. When interest rates are high, deposits move out of money-market mutual funds into regular transactions accounts, *ceteris paribus.*

T F 22. Savings deposits are time deposits.

Multiple Choice: *Select the correct answer.*

_____ 1. Which of the following sets the legal minimum-reserve ratio?
(a) The commercial banks.
(b) The U.S. Treasury.
(c) The Federal Reserve System.
(d) None of the above.

_____ 2. If the minimum-reserve ratio is 25 percent, the money multiplier is:
(a) 25.
(b) 5.
(c) 4.
(d) Not enough information is given to answer the question.

_____ 3. Which of the following is the correct way to calculate excess reserves?
(a) Total reserves minus required reserves.
(b) The minimum-reserve requirement times transactions account liabilities.
(c) Total reserves minus the legal minimum-reserve ratio.
(d) None of the above.

_____ 4. M1 refers to:
   (a) The money-supply concept.
   (b) Currency held by the public plus transactions accounts balances.
   (c) The smallest of the money-supply aggregates watched by the Fed.
   (d) All of the above.

_____ 5. The purpose of the legal minimum-reserve requirement is:
   (a) To provide safety to depositors.
   (b) To provide control of the money supply by the Fed.
   (c) To prevent bankers from calling in loans.
   (d) None of the above.

_____ 6. Which of the following is included in M2?
   (a) M1.
   (b) Treasury bills.
   (c) U.S. Savings bonds.
   (d) Bankers' acceptances.

_____ 7. Which of the following is included in M1?
   (a) Repurchase agreements.
   (b) Time deposits larger than $100,000.
   (c) U.S. savings bonds.
   (d) Transactions accounts.

_____ 8. Which of the following is included in M3?
   (a) Repurchase agreements.
   (b) Time deposits larger than $100,000.
   (c) M2.
   (d) All of the above.

_____ 9. Which of the following is the least liquid form of _L_?
   (a) Overnight eurodollars.
   (b) Treasury bills.
   (c) Money market mutual funds.
   (d) Time deposits larger than $100,000.

_____ 10. Which of the following appears in M2, but not M1?
   (a) Savings accounts.
   (b) Currency in circulation.
   (c) Transactions accounts.
   (d) Traveler's checks (nonbank).

_____ 11. The money supply will grow faster through deposit creation when:
   (a) People suddenly want to use cash instead of checks.
   (b) Consumers, businesses, and government suddenly have greater borrowing needs.
   (c) Banks suddenly perceive loans to be too risky and therefore buy government securities instead.
   (d) All of the above.

12. Which of the following could cause the money supply to fall even when the Federal Reserve tries to expand deposit creation capacity?
    (a) People and institutions borrow more.
    (b) The economy emerges from a recession into rapid growth.
    (c) The society moves to a cashless society.
    (d) Banks become conservative in making loans.

13. When you pay off a loan at the bank:
    (a) The money supply becomes smaller.
    (b) The money supply becomes larger.
    (c) There is no change in the money supply.
    (d) More information is needed to determine the money-supply effect.

14. Suppose a bank has no excess reserves when someone deposits $100. The bank will then be able to lend:
    (a) More than $1,000.
    (b) $100.
    (c) Less than $100.
    (d) Not enough information is given to determine the answer.

15. If none of the banks in the banking system have any excess reserves, but the Fed suddenly lowers the minimum legal reserve ratio from 16 percent to 12 percent, then:
    (a) The banks will then be able to make loans.
    (b) Excess reserves will then exist.
    (c) The Fed is engaging in an expansionary policy.
    (d) All of the above are the case.

16. Suppose the total amount of transactions account balances on the books of all of the banks in the system is $1 million and that the minimum-reserve ratio is 0.10. The amount of required reserves for the banking system is then:
    (a) $10,000,000.
    (b) $1,000,000.
    (c) $900,000.
    (d) $100,000.

17. Suppose that conditions remain as in Question 16 and the minimum-reserve requirement is raised to 20 percent. In order to meet the new requirement the banks in the system will need an *additional:*
    (a) $10,000,000 of reserves.
    (b) $1,000,000 of reserves.
    (c) $900,000 of reserves.
    (d) $100,000 of reserves.

18. If the banking system described in Question 16 (the reserve requirement is 0.10) has no excess reserves and you deposit $100 in cash:
    (a) Your bank can lend no more than $90.
    (b) Your bank can lend no more than $10.
    (c) Your bank can lend no more than $100.
    (d) Your bank can lend none of the above.

19. Given the situation in Question 18, all of the banks in the banking system together could expand loans by:
    (a) $1,000.
    (b) $900.
    (c) $100.
    (d) $10.

20. If the banks lend the maximum legal amount in Questions 18 and 19, the total maximum expansion in the money supply is:
    (a) $1,000.
    (b) $100.
    (c) $900.
    (d) None of the above.

21. When the minimum-reserve ratio is 10 percent, the money multiplier is:
    (a) 10.
    (b) 1.
    (c) 0.01.
    (d) None of the above.

22. Which of the following is a source of profits for banks?
    (a) Securities.
    (b) Reserves.
    (c) Cash in the vault.
    (d) All of the above.

23. The alternative measures of the money supply are all intended to reflect:
    (a) Variations in liquidity and accessibility of assets.
    (b) Whether deposits are domestic or international.
    (c) How often depositors use their accounts.
    (d) All of the above.

24. In Russia many consumers prefer to use sugar, flower, matches, and soap rather than rubles as:
    (a) Mediums of exchange.
    (b) Standards of value.
    (c) Stores of value.
    (d) All of the above.

25. For the Russians, using sugar, flower, matches, and soap rather than rubles allows them to:
    (a) Avoid long lines in stores.
    (b) Buy the items they wish on black markets.
    (c) Maintain wealth in a form which the government cannot tax or change.
    (d) All of the above.

26. Which of the following groupings contains a word that does not belong?
    (a) Coin, currency, transactions account balance.
    (b) M1, M2, L
    (c) Money multiplier, reserve ratio, aggregate demand.
    (d) Savings and loans, credit unions, banks.

Problems and Applications

Exercise 1

Use the information from the T-account in Table 13.1 to answer Questions 1-10.

Table 13.1. Bank of Arlington

Assets		Liabilities	
Loans	$1,000,000	Transaction accounts	$1,000,000
Securities	200,000	Ownership claims	500,000
Member bank reserves	200,000		
Other assets	100,000		
Total	$1,500,000	Total	$1,500,000

1. Suppose that the Bank of Arlington is just meeting its reserve requirement. The reserve requirement must be _____.
2. To be in a position to make loans, the Bank of Arlington must acquire some (required reserves, excess reserves).
3. If we assume that the reserve ratio is changed to 10 percent, the Bank of Arlington would have required reserves of _____ and excess reserves of _____.
4. With a 10 percent reserve ratio the Bank of Arlington is in a position to make new loans totaling _____.
5. Suppose the Bank of Arlington makes a loan of $100,000. The $100,000 is then spent so that it does not return to the Bank of Arlington but goes instead to the Bank of Cambridge. After this transaction, transactions account liabilities of the Bank of Arlington will be _____ ; its total reserves will be _____ ; its excess reserves will be _____ ; its required reserves will be _____.
6. The Bank of Cambridge had zero excess reserves before receiving the $100,000 deposit. Because of the 10 percent reserve requirement, the required reserves for the bank rise by _____ .
7. Excess reserves for the Bank of Cambridge after the $100,000 deposit in its transaction accounts are _____ .
8. If it makes the full amount of loans possible under the reserve requirement, the Bank of Cambridge will cause M1 to increase by _____ .
9. With these transactions the Bank of Arlington and the Bank of Cambridge make loans and create transactions account liabilities of _____.
10. If this process were to continue to the maximum, the amount of loans made on the basis of the $100,000 initial excess reserves of the Bank of Arlington would be _____, and the amount of transactions account liabilities created would be _____.

Exercise 2

This exercise is very much like Table 13.3 in the text (p. 268), but the reserve requirement has been changed. Assume all of the banks are in the same banking system.

1. Complete Table 13.2 on the basis of the following:
   $100 in cash is deposited in Bank A. (Assume cash is counted as reserves.)
   The reserve requirement is 0.10.
   The bank begins with zero excess reserves.

Table 13.2 Transactions-deposit creation

	Change in transactions accounts	Change in total reserves	Change in required reserves	Change in excess reserves	Change in lending capacity
If $100 in cash is deposited in Bank A, then Bank A acquires	$_____	$_____	$_____	$_____	$_____
If loan made and deposited in Bank B, then Bank B acquires	_____	_____	_____	_____	_____
If loan made and deposited in Bank C, then Bank C acquires	_____	_____	_____	_____	_____
If loan made and deposited elsewhere, then Bank D acquires	_____	_____	_____	_____	_____
If loan made and deposited elsewhere, then Bank E acquires	_____	_____	_____	_____	_____
If loan made and deposited elsewhere, then Bank F acquires	_____	_____	_____	_____	_____
If loan made and deposited elsewhere, then Bank G acquires	_____	_____	_____	_____	_____
And if process continues indefinitely, changes will total	_____	_____	_____	_____	_____

2. The money multiplier in Table 13.2 in the text was 5 and the money multiplier in this exercise is _____.

3. Suppose that the initial transaction had been a withdrawal of $100 in cash (reserves) and the banking system had been all loaned up (had no excess reserves). As a result of the initial withdrawal, _____ of reserves would have been lost. Required reserves would have been reduced by _____ and the banking system would be deficient by _____. Assuming no other way to get reserves, the banking system would ultimately have to call in loans of _____.

Common Errors

The first statement in each "common error" below is incorrect. Each incorrect statement is followed by a corrected version and an explanation.

1. Banks can't create money. WRONG!
   Banks can and do create money. RIGHT!
   It should be obvious by now that banks and other depository institutions are very important participants in the money-supply process. They create money by granting loans to borrowers and accomplish their role by adding to their customers' transactions accounts. The accounts are money just as much as the printed money in your wallet is money. The banks create (supply) money, but only in response to borrowers' demands for it. Without customers "demanding" loans, banks wouldn't be able to create money at all.

2. Banks hold your deposits in their vaults. WRONG!
   Banks don't hold your deposits in their vaults. (And neither do other depository institutions.) RIGHT!
   You can look at this two ways. First, when you deposit your paycheck there's nothing for the bank to "hold" in its vault, except the check, and that is returned to the person who wrote it. Second, if you deposited coin or cash, it's all put together and you can't distinguish any one person's deposit from any other person's deposit. Even then, when "cash in vault" becomes too large, much of it is shipped away by armored truck to the Federal Reserve Bank. (This is described in Chapter 13.) Thus, banks don't hold your deposits in their vaults.

■ ANSWERS ■

Key-Term Review

1. barter	4. required reserves	7. excess reserves	10. bank reserves
2. deposit creation	5. money	8. money supply (M1)	11. aggregate demand
3. transactions account	6. reserve ratio	9. money multiplier	

True or False

1. T	5. F	8. T	11. F	14. T	17. T	20. T
2. T	6. T	9. T	12. F	15. F	18. T	21. F
3. F	7. F	10. F	13. F	16. T	19. F	22. T
4. T						

Multiple Choice

1. c	5. b	9. b	13. a	17. d	20. c	23. a
2. c	6. a	10. a	14. d	18. a	21. a	24. d
3. a	7. d	11. b	15. d	19. b	22. a	25. d
4. d	8. d	12. d	16. d			

26. c Aggregate demand is not directly linked to the reserve ratio or the money multiplier. (a) Kinds of money, (b) money supply measures, (d) financial institutions.

Problems and Applications

Exercise 1

1. 0.20
2. excess reserves
3. $100,000; $100,000
4. $100,000
5. $1,000,000; $100,000; 0; $100,000
6. $10,000
7. $90,000
8. $90,000
9. $190,000
10. $1,000,000; $1,000,000

Exercise 2

1. **Table 13.2 Answer**

	Change in transactions accounts	Change in total reserves	Change in required reserves	Change in excess reserves	Change in lending capacity
If $100 in cash is deposited in Bank A, then Bank A acquires	$ 100.00	$100.00	$ 10.00	$90.00	$ 90.00
If loan made and deposited in Bank B, then Bank B acquires	90.00	90.00	9.00	81.00	81.00
If loan made and deposited in Bank C, then Bank C acquires	81.00	81.00	8.10	72.90	72.90
If loan made and deposited elsewhere, then Bank D acquires	72.90	72.90	7.29	65.61	65.61
If loan made and deposited elsewhere, then Bank E acquires	65.61	65.61	6.56	59.05	59.05
If loan made and deposited elsewhere, then Bank F acquires	59.05	59.05	5.91	53.15	53.15
If loan made and deposited elsewhere, then Bank G acquires	53.15	53.15	5.32	47.84	47.84
And if process continues indefinitely, changes will total	1,000.00		100.00		900.00

2. 10

3. $100; $10; $90; $900

CHAPTER 14

Monetary Policy

Quick Review

In the preceding chapter we saw how money was created, and we got some hints that money must be controlled. In this chapter we examine these questions:

- How does government control the amount of money in the economy?
- How does the money supply affect macroeconomic outcomes?

The answer to all of these questions begins with the Federal Reserve System. The Federal Reserve System is the central bank of the United States. All deposit institutions are subject to the reserve requirements imposed by it.

The Federal Reserve System has three basic tools with which to control the money supply: open-market operations, changes in the reserve requirement, and changes in the discount rate. Open-market operations, implemented by the Open Market Committee, are the most important. To increase the size of the money supply, the Open Market Committee orders the purchase of government securities (bonds) in the open market. These purchases increase bank reserves and lending potential.

The Fed could accomplish the same objective, although with less certainty, by lowering the discount rate. A lower discount rate encourages member banks to borrow reserves and acquire lending potential. The Fed can also modify reserve requirements. Reserve requirements, however, are not changed often or by large amounts. When the reserve requirement is raised, excess reserves are transformed into required reserves; when the reserve requirement is lowered, required reserves are transformed into excess reserves. In addition, there is an inverse relationship between the size of the reserve requirement and the size of the money multiplier.

Through its control of lending capacity the Fed can have an impact on aggregate demand. Increasing lending capacity increases the system's potential for creating money through the lending process to accommodate higher aggregate demand.

However, if fears of recession make aggregate demand unresponsive or if the aggregate supply curve is vertical, increased lending capacity may be ineffective or may translate into higher inflation rather than higher output.

A major debate in economic policy concerns how monetary policy should be applied. Keynesians suggest that monetary policy should be applied in a discretionary way so as to control or shift aggregate demand and, they hope, to achieve full employment. However, if market participants anticipate intervention, they can, it is argued, defeat the policy initiative, and so monetarists actually recommend that fixed rules of money growth be imposed. The Fed has chosen an eclectic policy between these two positions.

Learning Objectives

After reading Chapter 14 and doing the following exercises, you should:	True or false	Multiple choice	Problems and applications	Common errors	Pages in the text
1. Be familiar with the organization, structure, and purpose and functions of the Federal Reserve System.	2	8, 9, 12			276-278
2. Know how the reserve requirement can be changed to achieve a money-supply objective.	3, 5, 6, 7, 12	2, 3, 4, 5, 6, 9, 10, 16	1	1, 2	278-279
3. Know how the discount rate can be changed to achieve a given policy objective.	1, 4, 7	2, 10, 11, 16	3, 4	2	279-281
4. Know how the Open Market Committee can achieve a given policy objective by buying or selling securities.	8, 9, 10	2, 10, 16	2	2	282-294
5. Understand how the Fed's activities in the bond market alter portfolio decisions of bond sellers and buyers.	11, 13, 14	18			283
6. Understand how expansionary and restrictive monetary policy can be used to influence aggregate demand.	15, 18, 19, 20	1, 13, 14, 15	4		284-286
7. Understand how the slope of the aggregate supply curve determines whether more output or higher prices will result from a given policy initiative.	17, 18, 19	1, 13, 14	4		286-288
8. Be able to discuss the areas of disagreement between Keynesians, Monetarists, and the eclectic economists.	16, 20	1, 13, 15, 17, 19			288-289

Key-Term Review

Review the following terms; if you are not sure of the meaning of any term, write out the definition and check it against the Glossary in the text.

aggregate demand   discounting   money multiplier   open-market operations
aggregate supply   excess reserves   money supply (M1)   required reserves
discount rate   monetary policy

Fill in the blank following each of the statements below with the appropriate term from the list above.

1. When a member bank borrows from the Federal Reserve bank in its district, it is engaged in .... 1. _____

2. Those reserves a bank holds over and above the amount which is required are called .... 2. _____

3. The rate of interest that the Fed charges on loans to member banks is called the .... 3. _____

4. When the Fed buys or sells government securities, it is using .... 4. _____

5. Those reserves that a bank must hold against its demand liabilities are referred to as .... 5. _____

6. The _____ is the inverse of the .... 6. _____
   required-reserve ratio.

7. The discount rate, reserve requirements, and open-market operations are the Fed's instruments of .... 7. _____

8. The main function of the Federal Reserve System is to control the .... 8. _____

9. By controlling the money supply, the Fed causes shifts in .... 9. _____

10. A vertical _____ curve can thwart ..... 10. _____
    monetary policy by translating increased M1 into greater inflation rather than additional output.

True or False: *Circle your choice.*

T F 1. When commercial banks borrow from each other the process is called "discounting."

T F 2. The Federal Reserve banks hold deposits of banks and other business firms.

T F 3. All depository institutions are subject to reserve requirements established by the Federal Reserve System.

T F 4. The most powerful monetary policy tool available to the Fed is the power to change the discount rate.

T	F	5. If the Fed wishes to create the conditions under which the money supply can be increased, it can reduce the reserve requirement.
T	F	6. When the reserve requirement is increased, excess reserves are reduced.
T	F	7. The Fed changes the reserve requirement by changing the discount rate.
T	F	8. Banks that are short of reserves can acquire additional reserves by selling securities.
T	F	9. The buying and selling of federal government securities by the Fed is known as "open-market operations."
T	F	10. To increase the lending capacity of the banking system, the Fed buys securities.
T	F	11. The Fed's activities in the bond market influence bankers' portfolio decisions.
T	F	12. The size of the reserve requirement is positively related to the dollar volume of the transactions accounts on a bank's balance sheet.
T	F	13. People who hold idle money balances incur no costs.
T	F	14. When the Fed increases the supply of securities (by selling in the open market), interest rates rise.
T	F	15. When the Fed buys securities, causing interest rates to fall, investment spending increases, thus expanding GDP.
T	F	16. Consumer expectations regarding future price levels are important in determining the effectiveness of monetary policy.
T	F	17. If the aggregate supply curve is horizontal, an increase in the money supply will result in greater inflation, rather than higher output.
T	F	18. When the Fed increases lending capacity, the money supply will always increase.
T	F	19. During depressions, fear of lending and inability to find productive investments for which to borrow means that deposit creation may not result from additional lending capacity.
T	F	20. Whether restrictive monetary policy is effective or not depends on its ability to reduce aggregate demand.

Multiple Choice: *Select the correct answer.*

_____ 1. The effectiveness of monetary policy depends on which of the following?
(a) Responsiveness of aggregate demand to increases in the money supply (M1).
(b) The slope of the aggregate supply curve.
(c) The Fed's reserve requirement, discount rate, and open-market operations.
(d) All of the above.

_____ 2. Which of the following is *not* one of the tools of monetary policy used by the Fed?
(a) Expulsion from Fed membership.
(b) Changing the reserve requirement.
(c) Changing the discount rate.
(d) Performing open-market operations.

_____ 3. Suppose the banking system has $1 million of reserves when the reserve requirement is 0.20. What is the volume of transactions account liabilities in the system if there are no excess reserves to begin with?
(a) $200,000.
(b) $500,000.
(c) $5,000,000.
(d) $2,000,000.

4. Suppose the Fed raised the reserve requirement to 0.25 in Question 3. Then the banks in the system would be *deficient* in required reserves by:
   (a) $2,500,000.
   (b) $1,250,000.
   (c) $250,000.
   (d) $1,000,000.

5. Suppose the banking system is in the condition described in Question 3, and the Fed lowers the reserve requirement to 0.15. Then the banking system has:
   (a) Excess reserves of $250,000.
   (b) Required reserves of $750,000.
   (c) The potential to create 250,000 x 0.15 dollars of loans.
   (d) All of the above.

6. In Question 5, the money multiplier is:
   (a) 10 ÷ 0.15.
   (b) 0.15 ÷ 1.
   (c) (1)(0.15).
   (d) None of the above.

7. When the Fed wishes to increase the excess reserves of the member banks, it:
   (a) Buys securities.
   (b) Raises the discount rate.
   (c) Raises the reserve requirement.
   (d) None of the above.

8. Which of the following are services performed by the Federal Reserve banks?
   (a) Clearing checks between commercial banks.
   (b) Holding reserves of commercial banks.
   (c) Providing currency to commercial banks.
   (d) All of the above.

9. In which of the following forms can bank reserves be held?
   (a) Deposits at the district Federal Reserve bank.
   (b) Cash in the bank's own vault.
   (c) Deposits held at other commercial banks.
   (d) Both as deposits at the district Federal Reserve bank and as cash in the bank's own vault.

10. The Federal Reserve System can provide reserves to the banking system by all of the following except:
    (a) Buying securities in the open market.
    (b) Lending to member banks.
    (c) Insuring transaction account balances of less than $100,000.
    (d) Reducing the reserve requirements.

11. When the Fed raises the discount rate, this policy initiative:
    (a) Raises the cost of borrowing reserves to member banks.
    (b) Is a signal that the Fed is moving toward a slower growth rate for the money supply.
    (c) Is a signal that interest rates may rise generally.
    (d) Does all of the above.

12. Which of the following are subject to regulation by the Fed?
    (a) All commercial banks.
    (b) Savings and loan associations.
    (c) Savings banks.
    (d) All of the above.

13. Monetary policy is most effective when lending capacity is:
    (a) Not fully utilized and aggregate supply is vertical.
    (b) Not fully utilized and aggregate supply is horizontal.
    (c) Fully utilized and aggregate supply is vertical.
    (d) Fully utilized and aggregate supply is horizontal.

14. Banks and customers are most likely to be reluctant to use the full lending capacity made available by the Federal Reserve when the economy experiences:
    (a) Growth and low interest rates.
    (b) Growth and inflation rates higher than the interest rate.
    (c) High inflation rates.
    (d) A depression.

15. Monetary policy is most likely to result in inflation when the aggregate supply curve is:
    (a) Vertical and the Fed lowers the discount rate.
    (b) Vertical and the Fed raises the reserve requirement.
    (c) Horizontal and the Fed sells securities.
    (d) Horizontal and the Fed lowers the reserve ratio.

16. Which of the following best describes how the money supply is increased:
    (a) The Fed prints more currency.
    (b) The Fed raises the discount rate and the reserve requirement.
    (c) The Fed sells more securities.
    (d) Banks lend more excess reserves.

17. The monetary policy adopted by the Fed most closely resembles:
    (a) An eclectic policy.
    (b) A Keynesian policy.
    (c) A fixed-rule approach.
    (d) A laissez-faire policy.

18. The cost of holding idle balances is:
    (a) Nothing if you hold it in the form of cash.
    (b) Equal to a service charge collected by the bank for obtaining cash.
    (c) The return that could have been earned had the funds been lent out at interest.
    (d) None of the above.

19. The Fed adopted fixed money-supply targets as a policy goal from 1979 to 1982. Then the Fed abandoned the money-supply targets:
    (a) Because interest rates rose to undesired levels.
    (b) Because the economy went into a deep recession.
    (c) Because it wanted greater flexibility in policy making.
    (d) For all of the above reasons.

Problems and Applications

The first three exercises demonstrate how monetary policy might work in a hypothetical situation.

Exercise 1

This exercise is similar to the problems at the end of Chapter 14 in the text, which should help you understand the accounts for the entire banking system. The focus of this exercise is the reserve requirement.

Suppose the Fed wishes to expand M1. Carefully read the assumptions below and then work through the exercise step by step to achieve the policy objective. Assume:
- The banks in the system have initially $240 million of transactions account liabilities.
- The banking system has initially no excess reserves.
- The initial reserve requirement is 0.25.
- The banks make loans in the full amount of any excess reserves that they acquire.
- No cash is drained out of the system.

The combined balance sheet of the banks in the system is as shown in Table 14.1.

Table 14.1. Balance sheet of banking system when reserve requirement is 0.25
(millions of dollars)

Total reserves	$ 60	Transactions accounts	$240
Required, $60			
Excess, $0			
Securities	80		
Loans	100		
Total	$240	Total	$240

1. Suppose the Fed lowers the reserve requirement to 0.20. How many dollars of excess reserves does this create? $ _____.
2. How large are required reserves now? $ _____.
3. How large are total reserves? $ _____.
4. What is the additional lending capacity of the banking system due to the change in the reserve requirement from 0.25 to 0.20? $ _____.
5. If the banks fully utilize their new lending capacity, reconstruct the balance sheet in Table 14.2 to show the new totals for the accounts affected in the total banking system.

Table 14.2. Balance sheet of banking system when reserve requirement is 0.20
(millions of dollars)

Total reserves	$_____	Transactions accounts	$_____
Required, _____			
Excess, _____			
Securities	_____		
Loans	_____		
Total	$_____	Total	$_____

6. So far the money supply (M1) has expanded by $ _____.
7. Total reserves have gone up by $ _____.
8. Loans have gone up by $ _____.

Exercise 2

Like the problem at the end of Chapter 14 in the text, this exercise shows how the money supply can be changed. The focus of this exercise is open-market policy.

Suppose the Fed wants to expand the money supply using open-market operations and it is faced with the balance sheet of the banking system as shown in Table 14.3. Suppose further that:
- The banking system initially has no excess reserves.
- The reserve requirement is 0.20.
- The banks make loans in the full amount of any excess reserves that they acquire.
- No cash is drained out of the system.

Table 14.3. Balance sheet of banking system (millions of dollars)

Total reserves	$ 60	Transactions accounts	$300
Required, $60			
Excess, $0			
Securities	80		
Loans	160		
Total	$300	Total	$300

1. Suppose the Federal Open Market Committee orders the purchase of $10 million of securities from the commercial banking system. In Table 4.4 show the changes and new totals for the various accounts on the balance sheet of the commercial banks after this transaction but before any new loans are made or called in.

Table 14.4. Balance sheet of commercial banking system after the Fed buys $10 million of securities (millions of dollars)

Total reserves	$_____	Transactions accounts	$_____
Required, _____			
Excess, _____			
Securities	_____		
Loans	_____		
Total	$_____	Total	$_____

2. Suppose the banking system now expands its loans and transactions accounts by the maximum amount it can on the basis of its $_____ in excess reserves.
3. In Table 14.5 complete the balance sheet for the banking system showing the new totals for all of the accounts after loans have been made. (*Remember:* The reserve ratio is 0.20.)

228

Table 14.5. Balance sheet of banking system after expansion of loans and deposits (millions of dollars)

Total reserves	$_____	Transactions accounts	$_____
Required, _____			
Excess, _____			
Securities	_____		
Loans	_____		
Total	$_____	Total	$_____

4. As a result of the open-market operations, the money supply has expanded by a total of $ _____.

5. Total reserves have gone up by $ _____.

6. Loans have increased by $ _____.

Exercise 3

This exercise demonstrates what might happen when the Fed lowers the discount rate.

Suppose the Fed wants to expand the money supply by changing the discount rate. It is faced with the balance sheet of the banking system as shown in Table 14.6. Carefully read the assumptions below and then work through the exercise step by step to achieve the policy objective. Assume that:

- The banking system initially has no excess reserves.
- The initial reserve requirement is 0.20.
- The banks in the system respond to each percentage point drop in the discount rate by borrowing $2 million from the Fed.
- The banks make loans in the full amount of any excess reserves that they acquire.
- No cash is drained out of the system.

Table 14.6. Balance sheet of banking system (millions of dollars)

Total reserves	$ 70	Transactions accounts	$350
Required, $70			
Excess, $0			
Securities	70		
Loans	210		
Total	$350	Total	$350

1. Suppose that the Fed now lowers the discount rate by one percentage point and that the banking system responds as indicated in the third assumption above. As a result of this policy initiative, the banks in the system will now borrow $ _____ from the Fed, all of which is (excess, required) reserves. On the basis of this lending potential, the banks together can expand their loans by $ _____.

2. In Table 14.7 assume the banks have made the additional loans. Complete the balance sheet to show the final effect of the change in the discount rate.

229

Table 14.7. Final balance sheet of banking system (millions of dollars)

Total reserves	$_____	Transactions accounts	$_____
Required, _____			
Excess, _____			
Securities	_____		
Loans	_____	Discounts payable to Fed	_____
Total	$_____	Total	$_____

3. The effect of lowering the discount rate is an increase in the money supply of $ _____.

Exercise 4

The media often provide information about changes in policy by the Federal Reserve System. By using one of the articles in the text, this exercise will show the kind of information to look for. If your professor makes a newspaper assignment from the *Instructor's Manual*, this exercise will provide an example of how to do it.

Reread the Headline article on page 285 in chapter 14 entitled "Fed Lowers Key Rate to 3.5 Percent." Then answer the following questions:

1. What central monetary authority is mentioned in the article?

2. What phrase in the article indicates the monetary instrument that is being used by the central monetary authority?

3. Which instrument is being used:
    (a) Reserve requirement.
    (b) Open-market operations.
    (c) Discount rate.
    (d) Other (Specify:).

4. Which of the following *best* summarizes the effect of this monetary policy on the economy?
    (a) Interest rates should fall.
    (b) Investment spending should increase.
    (c) Income should increase.
    (d) All of the above.

5. Which of the following effects is most likely to result from the action of the central monetary authority described in the article?
    (a) Aggregate supply shifts leftward.
    (b) Aggregate supply shifts rightward.
    (c) Aggregate demand shifts leftward.
    (d) Aggregate demand shifts rightward.

6. Which of the following effects would be most likely as a result of the shift in 5, *ceteris paribus?*
    (a) Stagflation (higher unemployment rate and higher inflation).
    (b) Higher inflation and lower unemployment rate.
    (c) Lower inflation and higher unemployment rate.
    (d) Lower inflation and lower unemployment rate.

Common Errors

The first statement in each "common error" below is incorrect. Each incorrect statement is followed by a corrected version and an explanation.

1. Bank reserves are required for the safety of depositors' money. WRONG!
   Bank reserves are for control of the money supply. RIGHT!
   Many people have the idea that bank reserves provide for the safety of depositors' money. They don't. Reserves are for control of the money supply. The FDIC provides for safety of deposits by insuring them within limits. Reserves are not principally for depositors' safety.

2. Deposits of cash are necessary to start the process of lending and deposit creation. WRONG!
   To start the lending process, the banks must acquire reserves from outside of the banking system. RIGHT!
   Many find it difficult to understand that for deposit creation to occur, the banking system needs only to acquire reserves from outside the system. It may acquire reserves by selling a security to the Fed or by borrowing from the Fed. An individual bank, however, may acquire reserves from another bank. So to the extent that it has increased its reserves, another bank's reserves have shrunk. Thus, the system has no more reserves after the transaction than it had before, and so the system's lending capacity is unchanged.

■ ANSWERS ■

Key-Term Review

1. discounting	5. required reserves	8. money supply (M1)
2. excess reserves	6. money multiplier	9. aggregate demand
3. discount rate	7. monetary policy	10. aggregate supply
4. open-market operations		

True or False

1. F	4. F	7. F	10. T	13. F	16. T	19. T
2. F	5. T	8. T	11. T	14. T	17. F	20. T
3. T	6. T	9. T	12. T	15. T	18. F	

Multiple Choice

1. d	4. c	7. a	10. c	13. d	16. d	18. c
2. a	5. d	8. d	11. d	14. d	17. a	19. d
3. c	6. a	9. d	12. d	15. a		

Problems and Applications

Exercise 1

1. $12 million
2. $48 million
3. $60 million
4. $60 million

5. See Table 14.2 answer
6. $60 million
7. Zero
8. $60 million

Table 14.2 Answer (millions of dollars)

Total reserves	$ 60	Transactions accounts	$300
Required, $60			
Excess, $0			
Securities	80		
Loans	160		
Total	$300	Total	$300

Exercise 2

1. ### Table 14.4 Answer (millions of dollars)

Total reserves	$ 70	Transactions accounts	$300
Required, $60			
Excess, $10			
Securities	70		
Loans	160		
Total	$300	Total	$300

2. $10 million

3. ### Table 14.5 Answer (millions of dollars)

Total reserves	$ 70	Transactions accounts	$350
Required, $70			
Excess, $0			
Securities	70		
Loans	100		
Total	$210	Total	$350

4. $50 million
5. $10 million
6. $50 million

Exercise 3

1. $2 million; excess; $10 million

2. **Table 14.7 Answer (millions of dollars)**

Total reserves	$ 72	Transactions accounts	$360
Required, $72			
Excess, $0			
Securities	70		
Loans	220	Discounts payable to Fed	2
Total	$362	Total	$362

3. $10 million

Exercise 4

1. Federal Reserve
2. "The discount rate cut will help when it is passed on to consumers and businesses."
3. c
4. d
5. d
6. b Quantity rises along with price to reach the new equilibrium for demand and supply.

CHAPTER 15

Economic Growth

Quick Review

When an economy produces greater real GDP from one year to the next the process is called economic growth. Economic growth is desired by virtually all societies because it provides for possible improvements in the standard of living, and even though it has been studied for a long time, the nature of the process and possible limits to it are still debated. In this chapter we focus on the following concerns:

- How important is economic growth?
- How does an economy grow?
- What policies promote economic growth?

Economic growth in the short run means moving from a point inside the production-possibilities curve to a point on it. In the long run growth requires an outward shift of the whole curve. How does this outward shift occur? Can economic policy enhance the process?

Economists have identified several sources of growth including increases in the available factors of production. Strangely, these have not been found to be as important in the process as has the increased productivity factors. The most important sources of increased productivity (an increase in the amount of output per unit of input) appear to be the following:

- Higher skills
- More capital
- Improved management
- Technological advances

Savings and investment are obviously important to the growth process. Without saving, the required investment, research, and development could not occur. In addition, we frequently look to government policy to speed up the process. Policy makers have several "levers" that can be important in increasing the amount and kind of resources available, and in spurring the development of new technologies. Specifically, they can influence:

- Education and training incentives
- Immigration policy
- Investment incentives
- Saving incentives
- Budget deficits
- (De)regulation

The short-run focus of government policy is often to increase aggregate demand through greater government spending. When government uses resources that would otherwise be used by the private sector, the mix of output is definitely changed. This is referred to as "crowding out" of private output. If the rate of investment and economic growth are both slowed when government borrowing pushes interest rates up, this has a major impact on the mix of output that can be produced both in the present and in the future.

Learning Objectives

After reading Chapter 15 and doing the following exercises, you should:	True or false	Multiple choice	Problems and applications	Common errors	Pages in the text
1. Know the difference between short-run and long-run limits on economic growth.	2, 3, 4, 5, 7, 13, 14, 15	12, 13, 14, 15, 16, 17	1		294-295
2. Know that economic growth (decline) is measured using real GDP.		18			295
3. Be able to calculate the growth rate in real GDP.		3, 20	2, 3		295-296
4. Understand the importance of economic growth as an "exponential process."			3		296
5. Know why real GDP per capita is the common measure of living standards.	6, 16, 17	18, 19	2, 3		297
6. Be able to discuss productivity and the sources of productivity gains in the U.S. economy.	1, 8, 9, 11, 12	1, 2, 4, 5, 18, 22		1	298-301
7. Be able to discuss the way economic policy and external shocks can work to shift the aggregate supply curve.	10, 13, 14, 15	6, 7, 11, 13, 14	1, 3		301-306
8. Understand how (de)regulation and other types of government intervention affect factor and product markets.		7, 8, 9, 10, 21			301-306
9. Know when and how government deficit spending imposes opportunity costs on the economy.		23, 24, 25			304-305

Learning Objectives (cont'd.)	True or false	Multiple choice	Problems and applications	Common errors	Pages in the text
10. Develop a perspective on the desirability of the growth process.					306-307

Key-Term Review

Review the following terms; if you are not sure of the meaning of any term, write out the definition and check it against the Glossary in the text.

crowding out   growth rate   nominal GDP   productivity
economic growth   labor force   production possibilities   real GDP
GDP per capita   investment

Fill in the blank following each of the statements below with the appropriate term from the list above.

1. The dollar value of an economy's final output divided by total population is defined as .... 1. _____

2. Total output divided by the number of units of input is a measure of that input's .... 2. _____

3. The money value of GDP unadjusted for price changes is called .... 3. _____

4. An increase in real GDP is referred to as .... 4. _____

5. When nominal GDP is adjusted for price changes, the resulting aggregate is called .... 5. _____

6. In the 1970s the population grew much more slowly than the working-age population, which makes up the .... 6. _____

7. The percentage change in real GDP from one period to another is the _____ in real GDP. 7. _____

8. Increased factor productivity leads to an outward shift in the economy's .... 8. _____

9. _____ must occur if a nation's ...... 9. _____
capital stock is to grow.

10. _____ occurs when government ... 10. _____
borrowing absorbs saving that would otherwise have been used to finance private-
sector investment.

True or False: *Circle your choice.*

T F 1. The United States is among the leading Western countries in improving average yearly productivity.

T F 2. When an economy moves from a point within its production-possibilities curve to a point on its production-possibilities curve, no economic growth takes place.

T F 3. Once an economy is on its production-possibilities curve, further increases in output require an expansion of productive capacity.

T F 4. An increase in nominal GDP means there has been an outward shift in the production-possibilities curve.

T F 5. To achieve long-term economic growth requires an increase in potential GDP.

T F 6. Growth in GDP per capita is achieved when population grows more rapidly than GDP.

T F 7. Increases in the rate at which we utilize our productive capacity move the economy toward our production-possibilities curve.

T F 8. Since increased saving shifts aggregate demand to the left, it tends to inhibit improvements in productivity.

T F 9. Increases in the size of the labor force and capital stock have been less important than productivity advances in causing U.S. GDP to grow.

T F 10. Deregulation leads to a shift of the aggregate supply curve by lowering costs and releasing supplies of goods.

T F 11. Labor productivity is measured by the wage earned per hour of labor worked.

T F 12. Education leads to increased productivity of the labor force.

T F 13. A major goal of short-run economic policy is to increase economic growth.

T F 14. Long-run economic policy attempts to move the economy onto its production-possibilities curve.

T F 15. Short-run macroeconomic policies focus on managing aggregate supply.

T F 16. GDP per capita is a measure of productivity.

T F 17. GDP per worker is a measure of living standards.

Multiple Choice: *Select the correct answer.*

_____ 1. Which of the following would likely contribute to an improvement in the productivity of labor?
(a) Greater expenditures on training and education.
(b) Policies to stimulate the saving and investment process.
(c) Greater expenditures on research and development.
(d) All of the above.

_____ 2. Which of the following is thought to have been the *greatest* source of advances in productivity?
(a) Improvement in management.
(b) Increases in capital per worker.
(c) Spending on research and development.
(d) Improvements in the quality of labor.

3. A sustained net growth in real output of 3.5 percent per year will cause real output to double in about:
   (a) 10 years.
   (b) 20 years.
   (c) 30 years.
   (d) 35 years.

4. Which of the following may be cited as a cause of the U.S. economy's poor performance in advancing labor productivity?
   (a) A relatively low saving rate.
   (b) Changes in the age-sex composition of the labor force.
   (c) The trend away from manufacturing and toward services in our industrial structure.
   (d) All of the above.

5. Which of the following are sources of productivity increase?
   (a) Research and development.
   (b) Improvements in labor quality.
   (c) Capital investment.
   (d) All of the above.

6. Which of the following is the policy used to combat structural unemployment?
   (a) A decrease in tax rates for the purpose of increasing aggregate demand.
   (b) An increase in the discount rate.
   (c) Government intervention in labor markets for the purpose of holding wage increases down to 5.5 percent annually.
   (d) Job training programs.

7. Which of the following policies is a supply-side policy?
   (a) Tax cuts.
   (b) Deregulation.
   (c) Elimination of structural unemployment by job programs.
   (d) All of the above.

8. Unit labor costs depend on:
   (a) The wage rate.
   (b) The productivity of a worker.
   (c) Technological change.
   (d) All of the above.

9. Which of the following programs cause(s) unemployment?
   (a) Agricultural acreage restrictions by the government.
   (b) The minimum wage.
   (c) Price controls.
   (d) All of the above.

10. The method for eliminating structural unemployment when the economy is at full employment is through:
   (a) Fiscal policy.
   (b) Monetary policy.
   (c) Increasing the minimum wage.
   (d) Human-resource programs.

Using the diagram in Figure 15.1 answer Questions 11-13.

Figure 15.1. Aggregate demand and supply

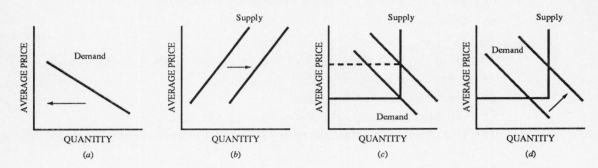

_____ 11. Which diagram would the Monetarists use to illustrate the effect of an increase in the quantity of money on the aggregate supply curve and aggregate demand curve?

_____ 12. Which diagram would the Keynesians use to illustrate the effects of an easier fiscal policy?

_____ 13. Which diagram illustrates the effects of supply-side policies?

_____ 14. A major goal of short-run macroeconomic policy is to:
(a) Shift the production-possibilities curve outward.
(b) Move toward the production possibilities curve.
(c) Shift the aggregate supply curve upward.
(d) Shift the aggregate demand curve downward.

_____ 15. Long-run macroeconomic policy:
(a) Shifts the production-possibilities curve outward.
(b) Shifts the aggregate supply curve upward.
(c) Shifts the aggregate demand curve upward.
(d) All of the above.

_____ 16. Economic growth in the long run:
(a) Shifts the production-possibilities curve outward.
(b) Moves the economy along the production-possibilities curve.
(c) Shifts the aggregate demand curve upward.
(d) None of the above.

_____ 17. Macroeconomic policies aimed at the long run instead of the short run are designed to:
(a) Increase capacity instead of increasing capacity utilization.
(b) Shift aggregate supply outward instead of shifting aggregate demand outward.
(c) Shift the production-possibilities curve instead of moving onto the production-possibilities curve.
(d) All of the above.

_____ 18. Which of the following is a measure of productivity?
(a) The ratio of current GDP to GDP in the base period.
(b) Percentage increase in GDP.
(c) GDP per capita.
(d) GDP per worker.

19. Which of the following is a measure of living standards?
    (a) The ratio of current GDP to GDP in the base period.
    (b) Investment as a percentage of GDP.
    (c) GDP per capita.
    (d) GDP per worker.

20. Which of the following measures the growth rate of GDP?
    (a) The ratio of the change in GDP to GDP in the previous year.
    (b) Investment as a percentage of GDP.
    (c) Real GDP.
    (d) GDP per worker.

21. Which of the following will benefit European economic growth after its integration in 1992?
    (a) Less competition.
    (b) More opportunities for specialization.
    (c) More powerful local government.
    (d) All of the above.

22. The sources of productivity growth include:
    (a) Higher skills.
    (b) More capital.
    (c) Improved management.
    (d) All of the above.

23. Crowding out occurs when the government:
    (a) Increases taxes, thus causing a decrease in consumption.
    (b) Issues debt, thus making it more difficult for the private sector to issue debt.
    (c) Prints money, which displaces currency.
    (d) Does all of the above.

24. "Crowding out" is most likely to occur:
    (a) When the federal government runs a surplus and pays off part of the debt.
    (b) When the federal government has a balanced budget but refinances a portion of the debt that matures.
    (c) When the federal government runs a deficit and raises taxes to generate more revenue.
    (d) When the federal government has run a deficit and sells bonds to make up the difference.

25. The "crowding out" hypothesis refers to the possibility that:
    (a) Foreigners will turn in the bonds they own and use the proceeds to purchase goods and services desired by U.S. residents.
    (b) State and local governments will sell the bonds they own and lower their taxes as a result.
    (c) The sale of bonds by the federal government will raise interest rates and cause firms to invest less.
    (d) The Federal Reserve System will be unwilling to lend to member banks because they own so many Treasury bonds.

Problems and Applications

Exercise 1

This exercise focuses on the supply-and-demand effects of the energy crisis that occurred in the early 1970s.

The energy crisis should have had an impact on the various markets listed below. Match the letter of the appropriate diagram in Figure 15.2 with each of the markets and events listed below and place it in the box marked "Shift." Then indicate with an arrow in the boxes "Price" and "Quantity" whether the equilibrium price and equilibrium quantity in each market should rise (↑) or fall (↓) because of the shift in demand or supply. Finally, list the determinant of demand or supply that changed. (*Hint:* The nonprice determinants of market demand are income, buyer expectations, the prices of related goods and availability of other goods, and the number of buyers. The nonprice determinants of market supply are technology, the price and availability of resources, expectations, taxes and subsidies, and the number of suppliers.) *Make sure you decide which market is affected before deciding which shift occurs.*

Figure 15.2

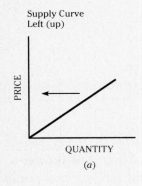

Supply Curve
Left (up)

(a)

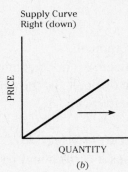

Supply Curve
Right (down)

(b)

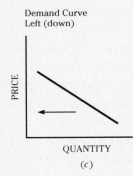

Demand Curve
Left (down)

(c)

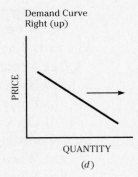

Demand Curve
Right (up)

(d)

1. **Market** — Shingles

   Change — OPEC announces it will increase the price of crude oil by 25 percent over the next six months. Crude oil is an input in the production of shingles.

Figure 15.3

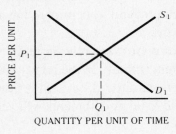

QUANTITY PER UNIT OF TIME

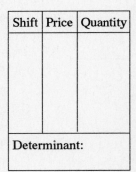

Shift	Price	Quantity
Determinant:		

2. **Market** **Change**
   Drilling rigs Government removes price controls on crude oil and the price of crude oil rises.

Figure 15.4

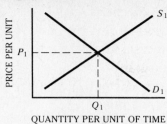

Shift	Price	Quantity
Determinant:		

3. **Market** **Change**
   Apartments in the suburbs Higher commuting costs convince the public it's better to live downtown.

Figure 15.5

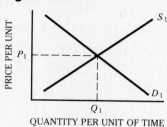

Shift	Price	Quantity
Determinant:		

4. **Market** **Change**
   Gas-run clothes dryers Canada and Mexico announce they will no longer sell the United States any natural gas.

Figure 15.6

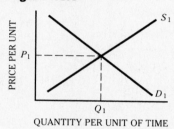
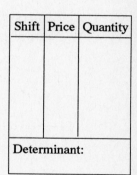

Shift	Price	Quantity
Determinant:		

5. **Market** **Change**
   Coal miners Government bans the use of crude oil in new electrical generating plants. New plants use coal.

Figure 15.7

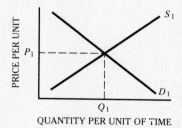

Shift	Price	Quantity
Determinant:		

6. **Market**
   Home
   insulation

   Change
   The *Farmer's Almanac* forecasts an unusually warm winter and the price of natural gas falls.

   Figure 15.8

   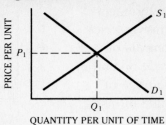

Shift	Price	Quantity
Determinant:		

7. **Market**
   Crude oil

   Change
   A huge oil deposit is discovered off the Atlantic coast.

   Figure 15.9

   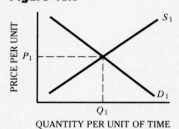

Shift	Price	Quantity
Determinant:		

8. **Market**
   Natural gas

   Change
   New technology improves the probability of hitting natural-gas wells.

   Figure 15.10

   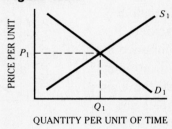

Shift	Price	Quantity
Determinant:		

9. **Market**
   Shrimp

   Change
   A Mexican oil well blows out in the Gulf of Mexico and the resulting oil slick damages commercial shrimp beds along the Texas coast.

   Figure 15.11

   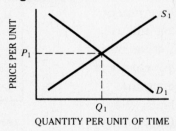

Shift	Price	Quantity
Determinant:		

10. **Market**
Marine
insurance

Change
The world
fleet of
supertankers
expands,
increasing the
probability
of collisions.

Figure 15.12

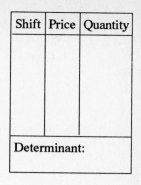

QUANTITY PER UNIT OF TIME

Shift	Price	Quantity
Determinant:		

Exercise 2

The following exercise gives practice in recognizing and computing geometric growth rates and the impacts on important macroeconomic indicators.

Assume that the population of a country is 1 million people in the year 2000 and that it is increasing at the rate of 10 percent per decade. Assume that food is produced at a rate of 1 million tons per year and that grows by 100,000 tons every decade.

1. In Figure 15.13 graph the tons of food per capita over a century.

Figure 15.13

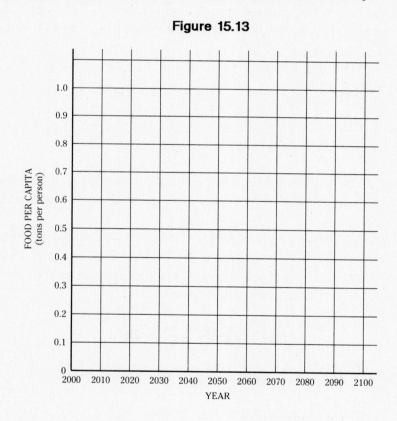

YEAR

2. T   F   The population growth is geometric.
3. After one century by what percentage has food consumption per capita declined as a result of the population increase? _____%

245

Exercise 3

The focus of this exercise is the value of investment in spurring economic growth. This exercise will help you with the second problem at the end of Chapter 15.

Suppose that every additional five percentage points in the investment rate (I/GDP) boosts economic growth by two percentage points. Assume also that all investment must be financed with household saving. Suppose the economy is currently characterized by the following data:

GDP:	$5 trillion
Consumption:	4 trillion
Saving:	1 trillion
Investment:	1 trillion

1. What is the current investment rate (I/GDP)? _____
2. If the goal is to raise the growth rate of income by one percentage point, by how much must investment increase? _____
3. By how much must consumption decline to permit the necessary growth in the investment rate to reach the 1% target? _____
4. How much does income increase in the first year due to the 1% growth rate? _____
5. Assuming that income each year in the future is 1% higher as a result of the one-year change in the investment rate, approximately how many years will it take before the economy recoups the amount of consumption goods given up to finance the increase in investment? _____

Common Errors

The first statement in the "common error" below is incorrect. The incorrect statement is followed by a corrected version and an explanation.

1. Labor productivity increases when more output is produced per dollar of wages. WRONG! Labor productivity increases when more units of product are produced per unit of labor. RIGHT!

    Productivity changes are not directly related to wage levels. Wage levels reflect a large number of influences embodied in the demand and supply curves for labor. Productivity, however, is a physical measure of the relation between units of product and the amount of labor needed to produce them.

■ANSWERS■

Key-Term Review

1. GDP per capita	4. economic growth	7. growth rate	9. investment
2. productivity	5. real GDP	8. production possibilities	10. crowding out
3. nominal GDP	6. labor force		

True or False

1. F	4. F	7. T	10. T	12. T	14. F	16. F
2. F	5. T	8. F	11. F	13. T	15. F	17. F
3. T	6. F	9. T				

Multiple Choice

1. d	5. d	9. d	13. b	17. d	20. a	23. b
2. c	6. d	10. d	14. b	18. d	21. b	24. d
3. b	7. d	11. c	15. a	19. c	22. d	25. c
4. d	8. d	12. d	16. a			

Problems and Applications

Exercise 1

	Shift	Price	Quantity
1.	a	↑	↓

Determinant: Price of a resource increase

	Shift	Price	Quantity
2.	d	↑	↑

Determinant: Price of a related good (complement), number of buyers, income

	Shift	Price	Quantity
3.	c	↓	↓

Determinant: Price of a related good (substitute, complement)

	Shift	Price	Quantity
4.	c	↓	↓

Determinant: Price of a related good (complement)

	Shift	Price	Quantity
5.	d	↑	↑

Determinant: Price of a related good (substitute)

	Shift	Price	Quantity
6.	c	↓	↓

Determinant: Price of a related good (substitute)

	Shift	Price	Quantity
7.	b	↓	↑

Determinant: Availability of number of suppliers

	Shift	Price	Quantity
8.	b	↓	↑

Determinant: Change in technology

	Shift	Price	Quantity
9.	a	↑	↓

Determinant: Price of resources rise, number of sellers

	Shift	Price	Quantity
10.	d	↑	↑

Determinant: Number of buyers

Exercise 2

Figure 15.13 Answer

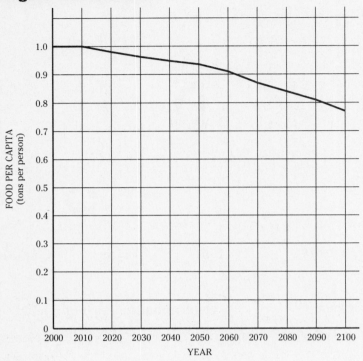

2. T
3. nearly 25 percent [(1 - 0.7711) x 100%]

Exercise 3

1. I/GDP is $\dfrac{\$1 \text{ trillion}}{\$5 \text{ trillion}} = 0.2$

2. To raise the income level by 1 percent the I/GDP ratio must rise to 22.5 percent.

   $\dfrac{X}{\$5 \text{ trillion}} = .225$ $X = \$1.125$ trillion

   Investment must go up by $1.125 trillion - $1.0 trillion = $0.125 trillion.

3. Saving must rise by the same amount ($0.125 trillion) as investment increases, so consumption must fall by that amount as well.

4. One percent of $5 trillion is $50 billion.

5. The economy gave up $0.125 trillion (or $125 billion) of consumption goods to raise the I/GDP ratio to 0.225. This is the amount to be recouped. Since the economy then grows by one percent more per year ($50 billion in the first year and increasingly larger amounts thereafter), it will take roughly 2.5 years (= $125 billion ÷ $50 billion) to make up the lost consumption.

CHAPTER 16

Theory and Reality

Quick Review

Designing economic policy for an economy as large and diverse as that of the United States is a very difficult job, and using the available tools in a complementary fashion to implement the policy adds to the complexity. It is thus appropriate that we consider the following questions:
- What is the ideal "package" of macro policies?
- How well does our macro performance live up to the promises of that package?
- What kinds of obstacles prevent us from achieving all of our economic goals?

We begin by noting that the president and Congress are responsible for designing and implementing economic policies to achieve our economic goals. One goal that is unanimously supported is that of eliminating the business cycle because achieving that goal alone would solve many additional problems all at once.

There are a number of policy tools or policy levers in the arsenal that can be used to fight upswings and downswings in the economy. Monetary policy tools (open-market operations, changing reserve requirements, etc.) and fiscal policy tools (changing taxes and spending) are the most powerful ones. Many economic resources are devoted to the study and development of economic policy.

Yet our policies seem to fail. Why? One reason is the lack of unanimity within the economics profession about how the economy works. There are several "groups" of economists that have been identified—Keynesians, Monetarists, and Supply-siders—who have somewhat different views about how to achieve economic stability:

1. *Recessions.* Modern Keynesians would increase the money supply, cut taxes, and increase government spending. Monetarists, on the other hand, believe these are quick fixes doomed to fail because the economy has a "natural" rate of unemployment that remains unchanged. They would prefer that the government follow a fixed policy. Supply-siders would focus on the more long-term policy of increasing incentives reduced through government intervention and cuts in marginal tax rates.

2. *Inflation.* While Keynesians would raise taxes and cut government spending, the Monetarists would cut the money supply to cure inflation. Supply-siders would provide more incentives to save, which would reduce consumption and simultaneously release more resources to increase productive capacity.

3. *Stagflation.* With stagflation the demand-side policies of the Keynesians and Monetarists are not as appropriate as supply-side policies of increasing some excise taxes, decreasing marginal tax rates, deregulation, and perhaps even the use of wage and price controls. When the stagflation is due to external shocks it may be particularly difficult for policy makers to respond.

These different prescriptions defy any unanimous view of the procedures for fine-tuning the economy.

Even if there were unanimous views about how to deal with various economic maladies, other serious problems plague us, too:

1. *Measurement problems.* It's difficult to measure what we want to know, to find current measurements when measurement is possible, or to make accurate forecasts even with current information.

2. *Design problems.* We don't know *exactly* how the economy responds to specific policies. Perverse reaction to government policies may actually worsen the problem the policy was intended to solve.

3. *Implementation problems.* It takes time for Congress and the president to agree on an appropriate plan of action. Four lags seem to prevent policies from being implemented quickly: recognition lag, lag in formulation of a response, lag in the response itself, and lag in the impact of the policy.

For all of these reasons the fine-tuning of economic performance rarely lives up to its theoretical potential. The issue then becomes whether or not government should have a hands-on policy of continual intervention or whether some fixed rules designed by government should be our policy.

Learning Objectives

After reading Chapter 16 and doing the following exercises, you should:	True or false	Multiple choice	Problems and applications	Common errors	Pages in the text
1. Know the three basic types of policies and each of the policy levers.	1, 3, 4	8, 15, 16, 17	3	1, 2	312-316
2. Know how the concept of opportunity cost defines the basic policy tradeoffs facing the economy.	10, 11	3, 23, 24	1, 2	1, 2	321
3. Be able to prescribe policies to eliminate a recession.	1, 6	1, 10, 12	1, 3		316-317
4. Be able to design policies to deal with inflation.	1, 6	5	1, 3		317
5. Be able to suggest policies to control stagflation.	1, 2, 9, 12, 17, 18	20	3	2	317-319
6. Know the general beliefs of several groups of economists.	13, 14, 15, 16	6, 7, 13, 15, 17, 18, 19			326-328

Learning Objectives (cont'd.)	True or false	Multiple choice	Problems and applications	Common errors	Pages in the text
7. Evaluate how effective policy makers have been in battling inflation and unemployment.		8, 9, 11, 14, 15, 16, 22, 24, 25	1	1, 2	312-316; 328
8. Be able to explain how measurement problems impede the development of effective policies.	5	2, 3, 4, 22, 24, 25	1, 2		322-323
9. Understand the design problems surrounding economic policy and the problems of forecasting.	8, 11	4, 22, 24, 25	1, 2		323
10. Recognize the lags involved in policy implementation.	7, 19	3, 4			323
11. Know the advantages and problems of rules and discretion in policy.		11, 18, 19	1		326-328

Key-Term Review

Review the following terms; if you are not sure of the meaning of any term, write out the definition and check it against the Glossary in the text.

automatic stabilizer	fiscal policy	money supply (M1)	structural unemployment
business cycle	fiscal year (FY)	multiplier	supply-side policy
fine-tuning	monetary policy	stagflation	

Fill in the blank following each of the statements below with the appropriate term from the list above.

1. Some believe that _____ of the economy ... is possible by making small changes in government taxes and spending, which is known as ....

   1. _____

   _____

2. Substantial implementation lags are experienced with fiscal policy, which can only be adjusted at the beginning of the_____ that begins each October 1.

   2. _____

3. Changes in fiscal policy have much larger economy-wide effects than the initial changes in government taxes and expenditures because of the_____ effect. ....

   3. _____

4. Fortunately many programs, such as unemployment compensation, offset the loss of income when jobs are lost and serve as a(n) _____ to the economy. 4. _____

5. Another policy that works through the aggregate-demand side is .... 5. _____

6. However, by increasing the_____ monetary policy may also contribute to_____ by causing inflation when unemployment is already too high. 6. _____
_____

7. Policy makers also have a difficult job in eliminating _____ which occurs .... when there is a mismatch between applicant qualifications and the skill requirements of available jobs. 7. _____

8. To alleviate that problem, _____ must be designed to provide incentives for people to work. 8. _____

9. Increased cyclical unemployment always accompanies the downswing in the .... 9. _____

True or False: *Circle your choice.*

T   F   1. To attain the economy's goals, fiscal and monetary policy should be consistent. For example, when the money supply is increased, fiscal policy should be expansionary.

T   F   2. When the economy is experiencing stagflation, it is appropriate to ease monetary policy and cut taxes.

T   F   3. "Fine-tuning" refers to the ability of policy makers to make small adjustments to the economy in order to attain economic goals.

T   F   4. A major change in the personal income tax during the 1980s was the reduction in marginal tax rates.

T   F   5. The reason it is said that the government tends to solve only those problems it can measure is that policy makers need information to show that something is wrong before they can act.

T   F   6. Either fiscal policy or monetary policy can be used in attempts to maintain levels of aggregate demand.

T   F   7. Automatic stabilizers have a substantial implementation lag due to the need for Congress to debate the problem after a recession begins.

T   F   8. Automatic stabilizers include the taxes and government expenditures over which Congress has discretionary authority.

T   F   9. Deregulation of financial institutions is an example of supply-side policy.

T   F   10. The shape of the aggregate demand curve is the most important limitation on the effectiveness of fiscal and monetary policies.

T   F   11. Marginal tax rates can be lowered and still result in greater tax revenues for government, *ceteris paribus.*

T   F   12. Increased immigration is a supply-side policy that shifts the aggregate supply curve upward.

T   F   13. The Tax Reform Act of 1986 was an example of both fiscal and supply-side policy.

T   F   14. The aggregate supply curve is vertical at the "natural" rate of unemployment.

T   F   15. Structural unemployment contributes to the rise in the aggregate supply curve.

T   F   16. Fine-tuning is used by Supply-siders.

T   F   17. When stagflation is caused by an external shock none of the macroeconomic levers provide a prescription to offset the shock.

T   F   18. Stagflation results when low inflation and low unemployment occur simultaneously.

T   F   19. The reason Congress fights over which communities and constituencies are to receive aid is an example of an implementation problem.

Multiple Choice: *Select the correct answer.*

_____ 1. The government's best policy to cure a recession is to:
(a) Expand the money supply and increase federal spending.
(b) Expand the money supply and lower federal spending.
(c) Contract the money supply and increase federal spending.
(d) Contract the money supply and lower federal spending.

_____ 2. Many economists argue that the CPI overstates inflation by two to three percentage points. From the point of view of those designing economic policy, this is an example of:
(a) A goal conflict.
(b) A measurement problem.
(c) A design problem.
(d) An implementation problem.

_____ 3. Which of the following is a reason that many economic policies fail, even if they are properly designed to achieve economic goals?
(a) Measurement difficulties prevent policy makers from correctly identifying what is happening in the economy.
(b) People often react in perverse ways that may counteract new government policies.
(c) There are important lags in response to policy.
(d) All of the above are reasons for economic policy failure.

_____ 4. Which of the following is the *appropriate order* in which lags cause policy actions to be tardy in their effects?
(a) Response design, recognition, impact, and implementation.
(b) Recognition, response design, implementation, and impact.
(c) Impact, implementation, recognition, and response design.
(d) Impact, recognition, response design, and implementation.

_____ 5. Why might Congress or the president hesitate to apply restrictive fiscal policies?
(a) Monetary policy is always more effective.
(b) Voters might become unemployed.
(c) Fiscal policy is too complex.
(d) Fiscal-year appropriations are not under the authority of Congress.

6. Which of the following groups of economists would argue that the American economy is inherently unstable because of its capitalist structure?
   (a) Neo-Keynesian.
   (b) Supply-siders.
   (c) Marxists.
   (d) Monetarists.

7. Which of the following groups feels that output and unemployment gravitate to their "natural" levels resulting in a vertical aggregate supply curve?
   (a) Keynesians.
   (b) Monetarists.
   (c) Fine tuners.
   (d) Supply siders.

8. Congress is responsible for:
   (a) Monetary policy.
   (b) Fiscal policy.
   (c) Monetary and fiscal policy.
   (d) Monetary, fiscal, and supply-side policy.

9. Which act established the following goals for the economy: 4 percent unemployment; 4 percent economic growth; 3 percent inflation?
   (a) The Gramm-Rudman Act of 1985.
   (b) The Employment Act of 1946.
   (c) The Employment and Balanced-Growth Act of 1978.
   (d) The Omnibus Reconciliation Act of 1988.

10. When the economy grows quickly out of a recession then automatically:
    (a) Tax revenues are reduced.
    (b) Government outlays are increased
    (c) Budget deficits become smaller.
    (d) All of the above.

11. From 1991 to 1992, Congress raised tax rates but government experienced a larger deficit because:
    (a) Discretionary policy and automatic stabilizers both increased tax rates.
    (b) Discretionary policy was overwhelmed by automatic stabilizers.
    (c) Automatic stabilizers were overwhelmed by discretionary policy.
    (d) Discretionary policy and automatic stabilizers both lowered government expenditures.

12. An easing of either monetary or fiscal policy will definitely result in greater output instead of inflation, *ceteris paribus,* if:
    (a) The aggregate supply curve is horizontal.
    (b) The aggregate supply curve is vertical.
    (c) The aggregate demand curve is horizontal.
    (d) The aggregate demand curve is vertical.

_____ 13. Which of the following is an example of supply-side policy:
    (a) Motor Carrier Act of 1980.
    (b) Gramm-Rudman-Hollings Act of 1985.
    (c) Fed imposes credit controls.
    (d) Discount rate increased in 1987.

_____ 14. The Tax Reform Act of 1986 represents the simultaneous use of:
    (a) Monetary and fiscal policy.
    (b) Monetary and supply-side policy.
    (c) Supply-side and fiscal policy.
    (d) Laissez-faire policy.

_____ 15. Which of the following is an example of fiscal policy:
    (a) Immigration law changes.
    (b) Deregulation of financial institutions.
    (c) Imposition of credit controls.
    (d) The Gramm-Rudman-Hollings Act.

_____ 16. Supply-side policy is designed to:
    (a) Move the economy from a point inside the production-possibilities curve to a point on it, and to shift the aggregate supply curve upward.
    (b) Move the economy from a point inside the production-possibilities curve to a point on it, and to shift the aggregate supply curve downward.
    (c) Shift the production-possibilities curve outward and to shift the aggregate supply curve upward.
    (d) Shift the production-possibilities curve outward and to shift the aggregate supply curve downward.

_____ 17. Which of the following can be both a supply-side policy initiative and a fiscal policy tool?
    (a) Tax cuts.
    (b) Deregulation.
    (c) Training programs.
    (d) Immigration law.

_____ 18. Which of the following is the Monetarist policy for fighting recession?
    (a) Increase government spending.
    (b) Expand the money supply at a faster rate.
    (c) Provide greater incentives.
    (d) Patience.

_____ 19. Which of the following is the Monetarist policy to fight inflation?
    (a) Cut the money supply.
    (b) Raise taxes.
    (c) Provide incentives for saving.
    (d) Cut government expenditures.

_____ 20. Which of the following would be recommended by Supply-siders to fight stagflation?
    (a) Raise tax rates.
    (b) Increase the money supply.
    (c) Deregulation.
    (d) Increase government expenditure.

21. The statement "I can't think of anything you can do to keep inflation down that is popular...It's completely different from fighting unemployment" is an example of:
    (a) A goal conflict.
    (b) A measurement problem.
    (c) A design problem.
    (d) An implementation problem.
22. The struggle over how the peace dividend from defense cutbacks is to be distributed is an example of:
    (a) A goal conflict.
    (b) A measurement problem.
    (c) A design problem.
    (d) An implementation problem.
23. The problem of deciding whether to provide aid to foreign countries when there are unresolved problems at home is an example of:
    (a) A goal conflict.
    (b) A measurement problem.
    (c) A design problem.
    (d) An implementation problem.
24. The debate over the shape of the aggregate supply curve contributes to:
    (a) A goal conflict.
    (b) A measurement problem.
    (c) A design problem.
    (d) An implementation problem.
25. The time it takes for Congress to deliberate over fiscal policy is an example of:
    (a) A goal conflict.
    (b) A measurement problem.
    (c) A design problem.
    (d) An implementation problem.

Problems and Applications

Exercise 1

This exercise shows the relationship between income and various economic aggregates that have been studied in Chapters 4-14.

Table 16.1 presents data on interest rates, government expenditures, taxes, exports, imports, investment, consumption, a price index, unemployment, and pollution for four levels of equilibrium income (GDP). These items appear frequently in newspaper articles about the economy. In the following questions you should be able to explain some of the relationships apparent in Table 16.1.

Table 16.1. Level of key economic indicators, by GDP level
(billions of dollars per year)

	30%	20%	10%	0%
Interest rate	30%	20%	10%	0%
Government expenditures	$100	$100	$100	$100
Taxes	$ 25	$ 75	$125	$175
Budget balance	$_____	$_____	$_____	$_____
Exports	$300	$300	$300	$300
Imports	$260	$280	$300	$320
Balance of trade	$_____	$_____	$_____	$_____
Investment	$ 10	$ 90	$170	$250
Consumption	$750	$790	$830	$870
Nominal GDP	$_____	$_____	$_____	$_____
Saving	$_____	$_____	$_____	$_____
Price index	1.00	1.00	1.02	1.10
Real GDP (constant dollars)	$_____	$_____	$_____	$_____
Unemployment rate	15%	7%	4%	3.5%
Pollution index	1.00	1.80	1.80	1.80

1. Compute the federal budget balance, balance of trade, nominal GDP, saving, and real GDP in Table 16.1, for each level of nominal GDP.
   (*Hint:* Remember the formula $C + I + G + [X - M] = $ GDP; see Chapter 4.)

2. Which of the following policies is the government most likely changing to reach each of the income levels in Table 16.1?
   (a) Fiscal policy.
   (b) Monetary policy.
   (c) Wage and price controls.
   (d) Labor policy.

3. Which of the following statements is *not* likely to explain why pollution changes as income changes, as indicated in Table 16.1?
   (a) Normal waste facilities are unable to handle the extra waste when the economy approaches its productive capacity.
   (b) When the economy grows, consumers have the income to dispose of waste more efficiently.
   (c) As income rises, people buy more houses; thus more land is cleared and streams are polluted.
   (d) Increased economic activity (higher GDP) naturally generates more waste.

4. Which of the following statements best explains why the amount paid in taxes might change as income changes, as shown in Table 16.1?
   (a) Taxpayers experience stagflation as income increases.
   (b) As taxpayers' incomes rise, their marginal tax rates rise.
   (c) The income tax is regressive.
   (d) Automatic stabilizers link taxes with income.

5. Which of the following statements best explains why imports change as income changes, as shown in Table 16.1?
   (a) People want to consume more foreign goods as their incomes rise.
   (b) People consume more domestic goods as their incomes rise.
   (c) Government buys fewer goods from domestic producers as incomes rise.
   (d) People consume fewer domestic goods as their incomes rise.
6. Which of the following statements best explains why exports *do not* change as GDP changes?
   (a) Exports are determined by the GDP of other countries.
   (b) Exports increase with GDP because firms can afford to produce more.
   (c) Exports decrease with GDP because people at home need goods and can pay for them.
   (d) Exports equal imports at all levels of income as the foreign exchange value of the dollar adjusts to bring them into equilibrium.
7. The reason that the price index changes as income changes, as shown in Table 16.1, is most likely that:
   (a) As people receive greater income, they can be more discriminating buyers and find the lowest prices.
   (b) As firms receive more orders, productivity rises allowing inflation to ease.
   (c) As people receive greater income, they spend it even when the economy is at full capacity, thus bidding up prices.
   (d) As businesses receive greater income, they have an incentive to expand capacity and must pass the cost of the increased capacity on to consumers in the form of higher prices.
8. The reason that unemployment changes as income changes, as shown in Table 16.1, is most likely that:
   (a) As income rises, people do not need jobs and leave the labor force.
   (b) As income rises, automatic stabilizers provide increased benefits to the unemployed, keeping them out of the labor force.
   (c) As income rises, inflation causes real income and employment to fall.
   (d) As income rises, aggregate demand rises, stimulating the derived demand for labor.
9. As income increases, the balance of trade worsens, which lowers the value of the dollar, because with higher income:
   (a) People buy more imports.
   (b) Businesses produce more goods for U.S. exports.
   (c) Businesses take goods out of export in order to sell them domestically.
   (d) None of the above is the case.

Exercise 2

This exercise shows the difficulties faced by policy makers because of the inevitable tradeoffs in the economy.

Table 16.2 presents data on government expenditure, taxes, exports, imports, a price index, unemployment, and pollution for four levels of equilibrium income (GDP). These items appear frequently in newspaper articles about the economy.

**Table 16.2. Level of key economic indicators, by GDP level
(billions of dollars per year)**

Indicator	Nominal GDP			
	$120	$160	$200	$240
Government expenditure	$ 0	$ 20	$ 35	$ 50
Taxes	$ 18	$ 24	$ 30	$ 36
Budget balance	$_____	$_____	$_____	$_____
Exports	$ 10	$ 10	$ 10	$ 10
Imports	$ 0	$ 10	$ 15	$ 20
Balance of trade	$_____	$_____	$_____	$_____
Price index	1.00	1.00	1.02	1.20
Real GDP (constant dollars)	$_____	$_____	$_____	$_____
Unemployment rate	15%	7%	4%	3.5%
Pollution index	1.00	1.10	1.80	1.90

1. Compute the federal budget balance, balance of trade, and real GDP in Table 16.2 for each level of nominal GDP.

2. What government expenditure level would best accomplish all of the following goals according to Table 16.2? $_____
   • Lowest taxes.
   • Largest trade surplus.
   • Lowest pollution.
   • Lowest inflation rate.

3. Which of the following might induce a policy maker to choose a higher government expenditure level than the one that answers Question 2?
   (a) High unemployment.
   (b) Government's inability to provide public goods and services.
   (c) Low real income.
   (d) All of the above.

4. What government expenditure level would best accomplish all of the following goals?
   $_____
   • Lowest unemployment rate.
   • Highest amount of public goods and services.
   • Highest real income.

5. For the policy that best satisfies the goals in Question 4, there would most likely be:
   (a) A recession.
   (b) Rapid economic growth accompanied by inflation.
   (c) Stagflation.
   (d) None of the above.

6. At what level of government expenditure is the value of the dollar in greatest danger? (*Note:* If there is a large trade deficit, the value of the dollar would fall.) $_____

7. Which government expenditure level would best accomplish all of the following goals?
   $_____
   - Balancing the federal budget.
   - Balancing the balance of trade.
   - Maintaining pollution at reasonably low levels.
   - Maintaining price stability.
8. At which government expenditure level does full employment occur? (Use 4 percent unemployment as full employment.) $_____.
9. If you were a policy maker faced with the alternatives in Table 16.2, would you be able to say that one of the alternative government expenditure levels was clearly best?
   _____

Exercise 3

This exercise tests your ability to choose the appropriate policy initiative to overcome various undesirable economic conditions.

Choose a policy from the list below that would be appropriate to correct the economic conditions at the top of Table 16.3. Mark the letter of each item only once in Table 16.3.

a. Deregulation.
b. Discount rate lowered.
c. Discount rate raised.
d. Government spending decreases.
e. Government spending increases.
f. Open-market operations (Fed buys government securities).
g. Open-market operations (Fed sells government securities).

h. Reserve requirement higher.
i. Reserve requirement lower.
j. Skill training and other labor market aids.
k. Tax cuts.
l. Tax incentives to alter the structure of supply and demand.
m. Tax incentives to encourage saving.
n. Tax increases.
o. Wage-price controls.

Table 16.3 Economic policies

	Recession	Inflation	Stagflation
Fiscal policy	1._____	6._____	
	2._____	7._____	
Monetary policy	3._____	8._____	
	4._____	9._____	
	5._____	10._____	
Supply-side policy		11._____	12._____
			13._____
			14._____
			15._____

260

Common Errors

The first statement in each "common error" below is incorrect. Each incorrect statement is followed by a corrected version and an explanation.

1. Fiscal and monetary policies should be consistently applied to stimulate the economy. WRONG!
   Fiscal and monetary policies must be tailored to the specific economic problems faced by the economy. RIGHT!

   The government sometimes needs to apply apparently contradictory monetary and fiscal policies in order to pursue contradictory goals. For example, an expansionary fiscal policy may be needed to stimulate the economy, but a contractionary monetary policy may be needed to raise interest rates so that foreign capital will be attracted to U.S. financial markets. A policy maker must weigh the various goals and decide on the appropriate mix of policies to best achieve them.

2. Fiscal, monetary, and stagflation policies are effective regardless of the current income level of the economy. WRONG!
   The state of the economy in relation to full employment is important in determining the effectiveness of the various policies. RIGHT!

   If the economy is experiencing inflation at full employment, wage-price controls will prove ineffective in curbing inflation. However, at relatively low levels of GNP, wage-price controls can be effective in holding down inflation. Work force policies are often more effective in matching people with jobs when many people are looking for work than when unemployment is low. It is easier for the government to increase expenditures to stimulate the economy when there is a recession than to cut expenditures to fight inflation.

■ANSWERS ■

Key-Term Review

1. fine tuning
   fiscal policy
2. fiscal year (FY)
3. multiplier
4. automatic stabilizer
5. monetary policy
6. money supply (M1)
   stagflation
7. structural unemployment
8. supply-side policy
9. business cycle

True or False

1. F	4. T	7. F	10. F	13. T	16. F	18. F
2. F	5. T	8. F	11. T	14. T	17. T	19. F
3. T	6. T	9. T	12. F	15. T		

Multiple Choice

1. a	5. b	9. c	13. a	17. a	20. c	23. a
2. b	6. c	10. c	14. c	18. d	21. a	24. c
3. d	7. b	11. b	15. d	19. a	22. a	25. d
4. b	8. b	12. a	16. d			

Problems and Applications

Exercise 1

1. **Table 16.1 Answer (billions of dollars per year)**

Interest rate	30%	20%	10%	0%
Budget balance	$ -75	$ -25	$ 25	$ 75
Balance of trade	40	20	0	-20
Nominal GDP	900	1,000	1,100	1,200
Saving	125	135	145	155
Real GDP (constant dollars)	900	1,000	1,078	1,091

At the 30 percent interest rate, the following calculations should have been made, in billions of dollars per year:

Budget balance = $25 - $100 = - $75
Balance of trade = $300 - $260 = $40
Nominal GDP = $750 + $10 + $100 + $40 = $900
Saving = (GNP - taxes) - consumption = $900 - $25 - $750 = $125

2. b	4. b	6. a	8. d
3. b	5. a	7. c	9. a

Exercise 2

1. **Table 16.2 Answer (billions of dollars per year)**

Indicator	Nominal GDP			
	$120	$160	$200	$240
Budget balance	$ 18	$ 4	$ -5	$ -14
Balance of trade	10	0	-5	-10
Real GDP (constant dollars)	120	160	196	200

2. $0   4. $50 billion   6. $50 billion   8. $35 billion
3. d   5. b   7. $20 billion   9. No

Exercise 3

1. Table 16.3 Answer

	Recession	Inflation	Stagflation
Fiscal	1. k Tax cuts 2. e Government spending increases	6. n Tax increases 7. d Government spending decreases	
Monetary policy	3. b Discount rate lowered 4. f Open-market operations (Fed buys government securities) 5. i Reserve requirement lower	8. c Discount rate raised 9. g Open-market operations (Fed sells government securities) 10. h Reserve requirement higher	
Supply-side policy		11. m Tax incentives to encourage saving	12. a Deregulation 13. l Tax incentive to alter the structure of supply and demand 14. o Wage-price controls 15. j Skill training and other labor market aids

CHAPTER 17

International Trade

Quick Review

Even the most casual observer of economic activity understands that trade between the United States and other nations is very important. In this chapter we ask some basic questions on trade, such as:

- What benefit, if any, do we get from international trade?
- How much harm do imports cause, and to whom?
- Should we protect ourselves from "unfair" trade by limiting some or all imports?

In recent decades the United States has become much more dependent on foreign trade than ever before. We export a wide variety of goods, especially agricultural products and capital goods, to many countries, and import from such advanced industrial nations as Japan and Germany and such poor countries as Bangladesh and Uruguay. Oil has become our most important import.

Countries are motivated to trade because by doing so they can produce together more total output than they could in the absence of trade. Specialization and trade allow both members of a trading partnership to consume beyond their respective production-possibility curves. That is, consumption possibilities exceed production possibilities when countries specialize and trade. The economic reason for this situation is rooted in what is called the "law of comparative advantage." This dictum says that as long as the opportunity costs of producing goods in two countries differ, it will always be possible for those countries to specialize and trade to their mutual advantage. Neither the absolute size of the countries nor their absolute costs of production are important. What does count is the relative (comparative) cost of producing alternative goods.

It is obvious that specialization and trade benefit trading nations. But special-interest groups often exert strong pressure *against* foreign trade. Those who would lose their markets and jobs to imported goods and foreign workers may oppose free trade.

The government may place a tariff or quota on imported goods or provide aid to the affected domestic industry. We have occasionally asked our trading partners to voluntarily limit their exports to us so as to ease the pressure on threatened firms and industries as well. The government has sometimes made assistance (cash, training, or relocation) available to those whose jobs were lost to foreign competition.

Learning Objectives

After reading Chapter 17 and doing the following exercises, you should:	True or false	Multiple choice	Problems and applications	Common errors	Pages in the text
1. Know some basic facts about U.S. trade patterns.	17, 18	15, 16, 17		4	334-336
2. Understand the macroeconomic impact of international trade.	3, 4, 5, 6, 7, 8		2		
3. Understand why specialization and trade increase both production possibilities and consumption possibilities.	9		1	3, 4	336-340
4. Be able to explain comparative advantage using opportunity costs.	10	1, 2, 3, 5, 7, 10, 11, 12	1	1	341-342
5. Know how to determine the limits to the terms of trade.	11	4, 13	2		342-344
6. Be able to calculate the gains from specialization and trade at a given exchange rate.		14	2		338-340
7. Be able to show how trade allows a country to consume beyond its production-possibilities curve.	9		1, 2		339
8. Recognize the sources of pressure that result in restricted trade.	12, 14			2	344-346
9. Know some of the arguments used by those wishing to restrict trade.	13	6, 8, 9		2	346
10. Be able to discuss tariffs and quotas as barriers to trade.	13, 14	6, 8		2, 3	
11. Know the basis for programs that provide assistance to workers displaced by imports.		9			350-351

Key-Term Review

Review the following terms; if you are not sure of the meaning of any term, write out the definition and check it against the Glossary in the text.

absolute advantage	exports	tariff
adjustment assistance	imports	terms of trade
comparative advantage	opportunity cost	trade deficit
consumption possibilities	production possibilities	trade surplus
equilibrium price	quota	voluntary restraint agreement (VRA)

Fill in the blank following each of the statements below with the appropriate term from the list above.

1. The slope of the production-possibilities curve indicates the quantity of one good that must be given up in order to produce one more unit of another good, or in other words, the .... 1. _____

2. Aggregate demand shifts to the left when _____ increase. .... 2. _____

3. When the opportunity cost of producing a good is lower in one country than in another, the first country is said to have a .... 3. _____

4. A country that can produce more of a good than another country with the same amount of resources is said to have an .... 4. _____

5. U.S. firms manufacture computers and produce agricultural goods and ship them to France. Computers and agricultural goods are U.S. .... 5. _____

6. The various combinations of two goods that a country can produce and consume without trade constitute its .... 6. _____

7. The various combinations of two goods that a country can consume when it engages in trade constitute .... 7. _____

8. An absolute limit imposed by a government on the quantity of a specific item that may be imported is called a .... 8. _____

9. A tax on imported goods is known as a .... 9. _____

10. Markets decide how much of one good from one country will trade for a unit of another good from another country. This ratio indicates the .... 10. _____

11. A country that imports more than it exports over a given period of time is said to have a ..... 11. _____

12. When a country's exports exceed its imports, it is said to have a .... 12. _____

267

13. Under a freely flexible exchange-rate system, the market price will approach the .... 13. _____

14. A quota placed by a country on its own exports is called a .... 14. _____

15. Workers who are aided because their jobs were lost when imported goods replaced domestically produced goods are said to receive .... 15. _____

True or False: *Circle your choice.*

T F 1. The main reason that countries specialize and trade with each other is that by doing so they can get things they cannot produce themselves.

T F 2. The trade balance is calculated by subtracting exports from imports.

T F 3. Any change in exports has a multiplier effect on the aggregate level of income, *ceteris paribus.*

T F 4. Any change in imports has a multiplier effect on the aggregate level of income, *ceteris paribus.*

T F 5. Positive net exports (exports exceed imports) tend to lower national income; negative net exports tend to raise the level of national income.

T F 6. If exports increase while imports remain constant, a trade surplus will increase.

T F 7. A trade deficit means that imports exceed exports over some relevant time period.

T F 8. Since one country's exports are another country's imports, overall world trade must balance.

T F 9. Specialization and trade allow countries to consume beyond their own respective production-possibility curves.

T F 10. If the opportunity costs of producing goods in two countries are the same, there is no incentive to trade.

T F 11. The terms at which countries will trade one good for another will occur between their respective domestic opportunity costs.

T F 12. Since free trade is beneficial to society as a whole, it benefits each individual group in society as well.

T F 13. From the consumer's point of view, quotas have the potential to inflict more damage than tariffs.

T F 14. The pressure for restrictions on trade tends to increase when the economy is operating near capacity.

T F 15. In countries where they are imposed, tariffs and quotas raise the price of imported goods to consumers.

T F 16. Voluntary restraint agreements are, in reality, "voluntary quotas."

T F 17. Bilateral trade balances refer to trade balances between two countries.

T F 18. Voluntary export restraints by Japanese auto manufacturers resulted in higher prices for automobiles purchased by U.S. consumers.

Multiple Choice: *Select the correct answer.*

_____ 1. Suppose the production of 1 ton of steel in the United States requires the same amount of resources as the production of 100 gallons of oil. In Canada, 2 tons of steel might require the same amount of resources as 200 gallons of oil. This means that:
   (a) The United States has the comparative advantage in steel.
   (b) Canada has the comparative advantage in steel.
   (c) The United States has an absolute advantage in steel.
   (d) None of the statements above is correct.

_____ 2. In Germany, suppose six cameras or four bicycles can be produced with one unit of labor. In Japan, suppose nine cameras or five bicycles can be produced with one unit of labor. Therefore:
   (a) Germany has an absolute advantage in the production of both goods.
   (b) Japan has a comparative advantage in the production of both goods.
   (c) Germany has a comparative advantage in the production of bicycles.
   (d) Japan has a comparative advantage in the production of bicycles.

_____ 3. Given the conditions listed in Question 2, what is the opportunity cost of producing one bicycle?
   (a) In Germany, 1.5 cameras.
   (b) In Germany, 2/3 camera.
   (c) In Japan, 5/9 camera.
   (d) In Japan, 8.1 cameras.

_____ 4. Given the conditions listed in Questions 2 and 3, the terms of trade at which these two goods would be traded between Germany and Japan would be one bicycle to:
   (a) More than 1.8 cameras.
   (b) More than 1.5 cameras but less than 1.8 cameras.
   (c) Less than 1.5 cameras.
   (d) None of the above, because Japan has an absolute advantage in both goods.

_____ 5. Suppose that France and the United States do not trade and that the competitive price of an ordinary bottle of wine is 20 francs in France and $2 in the United States; the price of wheat per bushel is 40 francs in France and $6 in the United States. This information is sufficient to enable us to state that:
   (a) France has a comparative advantage in the production of wine.
   (b) France has a comparative advantage in the production of wheat.
   (c) Neither country has a comparative advantage in the production of either good.
   (d) The United States has an absolute advantage in the production of both goods.

_____ 6. A person who accepts the arguments for freer trade:
   (a) Will oppose all tariffs, whatever the arguments in their favor.
   (b) Will favor tariffs because they will raise the real income of the countries levying them.
   (c) Could favor tariffs if he or she thought the objectives of policy served by such tariffs were more important than raising real income.
   (d) Will oppose all tariffs but will favor selective quotas.

7. To say that a country has a comparative advantage in the production of wine is to say that:
   (a) It can produce wine with fewer resources than any other country can.
   (b) Its opportunity cost of producing wine is greater than any other country's.
   (c) Its opportunity cost of producing wine is lower than any other country's.
   (d) The relative price of wine is higher in that country than in any other.

8. America's tariffs on foreign goods result in:
   (a) Lower domestic prices than those that would prevail in their absence.
   (b) A stimulus to efficient American firms that are not protected.
   (c) Higher employment and output in protected industries than would otherwise be the case.
   (d) A more efficient allocation of resources than would occur in their absence.

9. Adjustment assistance is designed to:
   (a) Ease the adjustment problems confronting consumers when a tariff or quota is levied.
   (b) Assist producers and those workers who are adversely affected by a reduction in tariffs or quotas.
   (c) Assist producers and those workers who are adversely affected by an increase in tariffs or quotas.
   (d) Increase the revenues received by the government.

Suppose the productivities of Japanese and U.S. producers are as indicated in Table 17.1. Refer to Table 17.1 in answering Questions 10-14.

Table 17.1. Output per worker-day in the
United States and Japan

Country	TV sets (per day)	Bicycles (per day)
Japan	2	10
United States	1	8

10. Which of the following statements is true?
    (a) The United States has an absolute advantage in the production of bicycles.
    (b) Japan has an absolute advantage in the production of bicycles only.
    (c) Japan has an absolute advantage in the production of TV sets only.
    (d) Japan has an absolute advantage in the production of both bicycles and TV sets.

11. Which of the following is a true statement?
    (a) The opportunity cost of TV sets is higher in Japan than in the United States.
    (b) The opportunity cost of TV sets is lower in Japan than in the United States.
    (c) It is impossible to tell anything about opportunity cost from the information given.
    (d) The United States has a comparative advantage in the production of TV sets.

12. Which of the following statements is true?
    (a) Japan has an absolute advantage in the production of both products but a comparative advantage in bicycles.
    (b) Japan has a comparative advantage in both products and an absolute advantage in the production of TV sets.
    (c) The United States has an absolute advantage in neither product but a comparative advantage in the production of bicycles.
    (d) The United States has an absolute advantage in neither product but a comparative advantage in TV sets.
13. Suppose the terms of trade are established in such a way that one TV set equals five bicycles. Which of the following statements would be true?
    (a) These terms of trade provide gains for the United States, but Japan is worse off.
    (b) These terms of trade provide gains for Japan, but the United States is worse off.
    (c) These terms of trade provide gains for the United States, and Japan is no worse off.
    (d) These terms of trade provide gains for Japan, and the United States is no worse off.
14. Which of the following terms of trade would provide gains for both countries?
    (a) One TV set equals five bicycles.
    (b) One TV set equals eight bicycles.
    (c) One TV set equals six bicycles.
    (d) None of the above would provide such gains.
15. Which of the following statements is correct?
    (a) The United States is becoming increasingly dependent on foreign trade.
    (b) The United States is becoming less dependent on foreign trade.
    (c) U.S. dependence on trade has remained relatively constant for the past decade.
    (d) There is no clear cut way to measure U.S. dependence on foreign trade.
16. When Japan "voluntarily" restrained automobile exports to the United States between 1981 and 1985:
    (a) U.S. auto producers became more profitable.
    (b) Firms importing Japanese cars became more profitable.
    (c) Consumers paid higher prices for both U.S. and Japanese cars.
    (d) All of the above were true.
17. Which of the following countries has the *lowest* export-to-GNP ratio?
    (a) The United States.
    (b) Japan.
    (c) Great Britain.
    (d) Canada.
18. Which of the following groupings contains a word or phrase that does not belong?
    (a) Imports, exports, trade balance.
    (b) Comparative advantage, absolute advantage, protectionism.
    (c) Quotas, tariffs, voluntary restraint agreements.
    (d) Production possibilities, consumption possibilities, terms of trade.

Problems and Applications

Exercise 1

This exercise shows how trade leads to gains by all trading partners through specialization and comparative advantage.

1. Suppose that Japan has 20 laborers in total and that the United States has 40 laborers. Suppose their productivities are as indicated in Table 17.2. (*Be careful:* The table tells you that a worker in Japan can produce two TV sets per day *or* ten bicycles per day, *not* two TV sets and ten bicycles!)

Table 17.2. Output per worker-day in the
United States and Japan

Country	TV sets (per day)	Bicycles (per day)
Japan	2	10
United States	1	8

Draw the production-possibilities curves for each country in Figure 17.1. Assume constant costs of production.

Figure 17.1

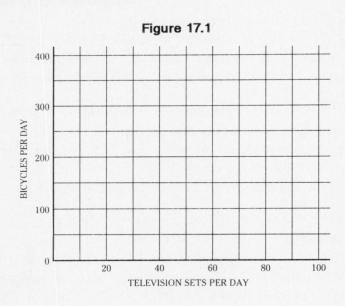

2. Suppose that before trade Japan uses 12 laborers to produce bicycles and 8 laborers to produce television sets; suppose also that in the United States 20 workers produce bicycles and 20 produce television sets. Complete Table 17.3.

272

**Table 17.3. Output produced and consumed
without trade**

Country	TV sets (per day)	Bicycles (per day)
Japan	___	___
United States	___	___
Total	___	___

3. Before trade, the total output of television sets is _____ ; of bicycles _____.
4. What is the opportunity cost of one television set in Japan?_____. In the United States?_____.
5. What is the opportunity cost of one bicycle in Japan?_____ . In the United States?_____.
6. If Japan and the United States specialize according to their respective comparative advantages, Japan will produce _____ and the United States will produce_____. They will do so because the opportunity cost of bicycles in terms of television sets is (lower, higher) in the United States than in Japan, and the opportunity cost of television sets in terms of bicycles is (lower, higher) in Japan than in the United States.
7. After specialization, the total output of television sets is _____ and the total output of bicycles is_____ . (*Hint:* Twenty Japanese produce only TV sets, and 40 Americans produce only bicycles.)
8. This output represents an increase of _____ bicycles and _____television sets over the prespecialization output. (*Hint:* Compare answers to Questions 3 and 7.)

Exercise 2

This exercise will help you understand how the terms of trade are determined. Refer to Exercise 1 for the data.

If Japan and the United States are to benefit from the increased production, trade must take place. The Japanese will be willing to trade television sets for bicycles as long as they get back more bicycles than they could get in their own country.

1. The terms of trade will be between one television set equals _____ bicycles and one television set equals _____ bicycles.
2. If the terms of trade were four bicycles equals one television set:
    (a) Neither country would buy bicycles but both would buy TV sets.
    (b) Neither country would buy TV sets but both would buy bicycles.
    (c) Both countries would buy bicycles and TV sets.
    (d) Neither country would buy TV sets or bicycles.
3. Suppose that the two countries agree that the terms of trade will be six bicycles equals one television set. Let Japan export 20 television sets per day to the United States. Complete

273

Table 17.4. Assume that Japan produces 40 television sets per day and the United States produces 320 bicycles.

Table 17.4. Consumption combination after trade

Country	TV sets (per day)	Bicycles (per day)
Japan	———	———
United States	———	———
Total	40	320

4. As a result of specialization and trade, the United States has the same quantity of television sets and _____ more bicycles per day. (Compare Tables 17.3 and 17.4.)
5. As a result of specialization and trade, Japan has the same number of bicycles and_____ more television sets per day.

Now suppose that at the exchange rate of 6 bicycles to 1 TV set, Japan would like to export 10 TV sets and import 60 bicycles per day. Suppose also that the United States desires to export 90 bicycles and import 15 television sets per day.

6. At these terms of trade there is a (shortage, surplus) of television sets.
7. At these terms of trade there is a (shortage, surplus) of bicycles.
8. Which of the following terms of trade would be more likely to result from this situation?
   (a) Five bicycles equal one television set.
   (b) Six bicycles equal one television set.
   (c) Seven bicycles equal one television set.

Common Errors

The first statement in each "common error" below is incorrect. Each incorrect statement is followed by a corrected version and an explanation.

1. A country must have an *absolute advantage* in order to gain from trade with another country. WRONG!
   A country must have a *comparative advantage* in order to gain from trade with another country. RIGHT!
       Mutually advantageous trade requires only that the opportunity costs of producing goods differ in the two countries. Another way of stating this is that the production-possibility curves of the two countries must have different slopes. These two circumstances are indicated in Figure 17.2.

Figure 17.2

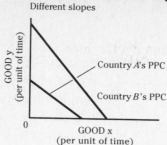

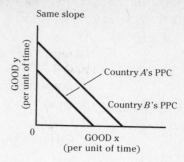

(a) Different slopes. Mutually advantageous trade *is* possible.

(b) Same slope. Mutually advantageous trade is *not* possible.

2. Foreign trade costs a country jobs. WRONG!
Although jobs may be lost, new ones will be created by the opportunities opened up with trade. RIGHT!

    When countries specialize and trade according to the law of comparative advantage, some particular workers and firms may be hurt by imports, but the economy as a whole gains by trade. More output per resource input will be attainable. Because the economy is able to reach full employment with trade as well as without trade, there is no reason to assume there will be fewer jobs.

3. A country is well off only as long as it exports more than it imports. WRONG!
Countries may, at times, be well off when they experience a trade surplus: they may also be well off when they have a trade deficit. RIGHT!

    Both trade deficits and trade surpluses can be problems if either situation persists for a long period of time. Trade surpluses mean that a country is giving more of its limited, precious resources in trade than it is acquiring from other countries. The currencies of deficit countries tend to depreciate, which means they will be unable to buy as many foreign goods with a unit of currency.

4. Countries tend to enter into trade to get things they cannot produce themselves. WRONG!
Countries very often trade for things they could produce themselves. RIGHT!

    Be careful! Countries often trade for things they could produce themselves, because the relative costs of domestic production would be prohibitive. Take baskets as an example. We could certainly produce baskets if we really wanted to. The technique is not difficult to learn and the materials are abundant. But baskets do not lend themselves to machine production, and hand labor is expensive. The cost in terms of goods forgone would be tremendous. (So would the price of the baskets.) We're better off specializing in something like computers, where we have a comparative advantage, and trading for baskets, where we clearly do not have a comparative advantage.

■ANSWERS ■

Key-Term Review

1. opportunity cost
2. imports
3. comparative advantage
4. absolute advantage
5. exports

6. production possibilities
7. consumption possibilities
8. quota
9. tariff
10. terms of trade

11. trade deficit
12. trade surplus
13. equilibrium price
14. voluntary restraint agreement (VRA)
15. adjustment assistance

True or False

1. F	4. T	7. T	10. T	13. T	16. T
2. F	5. F	8. T	11. T	14. F	17. T
3. T	6. T	9. T	12. F	15. T	18. T

Multiple Choice

1. d	4. b	7. c	10. d	13. c	16. d
2. c	5. b	8. c	11. b	14. c	17. a
3. a	6. c	9. b	12. c	15. a	18. b

Problems and Applications

Exercise 1

1. Figure 17.1 Answer

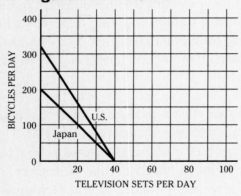

2. Table 17.3 Answer

Country	TV sets (per day)	Bicycles (per day)
Japan	16	120
United States	20	160
Total	36	280

3. 36; 280
4. 5 bicycles; 8 bicycles
5. one-fifth television set; one-eighth television set
6. television sets; bicycles; lower; lower
7. 40; 320
8. 40; 4

276

1. 5; 8
2. a

3. **Table 17.4 Answer**

Country	TV sets (per day)	Bicycles (per day)
Japan	20	120
United States	20	200
Total	40	320

4. 40
5. 4
6. shortage   The Japanese wish to export fewer (10) TV sets than Americans want (15).
7. surplus   The Americans wish to export more (90) bicycles than the Japanese want (60).
8. c